Okay? Okay!

Dennis James' Lifetime of Firsts

By Adam Nedeff

Okay? Okay! Dennis James' Lifetime of Firsts
© 2018. Adam Nedeff. All rights reserved.

All illustrations are copyright of their respective owners, and are also reproduced here in the spirit of publicity. Whilst we have made every effort to acknowledge specific credits whenever possible, we apologize for any omissions, and will undertake every effort to make any appropriate changes in future editions of this book if necessary.

No part of this book may be reproduced in any form or by any means, electronic, mechanical, digital, photocopying or recording, except for the inclusion in a review, without permission in writing from the publisher.

Published in the USA by:
BearManor Media
P O Box 71426
Albany, Georgia 31708
www.bearmanormedia.com

Printed in the United States of America
ISBN   978-1-62933-211-6 (paperback)

Book & cover design and layout by Darlene Swanson • www.van-garde.com

Contents

	Introduction and Acknowledgments vii	
Chapter 1:	Jersey Boy 1	
Chapter 2:	Signing On 11	
Chapter 3:	Section 8, Channel 5 23	
Chapter 4:	The Ringmaster 37	
Chapter 5:	Mother's Favorite 57	
Chapter 6:	All That Glitters, and Old Gold 73	
Chapter 7:	Look at Us, We're Walking! 83	
Chapter 8:	Hey Micki! 93	
Chapter 9:	A Lifetime of Work 105	
Chapter 10:	Don't Judge Me 129	
Chapter 11:	Clearing the Air 141	
Chapter 12:	The New Arrival 151	
Chapter 13:	Join the Club 165	
Chapter 14:	Way Out West 179	
Chapter 15:	In the Green 193	
Chapter 16:	Beating the Odds 209	
Chapter 17:	Here When You Need Him 221	
Chapter 18:	Dennis is Right 239	

Chapter 19:	Tune In, Tune Out	255
Chapter 20:	Telethon, and On and On	269
Chapter 21:	Acting Up	281
Chapter 22:	The Work Never Stopped	293
Appendix:	Dennis James' Resume	307
	Bibliography	313
	Index	319

Introduction and Acknowledgments

STU SHOSTAK MADE this book happen.

Stu Shostak, founder of Shokus Video and Shokus Internet Radio and host of *Stu's Show*, dedicated his February 18, 2015 broadcast to the life and times of Dennis James. His guests were two of Dennis' sons in the Los Angeles area, Randy and Brad (Dennis' oldest son, Dennis Jr., was over on the other side of the country), as well as Dennis' grandson, Colton. Stu graciously allowed me to sneak into the broadcast.

One of my hobbies for many years has been collecting photos of game show hosts, all neatly sorted and organized into their own dedicated albums lining the shelves of my bookcases. I asked Stu if I could come in just so

I could show the Dennis James album to his family and even get it autographed as a memento. The autographs honestly weren't that important to me, but I like the opportunity to show the performers—or in their absence, their families—that I value the work that they did.

Stu obliged and even let me answer a few questions on the show. After the program, I showed off the album, got the autographs, and started to tip my non-existent hat and head for the door.

Stu asked, "Adam, have you considered writing a book about Dennis?"

To be honest, the thought hadn't crossed my mind until Stu suggested it, and taking in everything that had just been discussed during the past two hours, I realized I really should be writing that book. Heck, not even me, necessarily. Somebody should be writing a book about Dennis—anybody.

He is often considered to be the first TV variety show host, first host of what would now be called an infomercial, first TV sports commentator, first network TV game show host, and the man who brought pro wrestling into the Big Time. He is also the man who popularized the telethon format for fundraising, the first man to appear in a videotaped commercial, the first cigarette spokesman to act on his conscience and walk away from the job, and the first man hired to host *The Price is Right* in 1972.

See what I mean? Isn't a guy like that entitled to a book about him? I thought so. It just took Stu Shostak bringing up that fairly obvious void that needed to be filled.

Much thanks, not just to Stu, but especially to Dennis' family, Randy, Brad, and Dennis' lovely wife, Micki, for sharing their memories, their father's treasures, and his vast collection of photos.

Thank you also to Dennis' friends and co-workers, who shared their memories and insights: Merrill Heatter, Tom Kennedy, Chris Korman, Elaine LaLanne, Gary Lortz, Craig MacEachern, and Peter Marshall.

Enjoy the book. Okay? Okay.

Chapter One
Jersey Boy

DR. ALLEN B. DuMont needed to hire *somebody*.

Dr. DuMont had set up his shingle in Upper Montclair, New Jersey in 1931, founding DuMont Laboratories to conduct experiments and develop equipment for a nascent idea called television.

A few years earlier, Dr. Philo T. Farnsworth, working out of a similar laboratory in San Francisco, California, used his image dissector camera tube to transmit a simple image of a straight line to an electronic receiver in a separate room. Television had been an idea that had existed for *decades*—a magazine illustration in the 1800s depicted a sporting event being shown on a screen over a fireplace—but Farnsworth was the one who made it happen. David Sarnoff, who was head of radio broadcasting for Radio Corporation of America (RCA), immediately recognized the potential of television and gave a $100,000 grant to a Westinghouse engineer to develop a functioning television unit.

Sarnoff and Farnsworth both hit a roadblock in the development of this new idea. Television operated on cathode ray tubes. All of the experimental television units built in the late 1920s used imported German tubes, which wore out after about thirty hours. At that point, there was nothing better, but tubes that needed replaced after only thirty hours meant that television wasn't really a commercially viable idea.

That's when the new kid on the block, Dr. Allen B. DuMont in New Jersey, stunned everybody by leapfrogging the more experienced inventors and engineers. DuMont Laboratories invented a cathode ray tube that would last more than 1,000 hours.

Despite his breakthrough, Dr. DuMont would always remain a self-employed underdog, financing his big ideas with his own money, no corporation and no research grants backing him up. When he made a deal with Paramount Pictures for company stock, Dr. DuMont officially went into the television business that he himself had made possible.

Dr. DuMont was still working on making cathode ray tubes last even longer, while his lab began producing and selling television sets—the DuMont Model 180—for $325. Not only did DuMont Laboratories begin selling televisions commercially, but Dr. DuMont received a license for two experimental TV stations, W2XVT in Passaic, New Jersey, and W2XWV in New York, New York.

Here's the problem Dr. DuMont was running into: many homes were not interested in television to begin with. A number of department stores bought the earliest batch of sets, just for the publicity that they could get from inviting shoppers to come in and look at it. Dr. DuMont's brother, Bruce, also managed to sell television sets to bars; his sales pitch was pointing out to bar owners that they were selling the same beer as the other bars, so why not install a television so that they had something to set their business apart?

If all those stores and bars were using television to drum up interest, something of interest had to be on television. They needed programs. Any programming would do. It just had to be something you could put on the screen, and preferably something low-cost, given Dr. DuMont's resources. The Paramount stock was nice but not a guaranteed cash flow. No matter what programming DuMont might put on the air, though, it needed a person on camera, didn't it?

Radio was the most logical resource for talent, but many radio performers dismissed television as an oddity or a novelty. The hundreds of sets in bars certainly didn't compare to the millions of radios in every American home. Radio presented a salary and security that television absolutely could not offer. Given a chance to perform on television, almost all radio performers said, "No thanks."

With one exception: a DuMont engineer, Lou Sposa, suggested to Dr. DuMont that his brother, a disc jockey down in Jersey City, might be the guy they were looking for to be the face of early television. His name was Demie Sposa.

At least it used to be. Demitrio Ernest Sposa, a construction executive, and his wife, Teresa Amoroso, had already brought two sons, Lou and Frank, into the world when, on August 24, 1917, they welcomed a third boy. The new baby was given a shortened form of his father's name and called Demie James Sposa.

Demie was raised in his family's Jersey City duplex. Demitrio and Teresa raised their family on the top level. Teresa's sister and her family lived on the bottom level. The families essentially functioned as a single unit, and Demie grew up in a large, happy Italian-American, Catholic home. He divided his childhood between Jersey City and Lake Parsipanny, New Jersey, where his father's construction business erected a summer home. In school, he was known as a natural athlete; a magazine article noted that he amassed quite a collection of trophies during high school. For a brief period, he trained to become a boxer. During the months away from school, Demie made extra money during the day as a lifeguard on the lake and then returned home to be with his family and soak in the cool nighttime breezes.

Demie Sposa, seated in the front of his boat, enjoyed the
New Jersey summer with his family, circa 1930.

Demie, and most of his family and friends, expected him to become a doctor. His school had voted him "Most Likely to Succeed in Medicine." Demie would later half-jokingly explain that in an Italian family, it was expected that somebody was to go to medical school and become a doctor. It was viewed as the height of achievement, and with neither Frank nor Lou showing any interest in the profession, Demie initially felt that the mantle fell upon him.

Demie finished high school and then attended St. Peter's College. While taking pre-med courses during the day, he was also quietly making his way to a night school for a course on radio broadcasting. Once he earned his degree from St. Peter's, he approached his parents and revealed he wanted to change his plans. He didn't want to start attending medical school. He wanted to try radio.

Demie Sposa as a young man, on the far left in this family portrait from the late 1930s.

Demie had shown some aptitude for performing as a child. When he graduated from elementary school, he brought tears to the audience's eyes with a stirring performance of the poem, "Over the Hill and to the Poorhouse," but hadn't actively pursued any further exploration of his talent after that one night. He never seemed particularly mesmerized by radio, either, at least, no more so than any other kid from the original generation to grow up with it, but some sort of broadcasting bug had bitten him, and Demie wanted to try it.

Demitrio wasn't completely on-board when he heard the idea, but he also wasn't about to stop his son from chasing this new interest. As Demie later said, "Dad knew the only cure for the type of affliction was to let the patient work it out of his system. A spell of hard knocks—a diet of coffee and buns—and in most cases, there was complete recovery."

There was no Dr. Sposa in the family, but Demitrio and Teresa weren't really disappointed by that. They were intrigued by their son's sudden passion for this new interest and supported it.

Demie couldn't hide his surprise at how gracefully they were taking it. As he remembered later, "I had expected my family to be disappointed that I was giving up medicine... but all my Dad said was, 'Look, this is your life.'"

His mom and dad weren't sure where broadcasting would take him, but Demie always threw himself into anything that grabbed his interest, and they knew that he'd try as hard as he could. In addition to his night school course on radio broadcasting, Demie took classes in dramatics, paying his way with a day job as a salesman in the dog department at Abercrombie and Fitch in New York.

Demie got hired by station WAAT in Jersey City and became something of a utility player for the station. He acted in the dramatic shows and filled in when a disc jockey took a few days off. After paying his dues, he quickly secured a full-time spot at WAAT as a disc jockey for $25 a week. Popular music was never really an interest to Demie, but it was a nice "in" while he figured out exactly what he wanted to do in the medium.

WAAT also showcased live music. One favorite at the station was an up-and-coming kid from Hoboken named Frank Sinatra. Sinatra had broken out as a star in 1935 with a knock-out performance on *Major Bowes' Amateur Hour*, the original radio talent search show, as part of a quartet called the Hoboken Four. Host/producer Edward Bowes was so dazzled by them that he kept booking the group to appear as contestants, under a different name each time so that the listening audience wouldn't catch on. Sinatra regularly sang on WAAT for free to promote his nightclub engagements all over the state.

Demie also reported the news on WAAT, an assignment that ended in disaster one day when he laughed at entirely the wrong time. Military action in Europe was becoming more aggressive, and Germany's invasion of Poland was the top story. As Demie reported the outbreak of what would become World War II, he began giggling. The worst part was that he couldn't explain what he found so funny because that would just make things worse. The script for the news report had several news stories on one page. As he reported the details of Germany's military action, his eyes darted down and looked ahead to the next story: "Jersey City police have found the body of a missing local man; he was found with six bullet holes in him. Police suspect foul play." Demie couldn't contain himself.

Demie had a lot to think about as he began making strides in the broadcasting business.

One day, WAAT owner Jimmy Shearer roped Demie into his office and asked in a way that Demie found rather off-putting, "Why don't you change your name? I don't want any Italian names on the station."

"My old man will kill me!" Dennis argued.

"I don't care. Change your name or you're fired."

Demie, realizing he had an argument he could make about the "no-Italian-names" edict, piped up, "What about Sinatra?"

"He has talent."

That was the end of the argument. Demie, almost out of spite, decided to give himself a name that was Americanized enough, but barely different from his real name: Demi Spay.

He talked it over with his brother Lou, who quickly talked his brother out of "Demi Spay" and suggested anglicizing his first name to Dennis, and lopping off his last name entirely. Demie James Sposa became known as "Dennis James."

He was Dennis James when he got the call from Dr. DuMont, asking if he'd join DuMont Laboratories. Unlike most of his colleagues, Dennis was willing to experiment. He saw it as a necessity for survival. Plenty of broadcasters had a forte, but Dennis saw that as detrimental in the long run. If a skillful sportscaster was suddenly unemployed, he might arrive at a station looking for a talented commercial pitchman, and what good did all of the sports casting experience do there? Likewise, a dramatic actor might depart from a radio station, but then find that the only stations hiring were looking for newscasters.

Dennis was so eager to take any opportunity that he almost made it a habit never to say "no." He got a call one day from a potential employer looking for a voice to help with an upcoming project.

"Have you ever done a slide presentation?" the man on the phone asked.

"Yes," Dennis answered. The truth was that not only had he never done one, he didn't know what a slide presentation was. Slide projectors weren't commercially available until the 1950s. Dennis may have been exposed to its predecessor, a device called the magic lantern, but even with that knowledge, Dennis may not have understood that the pictures were called slides.

He wasn't even asked to audition. He was hired immediately, just on the basis of saying he had done a slide presentation before. He was excited to learn that he'd be working with a renowned radio performer of the day, one whose voice was recognizable virtually everywhere. Dennis could put it on his resume that he had worked with a national radio star for a slide presentation, whatever that meant, and surely it would lead to more work.

Dennis, in what quickly became familiar surroundings, a recording studio, perhaps to narrate another slide presentation.

Dennis arrived at the studio and learned that this slide presentation was for a large corporation. He got some instructions from a producer, who clued him in to what a slide presentation was. He was told that he'd see a picture slide onto the screen in front of him. He'd read a marked section of his script, and when the bell rang, the picture would change. Dennis and the "big voice" would take turns reading the copy for each picture.

The big voice, in his own separate recording booth, went first. He read his part of the script, and then the bell sounded. Dennis started talking his way through a lengthy paragraph. When he reached the end, a bell sounded immediately and the picture changed.

Dennis thought, *Boy, that was a lot of copy, and I almost didn't finish it before the bell rang! I'd better talk faster.*

The big voice finished his slide, and Dennis started talking fast. He got it all in, *Just barely,* he thought, and the bell sounded again. The big voice took his turn, and the bell sounded. Dennis talked even faster. The big voice emerged from his booth.

"Young man!" he bellowed, "What are you doing?"

Dennis nervously stammered, "Well, that bell rings awfully soon each time."

The big voice was exasperated. "Young man, the bell rings when you stop talking!"

Dennis got the idea, and the rest of the presentation went smoothly . . . and slowly.

Dennis dreaded the idea of being committed to one skill and felt that the right way to approach a broadcasting career was to have as many irons in the proverbial fire as possible. DuMont's offer meant that he'd be doing a variety of programs. He'd be forced to learn multiple new skills on the job, and television was a skill that none of his more reticent peers would possess. How could he say "no"? He didn't.

Dennis became the first full-time on-air talent for DuMont in 1939. The New York World's Fair was happening that year. DuMont's rival, David Sarnoff, planned to use the fair to demonstrate television and officially begin regular television broadcasts on station W2XBS (now WNBC). Dr. DuMont followed suit, bringing five television sets to the fair to demonstrate television. Dennis even tagged along with him, a more natural salesman than the stilted scientist, Dennis helped put a friendly, personal face on DuMont's endeavors. He was DuMont's first on-air talent, and now, DuMont's first company-employed salesman. They were the first two of many "firsts" to come for Dennis.

CHAPTER TWO
SIGNING ON

TELEVISION HISTORY WAS happening on the 42nd floor of the DuMont Building on the corner of 53rd and Madison Avenue in New York City, in a 5-foot by 10-foot studio, barely large enough to qualify as a dining room in a small house, but just large enough to fill the 14-inch screen on a DuMont 180 model television set.

A camera fixed its view on a tiny elevator, as it ascended a 2-foot-tall model skyscraper. Dennis, standing in front of a faux-skyline that bore more than a passing resemblance to the standard-issue late night talk show sets of future decades, greeted whomever may have been looking in on that night's broadcast of *Television Roof.*

In later years, Dennis would refer to it as "Ed Sullivan without the acrobats." *Television Roof* (very briefly titled *Television Café*) was a variety show, which made sense. DuMont wanted to show off television's potential, and a variety of acts would certainly show a variety of possibilities.

The bulk of acts, though, were singers. That was a matter of practicality; they were the only ones who said yes. Singers all possessed a selection of songs they had already mastered and would lay out exactly what they were going to perform, so scripts weren't needed and rehearsals were minimal. Dennis, as a disc jockey, could use his radio connections as an incentive. When he moved from Jersey City to New York City to work for DuMont, he kept the promise he made himself to have multiple sources of experience. At the same time he was working for DuMont, he was at radio station WNEW for a disc jockey shift and another variety show. Although he was never interested in popular music—he mentally "tuned out" all the songs he played—he certainly knew that, as a disc jockey in America's top media market, he had something beneficial to offer potential guests for *Television Roof*. In lieu of pay, he could offer singers and musicians increased airplay on WNEW in exchange for an appearance on the program. The most attractive part of the offer to appear on an intimidating, untested medium was Dennis' repeated assurance to potential guests that nobody was watching.

That promise didn't sway everybody; even Dennis' former co-worker, Frank Sinatra, said no. A number of performers came on *Television Roof*, at least for practice, if not exposure. In 1939, there were only 300 television sets operating in New York City; there was no way to measure television audiences in that early stage. Between the more established programs available on radio and the experiments that NBC was conducting on the other functioning channel, and given that the earliest television sets sold to consumers were prone to breaking down periodically, Dennis estimated that the audience for *Television Roof* couldn't possibly have been more than 100 people. Still, he was as much in the business of selling television sets as he was in the business of hosting a television show. He took *Television Roof* seriously, and set out to present the best variety show possible—with no existing template for how to do that—in hopes of generating word of mouth about how interesting the new programs on this thing called television could be. His payday for that effort: $50 a week.

Dennis at the microphone for WNEW, his day job, while he and Dr. Dumont worked nights bringing television to life.

Exactly how long *Television Roof* lasted is difficult to determine. One source lists it as lasting only one year or so, but *The Billboard* (as the magazine was then known) was writing about recent episodes as late as the fall of 1943. The funny thing was that the term "variety show" hadn't occurred to anyone yet. *The Billboard* referred to *Television Roof* as "an experiment show."

It truly was an experiment in a few ways. *Television Roof* held a contest, which isn't usual now, but with so few televisions in use at that point, it was only a contest for DuMont employees. The winner, Trudy Wentz, got to be a guest announcer. Another employee, Lila Tirpak, appeared on the program because Allen DuMont went through the building one night and just asked employees point-blank if they could be on the show.

Because music was so heavily featured on the program, and because it was really the earliest forum for musical acts, it received regular attention from *The Billboard*, which, for a time, printed a weekly detailed recap of each episode, allowing us, decades later, to appreciate the program for what it was and what it offered. As time went by, more interest gathered in television, and in *Television Roof*. The program's scope broadened into a true variety show, although *Billboard*'s choice of words was perfectly apropos.

"The pie made from nine and twenty blackbirds had nothing on *Television Roof*, DuMont's weekly experimental show. At least that many persons of varied talent and experience have their fingers in the pie that they hope will someday be fit to set before a sponsor king. As a result of pooling time, talent, and technical skill on these programs, a satisfactory blend should evolve. Already improvements are evident and each week's previous mistake is eradicated. Not only are performers benefiting by their appearances before the cameras, but the directors are being developed from the ranks to aid in the shaping of future video shows." -Wanda Marvin, *The Billboard*

The August 4, 1943 episode included an employee from WNEW reviewing a book, including an interview with one of the book's subjects and even showing a short film related to the subject matter.

The September 15, 1943 program was a real spectrum: sportscaster Sam Taub showed some films of recent boxing matches and interviewed pugilist Harry Donovan about his career; Marian Ferrar and Lynn Russell, a Vaudeville team, demonstrated a new line of mending tape; The United States Marine Corps supplied a documentary short film about the South Pacific; Glorianne Lahr (daughter of Bert) made her television debut, performing sketch comedy and doing a few songs; a melodramatic sketch depicted the life of women whose men were overseas doing bombing expeditions (which, *The Billboard* noted, seemed awfully out of place); Sam Cuff wrapped up the program with maps of Europe and Asia, updating the audience on the recent progress made in World War II.

Chapter Two: Signing On

Dennis with *Television Roof* guest Lila Tirpak, who was booked for the show because she was a Dumont employee who happened to be in the building.

Television Roof unintentionally presented viewers with more than just a variety show. It gave viewers a chance to see the evolution of television as it was happening. Television was new for everybody, but DuMont's team had a particular learning curve: the company was run by scientists. They weren't businessmen and they weren't broadcasters, and with everybody still a little wary about television's potential—mainly, did it have any?—it was critically understaffed.

Dennis often started his workday by helping Dr. DuMont move packing cases and assorted clutter out of the studio until there was enough room to do the TV show. The facility was so tiny that when Fred Waring and His

Pennsylvanians, a popular Big Band at the time, were booked, some of the Pennsylvanians were sent home.

Then, there were the lights. Early television lights became the stuff of legend for pioneer broadcasters. Those who were brave enough to say "Me first," Dennis included, would never forget the 140° temperatures of the studios. The lights weren't spaced out in the studio, they were linked together in solid-state units, massive walls of bulbs that were blinding and overwhelming. It was akin to performing directly in front of the lights at a ballpark during a night game. It got so hot in the studio that even the most immaculately starched shirt collar was reduced to pulpy tissue by the end of a show. The make-up Dennis had to wear was a thick, dark brown spackle, a necessary evil while everybody searched for something better.

Small kinks had to be worked out program by program, and DuMont's team welcomed constructive criticism from all who offered. One review of *Television Roof* observed that female singers needed to be told not to wear light-colored blouses with dark skirts, because on the tiny black and white screens, the women appeared to be floating torsos. One critic noted how impressed he was one night when, at the conclusion of a singer's performance, the screen faded to black and the audio went silent, a conclusion that he said looked much better than the way the singers normally just nodded their heads and walked out of view of the camera at the end of a performance. The program's opening became more elaborate with more experience. The tiny elevator in the model skyscraper was now immediately followed by a film of Ted Flo Rito and His Orchestra performing in a club every week, creating a cabaret atmosphere for the viewers at home.

Dennis and his crew even came up with ways to make the straightforward act of introducing the performers a little bit more engaging. One night, Dennis was opening the program, when a pretty blonde interrupted him, eager to start performing. Dennis shooed her out, apologized for the disruption, and continued talking. At the start of the next act, a pretty blonde woman interrupted, again waiting to start her performance. Dennis shooed her out once more and continued the program. A few minutes later, a pretty blonde woman showed up, and Dennis got fed up, scolding her for her repeated intrusions. The pretty blonde insisted she had done no such thing, and revealed to the camera that "the pretty blonde" was actually three women, the lookalike McAuliff Sisters, who launched right into a song together.

Dennis on the tiny set of *Television Roof*, the medium's first variety show.

Dennis was doing more than *Television Roof* for DuMont. That 1800s magazine drawing's prognostication of a sporting event being shown on a screen over a fireplace was about to become reality: sporting events were about to make their way to television. Sports and television were practically made for each other, especially in those early days. Again, Dr. DuMont was looking for cost-effective programming, for the sake of just having *something* on the screen. Sports events were already taking place anyway, so no coordination was necessary on DuMont's end. The events certainly didn't require expensive sets, scripts, or rehearsals. You didn't even have to pay the athletes! Sports were the way to go.

"Television play-by-play commentator" is a strange trade when one thinks about it long enough. Sports on radio obviously required a play-by-play commentator, but a television viewer can see the action, so why is it also necessary for a voice to describe it? As Dennis explained later, when sports made the jump to television, play-by-play commentary was created because the feeling was the sports audience was so accustomed to hearing a voice that, if one wasn't describing the action, television viewers would think there was something wrong with their set.

Dennis provided commentary for the first boxing match ever on television, an outdoor fight held at a nearby field. He called the play-by-play live at the scene taking place atop the DuMont Building's roof. He followed all of the action through binoculars, while the camera situated next to him zoomed in as close as it could. Dennis laughed at himself and the rest of the DuMont crew as he remembered the event years later. To his own amusement and amazement, it simply did not occur to anybody at DuMont to run audio cables down to ringside so Dennis could cover the fight up close.

That same primitive technique was put to use for area football games. In the dead of winter, Dennis and the crew stood on the roof for the entire game to cover the action, including one horrible day when a blizzard struck the city. The skies became dark early that day, and the wind blew the snow right in Dennis' line of sight. He was calling play-by-play for a football game that he couldn't see.

To drum up some interest for televised sports, DuMont, in 1939, devised a second weekly program for Dennis to host, *Dennis James' Sports Parade*. The premise was that each week, Dennis would interview a professional athlete, and then take a lesson in the sport. If there was a basketball player, Dennis would shoot hoops for a few minutes. If a golfer was on the program, Dennis would putt a round.

Like *Television Roof* and its promise of increased radio airplay, *Dennis James' Sports Parade* was made possible through a promise that no one was watching, plus a little something in return. "Increased airplay" didn't mean anything to an athlete, obviously, but "free dinner" certainly did. It was a pledge that Dennis dreaded fulfilling. As he quickly found out, pro athletes could certainly put away a meal.

On one nightmarish evening, Dennis' guest was a professional wrestler, Man Mountain Dean. That evening's *Sports Parade* went rather well, but Dennis was horrified to learn after the program that Dean had eagerly told some of the other boys in the locker room about the TV show that paid for dinner—and they tagged along for the night. Dennis found himself buying dinner for nine large, hungry professional wrestlers, coughing up a bill that came to about $145, at a time when Dennis was only making $100 a week.

The skyline of New York adorns the set of a TV show for perhaps the first time. *Television Roof* established what would be a very familiar look for variety shows for years to come.

Professional wrestling gave Dennis more trouble on another week, when his guest was Bibber McCoy, a former Coast Guard Chief Petty Officer-turned-grappler, whom Dennis asked to apply a hold on him, so Dennis could see what it felt like. Professional wrestlers at that time operated under a code of conduct of sorts, called "kayfabe." Professional wrestling had been more spectacle than sport since shortly after the Civil War; ex-soldiers staged matches against each other in a town, allowing people to place bets on the favorite, wrestling a match where the underdog won, and then left town with all the money. "Kayfabe" basically meant that they never broke character; they were always "on," always acted as if they were fighting their next match to win, and that they had to make outsiders respect the sport by being as tough as they appeared. If a wrestler got into a bar fight on his off-time, a promoter probably wouldn't fire him for that, but if the wrestler lost that fight, for sure he'd be canned.

That last detail was important; they had to be truly tough and make sure that outsiders truly believed they were tough. When Dennis asked him to apply a hold, Bibber was duty-bound to really lock on that hold. Bibber applied a sleeper hold. Resembling a choke, a sleeper hold involves wrapping an arm around the neck of an opponent and applying pressure with a forearm, not on the throat, but on the side of the neck, where the carotid artery is located. Blood flow to the brain is cut off, and the opponent loses consciousness.

That's exactly what happened to Dennis. He passed right out in Bibber's arms. Bibber released the hold and Dennis crashed to the floor. The hold was so effective that Dennis didn't regain consciousness for fifteen minutes. The tiny audience tuning in just saw the camera fixed on Dennis, eyes shut, motionless, for fifteen minutes. Bibber tried bringing him around by shaking and slapping him, but when that proved ineffective, he gave Dennis a hard sock in the jaw, and that finally brought him around. Dennis, dazed and foggy, simply stood up, dusted himself off, and continued the program.

(In 1985, almost exactly the same incident occurred on Richard Belzer's talk show, *Hot Properties*, when he welcomed guest Hulk Hogan. Hogan demonstrated a front facelock, Belzer passed out, collapsed to the floor, and wounded the back of his head on impact. Belzer later filed a $5 million lawsuit, eventually collecting about $400,000 on settlement.)

In the early 1940s, filing a lawsuit never occurred to Dennis. He simply took the occasional passing out or punch in the face as an on-the-job hazard, one that just came with the territory. Perhaps even more remarkable was that the average broadcaster, after enduring such an incident, would probably have quietly thought to himself, *No more wrestling for me,* but Dennis went right back and stuck around for a while.

CHAPTER THREE
SECTION 8, CHANNEL 5

JULY 1, 1941 was a banner day for the television industry: The Federal Communications Commission (formerly the Federal Radio Commission) had set July 1 as the date when commercial television broadcasting could legally begin in the United States. Effectively, anybody who had a license to operate a television station could now use it for profit. The phrase "television experiment" was now "television business" and "television industry."

The party was interrupted fairly quickly. Five months later, on December 7, 1941, Japan attacked Pearl Harbor, and America entered World War II. The following month, President Franklin Roosevelt established the War Production Board, which was in charge of converting various industries from consumer needs to war effort needs. On April 1, 1942, the War Production Board issued a ban on further production of television sets for the home.

This didn't totally wreck television, of course. Commercial broadcasting could proceed as usual, but with many able-bodied men in the industry entering the war effort, and with the government's order meaning that television legally could not continue growing and expanding, the medium's progress seemed to freeze in place for the next three years. Low-frills experimental programming and filler material dominated the airwaves for the few hours a day that a station was on the air.

Dennis was drafted into the United States Army, formally joining on September 16, 1943, and getting stationed to a post in Texas, near the Gulf of Mexico. For years after, he bragged with a wink that "No Nazi war plane ever made it into Texas on my watch!"

At the time that Dennis entered the Army, he had been dating a young woman from New Jersey named Marion Greene. The courtship hadn't lasted very long, when they both decided that before Dennis left New York, they should get married. They tied the knot, but aside from the occasional weekend furlough, they wouldn't see each other again for two years.

With well-established credentials in television and radio, Dennis was immediately moved to Special Services, a division of the Army in charge of morale for the troops; specifically, organizing variety shows, something Dennis had already been doing for four years. Dennis would tour Army units around the country with a regular group of co-stars and some visiting celebrity guest stars.

He was in a mess hall one day eating with other troops, when another member of the unit began acting up at the table. All of his clowning around got the rest of the table's attention. The soldier sitting next to him, referencing a category of discharge from the military for mental unfitness, said, "You're a Section Eight!"

Dennis chimed in and said, "And the worst part is he's sitting with us in the first row!"

The light bulb flickered, and everybody pitched in to write a show called *First Row, Section Eight*. Dennis followed that one with *Sixteen Whacks and a WAC*, a sketch comedy show starring almost entirely men plus one woman. That was Dennis' main contribution to the war effort. He never saw active combat, except for the nights when he was put in charge of roaming from bar to bar in the area until he found actor/singer Sonny Tufts and dragging him back to the show.

What did you do in the war? Dennis and his co-stars cut up during a performance of *First Row, Section Eight*.

Dennis was honorably discharged in 1945 and was briefly reunited with

Marion and their infant son, Dennis Jr. He wanted to get his wife and son relocated to New York as fast as possible, so he went on the hunt for a new apartment.

Dennis later told the story of how he found a place. "Again, television was responsible. I sublet from a young couple who went along as entertainers with the RCA Jeep unit—the television demonstration outfit which my brother, Lou Sposa, who is a director, took out on tour. The apartment was a 5th-floor walk-up, $50 rent a month, at 35 West Fifty-Second Street."

The problem was that when it was time to return to New York, Marion didn't want to go back. She had been living with her mother and grandmother from the time that she became pregnant and found the arrangement comfortable. Dennis found an apartment in New York City suitable for a family of three, but Marion was unhappy and after an extremely brief stay, she returned home to her mother, taking Dennis Jr. with her. They remained separated until 1951, when Dennis finally filed for divorce on grounds of abandonment.

Abandonment was more than a legal term in this case; it was exactly what he was feeling. Before World War II, he was a successful and active performer, who made his living by experimenting. Now, he was in a family-sized apartment all by himself.

He remembered, "New York can be kind of a lonesome town, even when you think you know it. I was then chasing down every announcing job, commercial, or serial acting role I could find, trying to get re-established. Between times, I'd sit out on the stoop and look up and down that street. To the right were the swing joints. To the left was the fabulous and expensive Twenty-One Club. I'd wonder what New York held for me—which direction I'd be going."

At the end of 1945, Dennis had some justifiable trepidation about his future. Certainly, in the years he was gone, other people were covering the disc jockey shifts and hosting the variety shows. Dennis remembered years later that he was actually in quite a hurry to get back home. New York and

New Jersey didn't stop moving without him, and he returned to the area feeling that he needed to get caught up. If Dennis returned to civilian life with any fear at all of not being able to pick up where he left off, it was unfounded. World War II ended in the fall of 1945, the War Production Board quite logically was dissolved, and that meant the TV business was going to pick up where they left off. 1946 would be one of the busiest years of his life.

Dennis went from being a man in uniform to playing one on TV for his first TV job after World War II.

To start 1946, Dennis made history yet again, appearing in the first of what would now be known as an infomercial. A company called Wedgewood China had paid a local station in New York for a full 30-minute TV slot for promoting their new lines of plates and silverware. It was a little different in one sense from what we now think of as an infomercial; for one thing, it was written as a play.

Dennis elaborated later, "The whole half hour was a commercial and I starred as a soldier. The soldier was coming home from the war and he had seen Wedgewood china, and he was describing the Wedgewood china. A very interesting thing happened—they were going to run a piece of film on how the china is made from mud, and the film chain broke. They gave me a 'stretch' [signal] because everything was live, and I just kept on talking about mud. How they handle the mud in England and how they took this mud and developed it and how you were going to see it in a moment. I went on about mud for three and one-half minutes and I got an extra $25 for that."

DuMont welcomed back its former employee with ever-expanding arms. Dr. DuMont had continued conducting experiments and growing his budding television business despite the war. In 1944, his experimental New York station, W2XWV, was rechristened with call letters WABD (naming the station with his initials). Just before the end of the war, DuMont established a second experimental TV station, W3XWT, in Washington, DC.

DuMont's staff began experimenting with coaxial cable, hooking up the two stations and finding that they were capable of airing the same program across multiple stations—in other words, finding that they were capable of forming a television network. W3XWT was quickly renamed WTTG (after DuMont's chief engineer, Thomas T. Goldsmith), and plans were made for DuMont Network to begin commercial operations in the summer of 1946.

In preparation, DuMont continued doing experimental broadcasts and tinkering with assorted concepts for new shows. One new idea they were looking at was game shows, or "giveaway shows," as they were known at that point. Game/Giveaway shows were a fairly new concept in network broadcasting at that point. Local games had been a staple for stations from radio's earliest days, but national giveaway shows had only been around for about a decade. They were virtually always well-received, and in 1946, their popularity on radio exploded.

Chapter Three: Section 8, Channel 5

The speculative reasoning for the sudden boom was that Americans had sacrificed so much for the war effort, rationing gasoline, donating toys and appliances for scrap metal drives, and generally finding ways to do more with less, holding back on luxuries until the battle was finished. By 1946, with the war finally over and things going back to normal, numerous businesses and manufacturers needed to get the word out that goods were flowing and available for purchase again. Lavishing piles of goodies on happy people as a reward for winning a game was an easy way to spread that message, not to mention a thoroughly entertaining one. Giveaway shows were "in" in 1946.

CBS had already beaten DuMont to the punch for the historic footnote of airing the first TV game shows. On July 1, 1941, that day when commercial broadcasting officially began, a popular radio giveaway, *Truth or Consequences*, aired a special one-time-only television broadcast on WCBW, the CBS television station in New York. That same day, WCBW unveiled a prime-time game that would stick around for about a year and a half: *CBS Television Quiz*, in which host Gil Fates played a series of games with "contestants" who really weren't contestants; they were just a handful of Fates' friends who were able to come in that night.

DuMont, however, managed to land one first that CBS hadn't accomplished in due time. On May 29, 1946, as a one-time experiment, DuMont aired a special called *DuMont Beepstakes*, an odd program that pitted DuMont Network executives against each other in a game designed to resemble a car race. The executives were seated at large model cars, and their progress as they played the game was tracked by having their cars advance forward. The host of *DuMont Beepstakes* was—who else—Dennis James.

Three weeks later, WABD introduced its first regularly scheduled game show, *Cash and Carry*. The program was the brainchild of a producer named Art Stark. WABD didn't look very far for a host; Dennis James was already there.

Dennis minded the store for *Cash and Carry*.

Much like the infomercial that played out like a drama, *Cash and Carry* was a game show that looked like something else at first sight. The set was a grocery store. Dennis didn't wear a suit; he was decked out in an apron and a plaid button-down shirt; he was billed not as the host, but as the "store manager."

The shelves of the *Cash and Carry* supermarket were lined with rows and rows of sponsor Libby's food products. A contestant was asked to select one item from the shelf; each had a question and a dollar value attached; it could be $5, $10, or $15; a correct answer earned the money. In order to take fullest advantage of television's possibilities, all of the questions were visual questions. Even the show's closing credits were done in an eye-catching manner; the camera pulled out and viewers saw the "store" from seemingly outdoors, through a soaped-up window. A finger would pop up and write out a good-night message across the window.

Photos from Dennis' personal collection reveal that the show was a lot more involved than just questions and answers; all sorts of physical stunts and odd activities were woven into each episode. Contestants might have to balance something on their head during the game, or have to paint something on a bald man's head. For one game, two contestants were given baseball bats and had to use them to bust a floating helium balloon. For another game, bunches of grapes were hung from lines over the contestants' heads. The contestants had to eat all the grapes without using their hands or removing the grapes from the line. For a truly elaborate Country/Western-themed program, contestants even rode a mechanical bull.

The Billboard was looking in closely on DuMont's newest television project, and, as with the paper's week-by-week reviews of *Television Roof* a few years earlier, someone at *The Billboard* was interested in watching *Cash and Carry* just to see how the show would evolve from week to week.

On June 29, *The Billboard* said, "[*Cash and Carry*] is at least several hundred percent better than their first try, *Beepstakes*. All the questions were visual. Check. There was plenty of action in the answering of the questions. Check. However, less movement behind the store counter and more in full view of the audience would have helped. All the audience participation as before the camera, which is a negative since the folks at home should be keyed into the show... The members of the audience were really great fun this trip. That's a bit dangerous depending on the 'suckers' to supply all the humor. Dennis James, the emcee-storekeeper still doesn't know how to relax... Still, he had the show moving along at a rapid pace and there was no pause for empty reflection. Give him this vehicle week after week, and in no time flat he'll be as good as the best of them. He's clean cut and when he eases up, he'll be okay."

On July 20, *The Billboard* printed a second opinion, under the heading "Second Viewing." At that time, *The Billboard* said, "*Cash and Carry* has corrected most of its errors and it's now as good a visual audience participation seg [segment] as is being scanned on any of the metropolitan New York stations. Dennis James, the country grocer, doesn't punch anymore . . . That's progress, man!"

How far we've come. The pioneer television performers, like Dennis, had to face a blinding wall of lights for every broadcast for viewers to see the picture adequately.

Even as television was beginning to grow, the program still had a freewheeling, "Nobody is looking" spirit to it. Adding to that atmosphere were the practical jokes that the crew frequently played on Dennis during the show. It began with the August 29, 1946 episode, when Dennis got the idea to do a bit that would involve climbing into a bathtub for the start of the program. It was only when Dennis was in and it was too late to back out that he discovered that the crew had dumped about 4,000 ice cubes in the tub. That seemed to get the practical joke ball rolling for everyone on the show. Dennis later explained the evolution—and eventual demise—of the gags.

Chapter Three: Section 8, Channel 5

"It started on a day when I pretended to be late and the camera discovered me in a bubble bath. Then that fiendishly ingenious crew started to ad-lib. Every time I went on set, I knew I was due for a horror. One day they equipped a cash register with a spring strong enough to raise a bridge. When I opened it, the whole drawer shot across the stage. Another time, when I was sure I was safe, they used their electronic skill to wire a barber chair. The electric shock they gave me made me jump almost into the camera. But, the day the sandbags dropped within two inches of me, I laid down the law. I said 'Sure, your aim was good. Sure you missed me. But how did you know I wasn't going to move?'"

Dennis had a surprisingly easier time maintaining his sense of humor after a much more upsetting incident one night. Dennis and the contestant played the game, Dennis signed off, walked out of the studio smiling, and discovered that his car had been stolen while he was on the air. When an industry paper, *Radio Daily*, asked him about the incident, Dennis told him that his car was "a heap"; he was actually far more upset because he had stopped at a liquor store before the show that night, and his expensive bottles of Haig and Haig scotch were still in the backseat.

Audiences in New York liked the show well enough that when the DuMont Network formally launched on August 15, 1946, it stayed right where it was on Thursday night and ended up on the network. *Cash and Carry* became the first network television game show, and along with it, Dennis became the first network game show host.

The audience in Washington, DC took a liking to *Cash and Carry* as quickly as the New York audience was, and with DuMont always lagging behind NBC and CBS in terms of finances, they saw *Cash and Carry* as a potential solution to the problem . . . if the audience didn't mind.

In September, DuMont made a plea to viewers to write in and give them feedback. *Cash and Carry* did have a sponsor, Libby's, with Libby's products and the Libby's logo prominently visible on the set; but DuMont wanted viewers to let them how they would feel if *Cash and Carry* occasionally paused the game and cut away to messages from other sponsors; in other words, asking if it was okay to air commercial breaks during a television program. Only 148 viewers wrote in, but absolutely all of them granted permission, and suddenly DuMont had a new revenue source that they could explore.

What kind of game show is this? A look at some of the silliness that contestants—and Dennis—were subjected to on *Cash and Carry*.

Television was still so new that 148 was a reasonable sample size for such a survey. In fact, to give an idea of how small the viewing audience was in 1946, a regular feature of *Cash and Carry* (airing in prime time, mind you) was a guessing game involving a barrel. A large barrel with a question mark painted on it adorned the set, and every week, there was something hidden underneath it. Dennis announced a phone number for viewers to call in, and guess what was under the barrel? The first caller to solve the mystery won $5.

A New York man named Harry Dubin won almost every contest. He remembered later that the phone was never busy when he was called, and it finally got to a point that Dennis invited him to the studio and had him walk out and take a bow for the cameras on an episode of *Cash and Carry*.

Cash and Carry had a small audience, but then, so did everything at that point. The next few years would be crucial years for television, and Dennis, a tiny performing venue, and some larger-than-life personalities filling it, would play a role in ensuring the medium's success.

CHAPTER FOUR
THE RINGMASTER

DESPITE ALL THE progress Dennis was making in television, and despite the progress that he medium itself had made, Dennis was adamant about having as much work as possible, and continued fervently pursuing radio gigs even as more and more signs piled up that television was the way of the future.

In 1947, he served as announcer for an unusual radio show called *Lawyer Q*, an unusual fusion of drama, educational program, and game show. Twelve audience members were selected to serve as "jury" for a dramatized version of a case taken from actual court records. A regular cast, including actors Karl Swenson, Joseph Julian, Eleanor Audley, and Neil O'Malley, acted out the trial on each show. Afterward, the jury deliberated and issued their verdict. Interspersed with all this drama were time-outs for Dennis, assisted by an expert identified only as Lawyer Q (Malcolm Esterlin, a New York attorney) to explain bits of legal jargon, like a detailed explanation of the difference between slander and libel, or laying out semantics debates that frequently come up in trials—for example, is the statement "I can't live without you" inherently a marriage proposal? There was even a game segment in which audience members were quizzed about particulars of the law. At the end of the show, the audience-assembled jury announced their verdict, and they split a $60 cash prize if their verdict matched the verdict handed down in the actual trial. To put things in perspective, this was a full decade before the first version of *Divorce Court* premiered, and thirty-five years before *The People's Court* turned "courtroom shows" into a genre all their own. The show was produced and directed by Aaron Steiner. He and Dennis hit it off so well that Steiner became his personal manager after the series ended.

In July 1947, Dennis took over hosting chores for another radio show, *Can You Top This?*, an improvisational comedy show that predated *Whose Line is It Anyway* by several decades. "Senator" Ed Ford, an old Vaudeville comic, had previously been a panelist on a radio game called *Stop Me If You've Heard This One*, hosted by Milton Berle. Home listeners mailed in old jokes, and the comics on the panel interrupted and finished if any of them recognized the joke. Ford and his fellow comics had heard so many jokes and written so many of their own over the course of their careers that he conjured up *Can You Top This?* to show off what he and his friends were capable of.

Dennis introduced a joke mailed in by a home listener, and then announced the general subject of the joke. The panelists—usually Ford, cartoonist/writer Harry Hershfield, and actor/monologist Joe Laurie Jr.—had to tell a different joke about the same subject. All the laughs were measured on the Colgate-Palmolive Laugh Meter, and the home listener won a small prize for every panelist who failed to get a bigger laugh than the original joke.

Dennis did some reporting for DuMont, including what he later recalled as his saddest assignment: in the fall of 1947, many of the casualties from World War II were finally returned to the United States for proper burial. Dennis recalled that it was the only time in his career that he really couldn't think of anything to say. "I couldn't even say what a beautiful day it was, because it wasn't beautiful for those six hundred who couldn't see it."

He's got this. With time and experience accumulating, Dennis relaxed a little bit during some jobs.

Dennis also became the live reporter on the scene for ABC Radio with coverage of the New York premieres of major motion pictures. In the late 1940s, television was still regarded as "the enemy" in the film business. That attitude didn't really start to change until 1950, when a few of the smaller film studios began selling off their low-budget B-westerns to local stations and it was discovered that movies and TV were a perfect fit. For the moment, though, the film industry avoided TV, but liked radio just fine. Dennis and actress Anne Jeffreys were ABC Radio's correspondents, walking the red carpet and getting a word with the stars as they entered the theater.

If Dennis on radio and Dennis on television wasn't quite good enough, people could go down to their local movie house for Dennis before the feature presentation. Dennis was one of a number of voices heard on the newsreels that gave audiences their earliest chances to *see* the news instead of just reading it or listening to it. Paramount News was a weekly round-up of top stories assembled by the movie studio, with a variety of narrators assigned to different categories. Dennis was Paramount's go-to man for sports coverage and light news. He covered the 1949 Cleveland Indians, the invention of the world's smallest working automobile (it ran on an engine the size of a matchbox), the Daytona Motorcycle Derby, ski conditions in Alberta, and the retirement of Joe Louis.

"Joe Louis, longest-reigning monarch in heavyweight boxing history! Joe Louis, the fighter with an atomic bomb in each fist, retires undefeated just shy of his thirty-fifth birthday! He makes official a statement on his retirement. Acclaimed by his race and by legions of sports followers, the Bomber rolls from sharecropper days in Alabama and Detroit slums to fistic greatness! From 1934, when his professional career began, Joe's lethal fists rapidly carried him up the pugilistic ladder! In June of '37, he KO'ed champion Jimmy Braddock. Only 23, he became the youngest fighter ever to win the heavyweight title! And Louis went on to defend the championship more times than anyone else before him! Twenty-five bouts . . . twenty-one KO's."

On March 28, 1948, DuMont was finally secure enough with its remote broadcasting capabilities to venture completely outside for an event. Dennis, decked out in a top hat and tails, hosted DuMont's first live broadcast of a parade, specifically, the Easter parade, taking place that year a scant two months before the Fred Astaire/Judy Garland musical was released.

In 1948, Dennis was part of yet another first, television's first coverage of a political convention. He was on the floor during the Democratic National Convention in Baltimore, as President Harry Truman secured the nomination for his own first term. He would defeat Thomas Dewey and Strom Thurmond that November in one of the biggest upsets in American election history.

Because of television's limited resources, sports were still the preferred programming of choice. Again, no scripts, no actors, no rehearsals. Dennis sought to capitalize on that himself by reviving his *Sports Parade* concept from the late 1930s. He called the new program *Sports Den*, but it contained the same elements: an interview with a sports star followed by a detailed demonstration of their specialty. Dennis offered it to local stations as a syndicated program. Local stations that needed to fill the broadcast day could have a show, and Dennis could provide them with a format that cost next-to-nothing to produce.

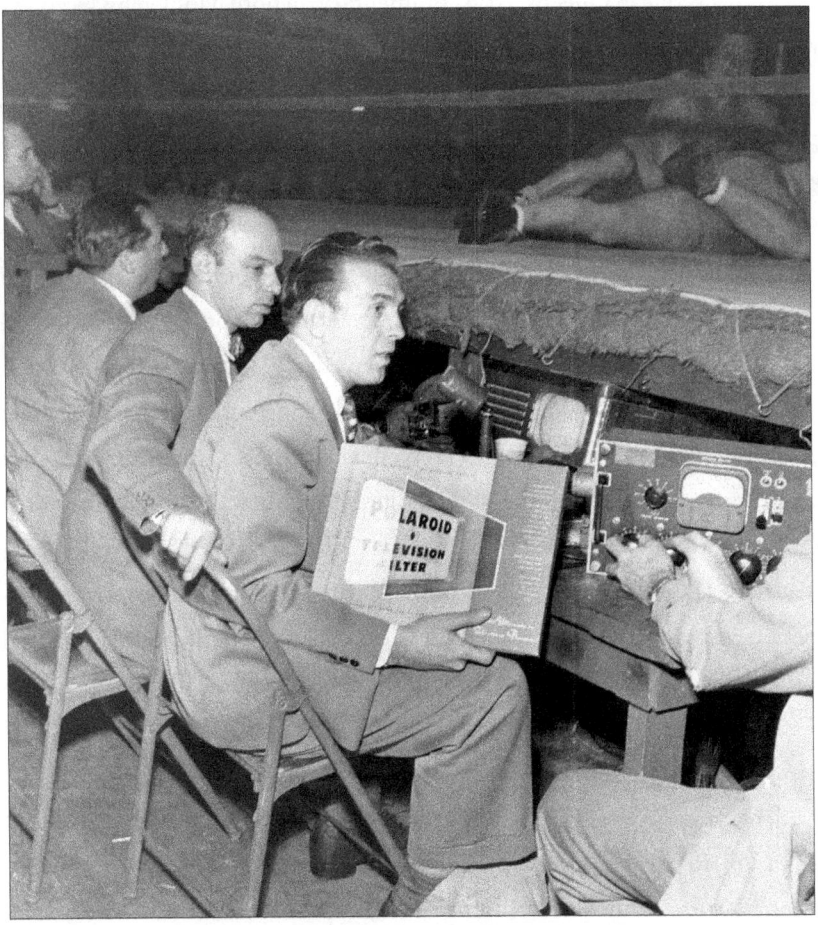

The best friend Mother ever had in professional wrestling.
Dennis called the action live from ringside.

For sheer cost-effectiveness in television, though, two sports seemed more ideal than the rest: wrestling and boxing. Both were indoor sports, which meant the events weren't at the whims of weather and they could be lit with the same studio lights as other programs. Even better, a ring was considerably smaller than a 100-yard field; wrestling and boxing only required one camera. In fall 1948, the DuMont Network weekly line-up included *Boxing from Jamaica Arena* and *Wrestling from Jamaica Arena*, both emanating from a venue in Queens, with commentary on both handled by, as you've probably guessed, Dennis James.

While boxing was fundamentally the same sport it had always been, professional wrestling had undergone an impressive metamorphosis in the previous sixty years. Just before the turn of the century, master showman P.T. Barnum had begun including wrestling matches in his circus tents. He had his wrestlers dress outlandishly in eye-catching outfits that they would shed just before the bell, and Barnum began concocting sideshow-like names and fictitious biographies for his wrestlers. Hiram and Barney Davis of Connecticut, for example, became Waino and Plutanor, the Wild Men of Borneo. Barnum's contests were fixed as a means of generating interest in future rematches with the same competitors. It was the dawn of what the world came to think of as professional wrestling. In the ensuing years, wrestling's popularity ebbed and flowed. In 1930s, a drunk sportswriter accidentally published the results of the next day's matches, and wrestling fell out of favor. Unlike other sports, which were thriving on radio, wrestling on the radio never really attracted an audience. The problem with professional wrestling was that you really *had* to see it.

That was the world Dennis found himself thrust into, when Dr. DuMont asked him to provide commentary for his new batch of weekly sports events. Dennis agreed while quietly hiding a handicap from his boss: he knew *nothing* about wrestling. Feeling the need to familiarize himself, Dennis got a ticket and headed to an arena to watch professional wrestling for the first time. Over the next few hours, Dennis was gobsmacked by the outlandish characters, their costumes, their wild-eyed, raucous behavior, the way that they flew around the ring for what was supposed to be a fight. He was expected to take this stuff seriously?

Wrestling from Jamaica Arena hit the airwaves in 1948, and Dennis James' unique approach to commentary not only solved his own problems, it proved to solve professional wrestling's problems, too. It had never experienced the kind of popularity that it would enjoy with Dennis James behind the mike.

As he later explained, "I bought a book. It was written by Frank Gotch, the Jack Dempsey of wrestling, and thank heaven, it was well-illustrated. I'd sit at ringside thumbing through the pages. When I found a hold on the mat which matched the picture in the book, I named it."

This didn't completely solve the problem. Dennis could only call the holds, he couldn't really elaborate on what the holds did, how it affected the match, or any other details. He just said, "That's a hammerlock . . . that's a wristlock . . . that's a clothesline." If any wrestling fans were tuning into the program, Dennis was only telling them what they already knew. It would be the same as a football commentator saying, "That's a tackle, that's a touchdown." Your audience *knows* that. Why are you telling them?

Dennis, being a fan of other sports himself, knew how irritating he'd find it if he was listening to a sportscaster who was just saying what he already knew, so he came up with a clever way of disguising his inexperience. He began talking to "Mother."

"Okay, Mother, this is a hammerlock. All right, now, Mom, do you see that? He's applying a stepover toehold."

Dennis had truly given this some thought. The television sets in bars were being watched mostly by men. They didn't need to be told anything about wrestling, but sets were starting to make their way into family homes. If the set was tuned to wrestling, it was almost certainly tuned there by the man of the house. If he was a married man, and this was after all, a nighttime program, his wife had to be in the room with him, looking on curiously. She had probably never seen wrestling in her life.

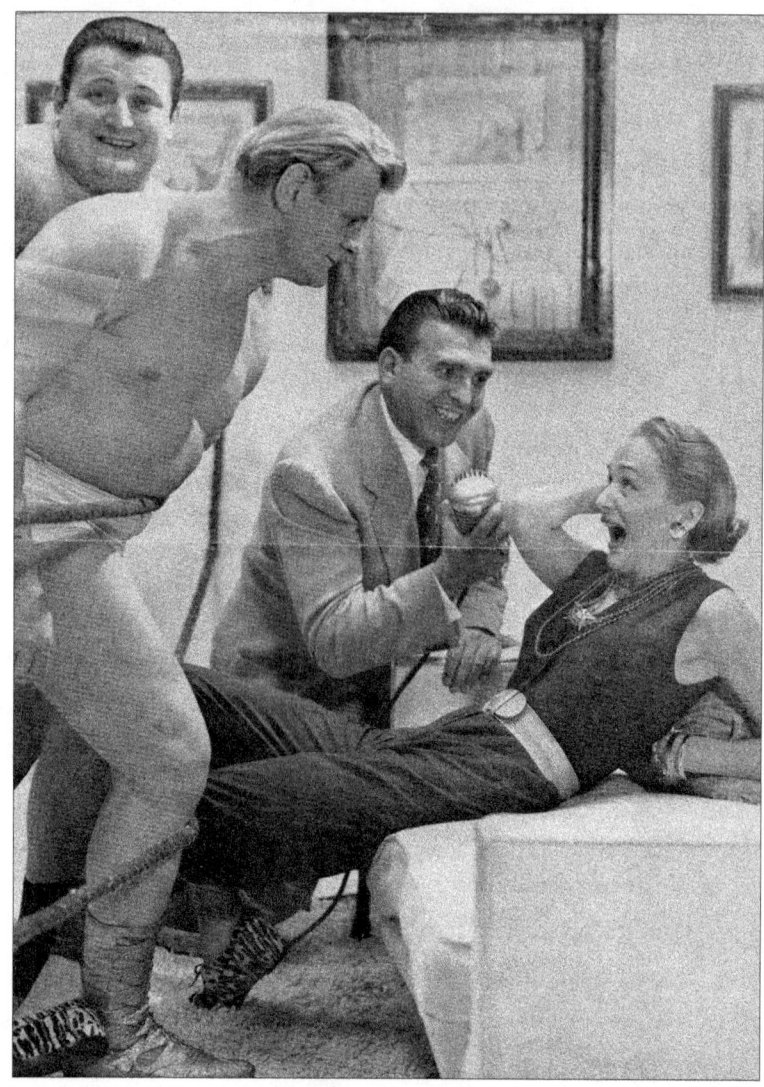

Grapplers Tarzan Hewett and Gene Stanlee helped Dennis pay a weekly visit to "Mother." Hewett actually had an acrimonious relationship with Dennis during wrestling's early days on television, but changed his mind when he saw the impact that the commentary would have on the wrestling business.

Chapter Four: The Ringmaster

If she was going to be stuck watching this alien activity on the screen in her living room, Dennis reasoned that he could give her all the help he could and she'd never know that he was just as clueless as she was about what was going on. As a nice bonus, Dennis figured the missus would turn to her husband after Dennis called a particularly esoteric hold, like an Argentine leg lock or a cross-face chicken wing, and ask, "Honey, is that right?" Husband would get a *little* bit of a confidence boost by nodding his head and saying "Of course."

Dennis, with a salesman's mind, reasoned that women had to like wrestling. Two and three television sets in most homes would one day become commonplace, but in the late 1940s, if there was a set in the house at all, there was only one. If a husband and wife couldn't agree on what to watch, television was going to make married life miserable, so Dennis did everything he could to make women enjoy wrestling.

There was also the issue of Dennis not being able to take it seriously. The Red Devil stepped in the ring wearing a stocking cap stuffed with "horns." Hairy The Ape came to the ring in a cage. When it was declared that Hairy the Ape was too wild to wrestle in one town in New Jersey and got himself barred, he snuck into town under a hood, calling himself The Masked Marvel. Repulsive Rogan, covered with tattoos, had a dancing girl who gyrated for his pleasure as he wrestled. The showmanship was so transparent to Dennis, and he was no actor, at least, not enough of an actor that he felt he could pull it off if he tried to portray it as a legitimate sporting event. So he had a little fun with it.

He brought some accessories to ringside and added sound effects to the matches. He brought a dog toy called a crackle bone, and when one wrestler twisted his opponent's limb, Dennis bent the crackle bone, causing a painful-sounding snap. When a wrestler cheated by grabbing his opponent's tights for leverage, Dennis ripped a lampshade. For a wishbone or any other hold that involved stretching a leg, he turned a ratchet wheel. Rubbing an inflated balloon made just the right noise for anything involving contact with the chest. When a wrestler did a ribcage-crunching move like an avalanche or a bear hug, he collapsed a small strawberry box. When a wrestler went airborne for a move and came crashing down, the audience heard a slide whistle. It looked like a wrestling match, but with him at the microphone, it sounded more like Looney Tunes.

Dennis and his crackle bone amplify the action on Dumont's wrestling broadcasts.

Chapter Four: The Ringmaster

If Dennis wasn't adding sound effects, he was doing little things mainly to amuse himself. As a challenge one night, he called an entire match in rhymes. "They're out of the ring and now they're back, and when they go, two heads will crack!"

A simpler rhyme became a catch phrase throughout the nation. Instead of saying "wrestling," Dennis often introduced the program as "Grunts, groans, and cracking bones."

On one evening, a second camera stationed on the roof got a beautiful shot of the night sky. Dennis had the director superimpose the shot of the ring onto the zoomed-in shot from the outdoor camera. The wrestlers in the ring had no idea that they were competing on the surface of the moon.

During another show in a sold-out arena, Dennis became aware of a young woman watching the matches while perched on a fire escape. He told the director to superimpose a shot of him on a shot of the woman. The viewers saw him apparently seated on the fire escape and carrying on a chat with a woman who wouldn't talk to him.

In between matches, Dennis conducted extended interviews with the fans at ringside. A number of devoted fans turned up week after week and became just as familiar to the viewers as the grapplers. A number of the men in Queens were unusually debonair Nathan Detroit types in their best suits and fedoras for the evening. Dennis developed a rapport with them and even a running gag: when somebody complimented Dennis' tie, he took it right off and handed it to the guy. (Spotting a chance at some great free advertising, a local clothier furnished him with as many neckties as he needed.) The shtick earned him the title "Mr. Tele-Tie of 1950" from the National Tie Institute, an organization that actually existed.

The women were plainer-looking but made up for it with sheer animation, springing to life when a heel—the bad guy in the match—got away with something behind the referee's back, screaming bloody murder and shaking her fists.

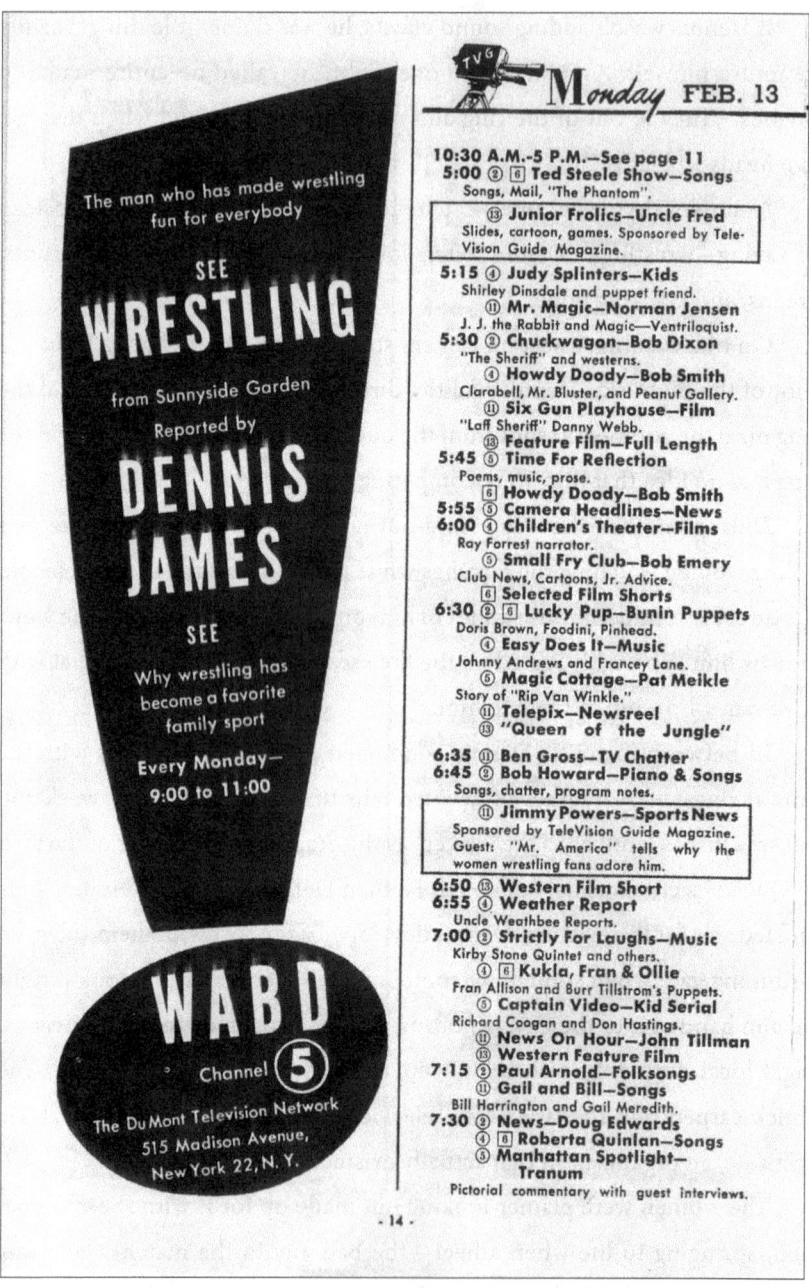

The more things change. Even in 1950, Monday night was wrestling night on American television.

Chapter Four: The Ringmaster

Among the colorful congregation was one little old lady who stood out from all the rest: "Hatpin Mary," as Dennis dubbed her. When she saw a wrestler she couldn't stand, she'd sneak up to ringside, remove the decorative pin from her hat, and give him a prod in his posterior. The wrestlers put on a show of complaining heartily, but the truth is, they tolerated Hatpin Mary because in front of a national audience, a jab in the keister was practically a seal of approval. If Hatpin Mary hated you, you *must* be somebody important.

Dennis' smirking, sideways approach to covering professional wrestling wasn't totally appreciated by the combatants he was covering. They were tough guys (as strange as it sounds in a predetermined sport, legitimate tough guys have always been preferred by the pro wrestling business; they could "protect the business" if, say, a crazed fan tried to prove himself with a sneak attack) and they didn't appreciate being treated like punch lines to Dennis' joke.

Chief among Dennis' detractors were the Garibaldi family: Gino, Chick, Tony, Joe, and Ralph, five Italian-American brothers who were among the last of the old school, the men who broke into the business on the grounds of pure wrestling technique and toughness, just before P.T. Barnum's showmanship strategy became standard operating procedure.

They hated Dennis, but only until the night when Gino's twenty-year-old son (and tag team partner), Leo, was rushed to the hospital, having apparently developed polio. While the Garibaldis waited at the hospital to get the prognosis, Dennis went on the air that night, briefed the audience on what had happened, and led the fans in the Jamaica Arena in a prayer for the boy's health. Leo recovered, and from that day forward, in the eyes of the Garibaldi family, Dennis James could do no wrong.

This didn't make all of the old guard entirely happy. A number of older wrestlers were just miserable at how strangely non-violent wrestling was becoming. One told a reporter, "It ain't wrestling the way I remember it. For one thing, wrestlers don't bleed anymore. You take Strangler Lewis. He whipped Jim Londos twenty times—and he bled a quart every time he done it. But these [new] wrestlers—there just ain't no blood in them at all!"

Who cares if there's blood? Dennis wondered. *This was fun.* He told the same reporter, "Today's wrestling is full of high action—and low comedy. You can't beat a combination like that."

Apparently not. Wrestling grew so big that Dennis found himself appearing in a movie about the pseudo-sport, making his feature film debut in *Mister Universe*. Call it typecasting, but he played the role of a professional wrestling commentator named Dennis James. The movie starred Vince Edwards—later TV's Dr. Ben Casey—as Tommy Tomkins, a Mister Universe winner, who naively joins the stable of wrestlers overseen by a corrupt promoter. Dennis was on the mic for all of Tomkins' matches in the film, and for a nice of touch of realism, all of the other wrestlers in the film were actual stars that James covered for DuMont, including The Missing Link, Chief Flying Mare, Gorilla Hogan, Newton the Teuton, Delightful Dave, Gregorivitch the Magnificent, and The Hoboken Turk. An eighteen-year-old girl named Joan Rivers was an uncredited extra, as one of Tomkins' devoted fans.

While Dennis won over some of the wrestlers through family, he won over plenty of others with fortune. His approach to professional wrestling, as counterintuitive as it seemed to the entire locker room, was garnering big TV audiences. The increased name recognition meant bigger paydays from promoters from city to city, and a number of wrestlers liked him just fine once they realized they were each on track to pull in $200,000 in 1949. He was turning wrestling into big business.

> "Not much doubt that DuMont's Dennis James is doing the best job among Manhattan's television sports commentators. James does the wrestling and boxing from the Jerome and Jamaica (L.I.) Arenas. It is on the groaners that James particularly shines due to his basic knowledge of wrestling besides a sense of humor that permits him to kid both the participants and himself. James

has had a definite part in popularizing wrestling on the screen and a poll of viewers might surprise as to the number of its regular followers." -*Variety*

The wrestlers' appreciation for Dennis saved the broadcaster's neck one night. After a show, he agreed to drive Maurice Tillet, one of the combatants, home. Tillet was a French immigrant who suffered from acromegaly, a tumor growth on his pituitary gland that caused him to grow continuously throughout his entire life, causing him to become overgrown and disfigured. (The same ailment later afflicted wrestling legend Andre the Giant.) The disfigurement gave Tillet a unique and memorable appearance: he went by the name The French Angel, because the name so starkly contrasted with his large, monstrous look. (Photos of Tillet, The French Angel, were later allegedly used by character designers at DreamWorks to create the appearance of the animated character, Shrek.)

Dennis became aware of another driver tailgating him and honking his horn repeatedly. He was aware that the guy wanted a confrontation and wouldn't back off until he got one. When he pulled off to the side of the road, the other driver pulled off right behind him, and Dennis prepared to get out of the car.

Tillet calmly told him, "Wait here." At 270 pounds of muscle with a fearsome grimace, he stepped out of the car, stood on the other driver's hood, peered through his windshield, and asked "Do we have a problem?"

The other driver timidly shook his head and said, "No." Tillet stepped down from the hood, got back in Dennis' car, and they took off. There's no telling what started the other driver's road rage, but they didn't see him for the rest of the night.

Local promoters paid top dollar for wrestling, and so did sponsors. Polaroid heavily marketed television filters (a transparent sheet that could be affixed to a television screen to prevent glare) on DuMont's wrestling events, and sales doubled, in part because of the unique deal Polaroid made with store owners who agreed to stock their television filters. Any store that agreed to stock 250 filters would receive a free national commercial, given by Dennis James during a break in the matches. National Brewing Company (makers of Colt 45 and National Bohemian Beer) bought commercial time during the wrestling matches and later reported that the fastest growth that the company ever experienced was during the two years that they sponsored Dennis James' wrestling matches.

Polaroid, one of the sponsors that first discovered the power of television when they bankrolled Dumont wrestling. The wrestlers themselves would discover the power of television when they saw their paychecks.

For a brief period, pro wrestling even enjoyed a rare moment of critical praise. Writers wrote glowingly of the matches with Dennis on commentary. The New York Critics' Circle even gave him an award for "Outstanding New Personality" in 1948, even though he was virtually the only face on television that year who was most decidedly *not* a "new" personality in the medium; he had been at it for ten years.

When *The New York Times* took stock of the new crop of performers on the emerging television landscape, they saw Dennis as an ideal. The paper said, "Possibly it is of significance that most of the new personalities that television already has brought to the fore are not singers or actors. Most of them are to be found in the ranks of announcers or commentators on various subjects. And in every case, their success is due in large measure to their realization that the audience in television does have a well-developed critical faculty, that too much talk is not only unnecessary but dangerous from the standpoint of their own box office appeal. In this category belongs a young announcer named Dennis James, who has achieved a measure of renown from announcing, of all things, wrestling matches. His specialty is the casual and dry ad-lib, scoffing at the utter nonsense going on in the ring beneath him. He supplements this with his own special sound effects that make the 'bone crushing' in the ring sound as if a leg were being torn off."

Another publication taking notice was *Television Guide*, the original New York regional publication that would expand nationally into *TV Guide* in 1952. In 1948, *Television Guide* took a reader poll and named Dennis TV's Top Sports Announcer.

Dennis' tact of gearing wrestling toward women was working far beyond anybody's expectations. The earliest reports on ratings and demographics for television found that for televised professional wrestling, female viewers outnumbered males three-to-one.

That demographic had a direct impact on the look of professional wrestling, and specifically of professional wrestlers. In the 1930s and 1940s, wrestling promoters only sought out guys who looked like they could win a fight, and it showed. They were stocky, burly, snarling jocks with beer bellies, hairy meat hooks hanging from tree trunk arms, and faces decorated by a smashed nose and cauliflower ears.

When those demographics reports came in and wrestling promoters found out that televised bouts were garnering an audience that was 75% female, they realized they needed to do something to keep that massive audience from going adrift. All of a sudden, looks mattered in the wrestling business. There would always be room for the freaks and the grunts, but these women needed some eye candy.

Dennis autographed a copy of the record album he released, *Mother O' Mine*, during the prime of his wrestling commentary career. Capitalizing on his catchphrase, the album included the songs "My Mother," "Songs My Mother Taught Me," "To a Mother," and an ode to Abraham Lincoln's mother, "Nancy Hanks."

Antonino "Argentina" Rocca, an Italian-born star of soccer and rugby in Argentina, came to America after World War II and trained for wrestling. A gifted singer (he was close friends with NBC Orchestra maestro Arturo Toscanini), Rocca left his mark on professional wrestling with an innovative style that involved high jumps and flying from the top rope onto his opponents. He wrestled barefooted, which he used to his advantage for a stunning display of flexibility in which he taunted his opponents by slapping them across the face with his toes. His chiseled physique was unlike anything seen in wrestling before he arrived, with a hairstyle and face that compelled a few writers to compare him to Rudolph Valentino.

"Nature Boy" Buddy Rogers had a deep tan and bleached blonde locks. His physique was a more natural-looking build, but women were drawn to him by his confidence—or rather, arrogance. After easily dispatching opponents with underhanded tactics or outright cheating, he'd smugly say of his winning ways, "To a nicer guy, it couldn't happen."

Gene Stanlee, a former Mr. America, ". . . struts around the ring like a Hollywood ham warmed over," as Dennis once eloquently put it. Stanlee catered his act to the women more directly than anyone else, blowing kisses to the ladies in the crowd every time he stretched his opponent across the mat.

The new look of pro wrestling traced itself directly back to Dennis and what he saw as an urgent need to lure in the fairer sex, but it was about more than "Ladies Night." His quirky presentation, with sound effects, camera tricks, and sly jokes, meant that more than ever, professional wrestling was a spectacle.

In an essay in 1950, at the height of this Golden Age of wrestling, Dennis wrote, "Women in their fifties have grabbed for bits of clothing belonging to their heroes. In the arena, wrestlers like Buddy Rogers are mobbed like the Sinatra of old. Today, wrestlers are concerned not about their physical condition, but about new means of self-exploitation in the form of madcap showmanship, for that's what sells."

Television had reached out to wrestling, but now, to survive, wrestling had to reach out to television. Wrestling characters were more than names and unusual biographies. Lord Carlton entered the ring with his butler of course, conducting himself as if making a rare appearance at a formal affair. He walked to the ring with a monocle and flowing cape, bowing to the audience as though they were royalty. Ali Baba, a California aristocrat who owned vast acres of vineyards, sported a bright red fez and a nine-inch handlebar moustache.

The toast of the coast, Gorgeous George, with bobby pins holding together his bleached mane, and sequined robes that made Liberace green with envy, plus a butler to dust off his shoulders when a common person like a referee laid his filthy hands on George, and an oxygen tank filled with fresh California air for George to inhale so he didn't have to suffer breathing the same air as the disgusting fans on the east coast.

Of course, the more the wrestlers drew attention to themselves, the more people looked at pro wrestling with a raised eyebrow. "Was this stuff really a sport?" they asked.

Dennis was one of the people who heard that question over and over again. He didn't exactly say "no." He respected the boundaries set by the code of kayfabe, but his ready answer when somebody asked him was, "It's a show."

Dennis would know. He was the one who made it that way.

CHAPTER FIVE
MOTHER'S FAVORITE

By 1948, TELEVISION had not quite yet outgrown some of its early limitations. It was still working with low budgets, which made it difficult to attract top-shelf actors and writers, and it was a medium that could only accommodate amateurs at the moment.

Fortunately, there was a radio format involving amateurs that seemed just perfect for television. *Major Bowes' Amateur Hour* had concluded its run in 1945. Major Bowes, in failing health, had been gradually easing himself away from the program in its final years, alternating hosting duties with actor Jay C. Flippen, and with Ted Mack, who had been working behind the scenes as Bowes' own personal talent scout.

Bowes passed away in 1946, but Ted Mack was determined that the format that Bowes created could survive. Mack made a deal with Old Gold cigarettes and DuMont to revive the show, under the title *Ted Mack's Original Amateur Hour*, making its television debut on January 18, 1948. It was actually Old Gold that had been the catalyst in getting the revival on the air. At the time, Old Gold was sponsoring a popular radio game show called *Stop the Music*. *Stop the Music* had become a national craze while at the same time being a stunningly inexpensive program to produce, as most game shows were. Old Gold was so delighted at the results they were getting with such a minor investment that they decided to give full sponsorship to a second show, when they learned that *Ted Mack's Original Amateur Hour* was in search of a sponsor and a network, Old Gold research determined that the show would be similarly inexpensive, but that it would probably attract an audience consisting almost entirely of demographics that didn't listen to *Stop the Music*, which meant that for a still-low investment, Old Gold would have full sponsorship of a hit radio show and a hit TV show. The sponsor closed the deal with the producers and with DuMont and got *Amateur Hour* back on the air, but with the new name.

A decade after Frank Sinatra had launched his career under Major Bowes' watch, Frank's old co-worker, Dennis, started a new weekly gig serving as the commercial announcer. Dennis had signed a ten-year, $300,000-a-year agreement with Old Gold cigarettes to serve as their pitchman for television advertising. Old Gold would be the permanent sponsor for *Ted Mack's Original Amateur Hour*, so Dennis would appear on that show for the next seven years.

An article in *Sponsor* magazine laid out the story of how the advertising agency for Old Gold, Lennen and Mitchell (ironically, they went by the abbreviation LandM, also the name of an Old Gold competitor), came upon Dennis James to serve as the Old Gold spokesman, and how the commercials evolved.

When cigarette advertising on television was big business, Dennis did the biggest business of all, as a pitchman for Old Gold.

Sponsor said, "Lennen and Mitchell believe that everything done before television cameras should be designed specifically for the medium. For the TV *Amateur Hour* commercials [*Ted Mack's Original Amateur Hour*], therefore, L&M selected a man who at that time was already a rising television personality, Dennis James. Dennis James is the ingenious voice behind the scenes who put bounce into DuMont wrestling telecasts by proceeding on the logical assumption that wrestling is a branch of the theatre rather than a pure competitive sport... On the TV *Amateur Hour*, the friendly and humorous James personality was ideal.

"To put that personality in the right framework, the agency devised a living room set complete with an easy chair, end table, and book shelf backdrop. James was to sit in the easy chair, look into the living rooms of viewers, and talk directly to them about his favorite cigarette. The lines written for James by the Lennen and Mitchell copy chief would require no shouting or orating; they were merely a hello from one smoker to another."

The commercials got more ornate, as the company grew in stature and television grew in popularity. For one, Dennis was joined by a beautiful blonde model, who appeared as a cigarette girl. She had one line—"Cigars, cigarettes"—but television merited a slightly different performance than the live stage or a radio commercial, so he took an extra moment before they went on the air to coach her on her delivery. The young lady was named Grace Kelly.

"For a change of pace, the L&M radio men wanted an additional commercial format involving Dennis James and talent from the show. At first, commercials were tried in which James and girl quartets sang the praises of Old Golds together. Then, the TV art department struck gold for Old Gold. In this case, gold was a cigarette pack that danced. The way the dancing cigarette pack evolved from an idea to one of the most effective commercials in TV reveals how closely all the members of the radio department work together.

"The basic idea was to have a girl dressed in a cigarette pack from the hips up do a dance routine in front of the camera. But how would you get the selling punch into this routine? . . . [T]he dance music [was] muted sufficiently so that Dennis James could speak through the music and make periodic comments tied in with the dance, yet referring directly to Old Golds."

During that time on *Ted Mack's Original Amateur Hour*, Dennis stood on the sidelines and watched new stars emerge. Seven-year-old Gladys Knight was the big winner on one evening. Irene Cara was eight years old when she appeared. A group called The Teen Tones performed a doo-wop number, and one of them, Robert Klein, went on to greater fame as a stand-up comic and actor. Some performers wouldn't be remembered for their talents on stage. Louis Wolcott played the violin for a show in 1949, about a decade before changing his name to Louis Farrakhan.

The talent on display wasn't always so stellar, and Dennis was amused at the way the program turned out one night. With the audience in the studio being encouraged to vote for their favorite act, he collected 125 votes. A women's club was in the audience and a member candidly said that her group enjoyed the commercials more than any of the performances.

Don't blink! Dennis hosted *Dennis James' Carnival* for one night only on WCBS.

Dennis was so successful during his career that he was afforded the luxury of laughing off the few failures he had. On October 31, 1948, WCBS in New York aired the debut broadcast of *Dennis James' Carnival*, sponsored by General Electric. It was a variety show with a circus/carnival atmosphere, starring Dennis as host and "ringmaster." For the big debut, the show booked Risko the juggler, fire dancers Leonardo and Zola, and Dagmar, a "dumb blonde"-style comic actress, doing a fortune teller act. If you've never heard of *Dennis James' Carnival*, don't feel bad; neither did the people who owned televisions in 1948. *Dennis James' Carnival* was pulled off the air after one broadcast. When it returned two weeks later, it had been renamed *The Eyes Have It*, Dennis had been replaced by Paul Gallico, and the circus theme was replaced by a more straightforward variety show concept. In other words, WCBS had thrown away everything but the time slot.

Show business can take the most unexpected twists and turns, and Dennis was about to discover that first-hand, when his impressive aptitude for tongue-in-cheek professional wrestling commentary led directly to being appointed for a new daytime variety show. In 1948, the new show attracted quite a bit of controversy.

To explain why, you need to know what television before 6:00 p.m. looked like before November 1948. On Fridays at 1:00 p.m., NBC aired *The Swift Home Service Club* for 30 minutes. Weekdays at 5:30 p.m., *Howdy Doody* came on. Over on CBS, *Vanity Fair* and a game show called *Missus Goes a' Shopping* filled an hour at 1:00 p.m. The barely functioning ABC Network showed old cartoons or a program called *The Singing Lady* at 5:30 p.m., and that was *all* of daytime television in 1948.

Radio was chockfull of options for listening pleasure during the daytime hours, but the notion of airing television programs during the day was met with great resistance, not because of low budgets or limited resources, but due to, of all things, the moral implications.

In 1948, the target audience for any daytime programming that the network might consider was obviously housewives. Housewives could certainly listen to the radio while ironing the laundry and dusting the living room, but television would require the wife to sit down on the couch and devote her attention to the screen for at least thirty minutes. There was a very real concern in 1948 that houses across America would fall into a state of disrepair if daytime television became popular enough for the average housewife to grow neglectful of her duties. NBC and CBS offerings at 1:00 p.m. were acceptable because that could serve as a nice companion while she took her lunch break, but other than that, the feeling was that women really shouldn't be encouraged to watch television.

Television executives and critics alike openly mocked that concern. Jack Gould of *The New York Times*, with tongue firmly affixed in cheek, wrote, "Just what Dr. DuMont is going to do to our way of life is still uncertain. The idea of a nation of housewives sitting mute before the video machines when they should be tidying up the premises or preparing the formula is not something to be grasped hurriedly. Obviously it is matter fraught with peril of the darkest sort."

Dr. DuMont's upcoming daytime endeavor was actually a well-connected husband's idea of a gift for his wife. James Hill, president of the Sterling Drug Company (Double Danderine shampoo, Phillips Toothpaste, Bayer Aspirin), reached out to Dennis with a phone call. After explaining who he was, Hill told him, "You've turned my wife into a wrestling fan. She's crazy about you—and, if she is, other women must feel the same way. Plan a show for me. Something to break up the monotony of housekeeping chores."

DuMont Network's new program, their first attempt at a daytime show of any kind, would thumb their noses at overly moral naysayers extra-hard with a daytime variety show—the first variety show on daytime TV—combining elements of game show, talk show, and sketch comedy. Dennis' brother, Lou Sposa, committed to direct the new show (the previous year, he had written the first how-to book for directing a television program) and Dennis, who had concocted the format himself, decided that, despite the many commitments he already had—wrestling, boxing, and *Ted Mack's Original Amateur Hour*—he could spare the half-hour every afternoon to host this new show.

Dennis had quite understandably become the "go-to guy" for DuMont, and even if Sterling Drug Company hadn't reached out to him directly to take the initiative in creating a daytime show, he probably would have wound up hosting DuMont's first daytime TV show anyway. He attracted the original audiences to DuMont with *Television Roof*, he attracted a viable audience to prime time with *Cash and Carry*, and he attracted new and massive audiences to professional wrestling and boxing. Now, he would help DuMont attract an audience to the network during daytime hours.

Dennis and his brother, Lou Sposa. As Dennis made his name in front of the camera, Lou made his name behind it as a director.

Not only that, he helped supply a title. Dennis had endeared himself to women across the country with his comments to "Mother" during wrestling matches, and now he'd be hosting a program dedicated to the American housewives, many of whom were mothers. With him hosting the new project, the show would be titled *Okay Mother*. The program set sail on November 1, 1948, with no commercial underwriting; Sterling Drug Company may have asked for the show, but they were savvy about spending their money. They wanted to see how the primary weeks looked before committing to it.

Chapter Five: Mother's Favorite

"Okay, mother! It's your time of day!
Okay, mother! Time to have your say!
The Problem Playhouse lets you share your views,
A guest consultant, with all the latest news!
So join in the fun…everyone!
With laughs, problems, and funny games,
So okay, mother! Okay, mother!
We're presenting Dennis James!"

The program aired at 1:00, that same daily "lunch break" slot that NBC and CBS were using for their female programming. Each presentation of *Okay Mother* started with exactly the kind of welcome that the nation's worrywarts got stomachaches from. Dennis would come out, greet the all-female studio audience, and tell the women at home to forget about the chores and the other household concerns. "No dishes to do, no lunches to prepare." This was *her* time to relax, forget her cares, and enjoy herself for thirty minutes.

Separating *Okay Mother* from the programming choices on the other channels was that Dennis really hammered home the fact that this program was on mom's side. After singing onstage the peppy opening theme, he belted out a short poem, with some assistance from the studio audience.

"WHO'S THE GAL WHO MAKES THE LEMONADE?"
"MOTHER!!!"
"WHO'S THE ONE WE'D NEVER TRADE?"
"MOTHER!!!"

Each program included a game segment called "Mothergrams." Dennis read a short rhyme written from the point of view of a famous person's mother. Audience members raised their hands for a chance to answer, with a prize awarded for correctly guessing the famous person's identity.

"This mother was proud, thought the skies would be sunny,
For her son was the first chap in charge of our money.

It afterward seemed as if fortune was cruel.
At the height of his fame, he was killed in a duel."

Dennis added another job to his already loaded workday. *Okay Mother* would be a gold mine for Sterling Drug Company.

(The answer, of course, was Alexander Hamilton, with a bottle of lighter fluid going to the lucky lady in the audience.)

Dennis' skill for improvisational poetry, which he had honed so well during professional wrestling matches, became a daily feature of *Okay Mother*. He went in the audience and encouraged women to say a fact about themselves. He then used that fact as the opening line of a short poem. If he drew a blank and couldn't come up with a second line, the woman won a small prize.

Every day, Dennis read a letter from a home viewer, speaking the praises of her own mother. That mother, named Mother of the Day, received a small prize, and at the end of the week, he awarded Mother of the Week (his favorite letter of that week) a larger prize.

Chapter Five: Mother's Favorite

"Problem Playhouse," another daily feature of the program, saw Dennis and his lovely assistant, Julia Meade (later a popular singer and commercial spokeswoman) act out a small household scene, with Julia playing "Mother" and Dennis acting in the role of the husband, or more often, Mother's little boy.

In the surviving kinescope of the program, Dennis and Julia act out a scene where he plays in the sprinkler wearing his good pants, and then lies to his mom about what happened. He plays the skit for laughs, doing a silly upper-register voice for the little boy, rattling off puns in his dialogue ("Daddy does it all the time, the neighbor said so! He says Daddy is all wet!"), and going for broad physical humor, plopping across Julia's lap when she threatens to spank him.

At the end of the skit, Dennis abruptly straightens up and leads the audience in a discussion about whether or not spanking is an appropriate punishment. On other occasions, he augmented the discussion with guests, including child psychologists and home care experts.

Okay Mother didn't condescend. Dennis allowed the women in the audience to speak their minds. It also celebrated the efforts that a housewife was giving from day to day. It was really the first time that women were given any sense of empowerment from watching television.

"The whole idea of the program is to put Mother on a pedestal, where she belongs," Dennis explained to a reporter. In case he fell short of that objective, there was a harsh critic nearby to keep him in check. His own mother was in the studio audience for *Okay Mother* nearly every day.

The results: after only six weeks on the air, Sterling Drug Inc. signed an unheard-of ten-year pact to become the only sponsor of *Okay Mother*. The price tag of the deal included a $2,225,000 talent fee to be divided among Dennis, his brother Lou Sposa, who directed the program, and assistant Julia Meade over the next decade. Dennis treated himself to a 33-foot yacht, which he named *Okay Mother*. As a bonus, he pocketed yet another first: first sponsored daytime television program.

The membership card for "Mothers Incorporated," the official fan club for *Okay Mother*.

2,000 "Mother of the Day" letters were written to Dennis every week, less than a decade after he was struggling to assure singers that nobody actually watched television. The program immediately became tops in the 1:00 p.m. time slot. Within a year of its debut, it was doing what seemed completely unthinkable; it became the first afternoon TV show to draw higher ratings than radio, and it was crushing the medium, regularly attracting double the audience of any radio show airing at 1:00 p.m. Its 5.2 Hooper rating (the precursor to the Neilsen Ratings Service) was strong enough to put *Okay Mother* ahead of even a handful of prime-time shows.

10,000 viewers wrote in for memberships in Mothers, Incorporated, the show's official fan club. Not only did it prove that the show was a hit, it was sufficient proof that daytime television was a viable enterprise, and too financially enticing for sponsors and networks to give any mind to the future of the nation, as seen by America's pessimists. Sterling Drug, Inc. was so impressed that they began cutting back on radio advertising. *Okay Mother* was getting the job done just fine for them.

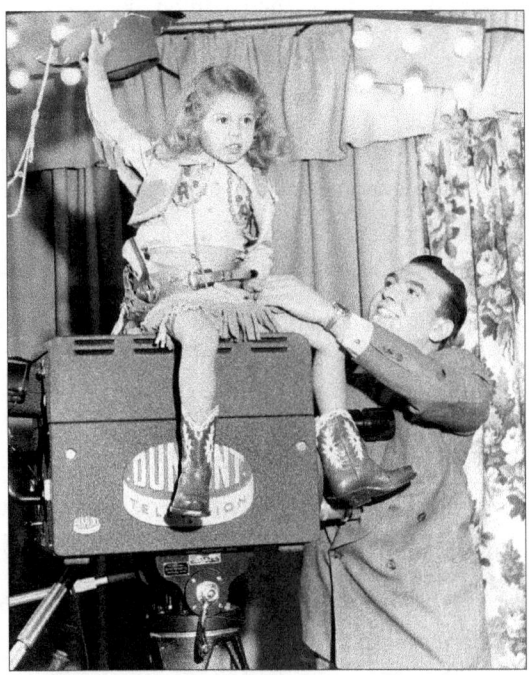

You didn't have to be a mother to have fun on *Okay Mother*. Dennis plays with a visitor to the set.

DuMont sales director Tom Gallery beamed, "Daytime television's pioneering days are over; it's definitely got to be counted among effective selling media."

Okay Mother performed so strongly that DuMont expanded its daytime programming to a three-hour block that stretched all the way to 4:00 p.m. DuMont called it *Mid-Day Matinee*, kicked off by Dennis and all the members of Mothers, Inc. every weekday.

Dennis was put in even more demand by the success of *Okay Mother*. He was handsome, articulate, and confident, without seeming like an intimidating presence to women; he was more of a pal to them. On his off-days, he made himself available as a pageant host for hire, traveling on the weekends to towns across the country to crown Miss This or The Queen of That. This as he continued steering more women toward professional wrestling with his sparkling commentary. Nearly every mention of Dennis in the press at this point made note of how darn much women liked him; other broadcasters talked *to* women. Dennis found a way to talk with them. He bonded with his audience.

DuMont itself was in more demand. With so many minds hard at work, and with Dennis' hit program generating some revenue that could help get some results, DuMont achieved a new technical breakthrough in the spring of 1949. It unveiled a new vehicle called a Telecruiser, a small bus equipped with three cameras, a control united, a power generator, and microphones. It was the first mobile unit in television, a concept that would soon become a standard throughout television, from the major networks down to the smallest of small market stations. The notion that a news crew could report a story within moments and do so live from the scene was a big accomplishment. Fittingly, given his resume up to this point, Dennis got the nod to serve as reporter the first time that the Telecruiser would put to use, making him television's first field reporter.

His ubiquitous nature in the early days of television was helping him amass quite a collection of nicknames. A number of DuMont co-workers called him "The Human Test Pattern." *Television Daily* called him "Mr. Versatelevision." A few writers piggybacked off his catchphrase and took to calling him "Mother's Boy" or "Mother's Helper." Writer Sid White dubbed him a "Wrestlinguist." He was amassing honor after honor, too. *TV Digest* named him Favorite Women's Program Personality. *TV Guide* (still only a regional publication at that time) called him TV's Outstanding Personality. *TV World* named him Most Popular Male Personality.

Chapter Five: Mother's Favorite

Dennis and his guests cut a little bit loose during the Problem Playhouse on *Okay Mother.*

Meanwhile, back at the DuMont Building, Dr. DuMont finally overhauled the living room-sized studios for his television programs, knocking down walls and expanding the facilities to something a little more suited for his growing network. DuMont proudly explained that the reason the change was finally made was because too many women were showing up for *Okay Mother*. After weeks and weeks of having to turn away the overflow, DuMont decided it was better to accommodate the expanding audience. In a funny twist of fate, major rainstorms hit New York City the week that reconstruction was finished. Women who hadn't been planning on going to *Okay Mother* went to the DuMont Building just to get out of the rain. Even with the expanded facilities, the show still had an overflow audience that had to be turned away each day until the storms settled.

Fittingly, in the fall of 1949, a year after the debut of *Okay Mother*, Dennis co-hosted a DuMont prime time special, trumpeting the opening of a new television receiver plant in East Paterson, New Jersey. Dennis interviewed workers and executives as he guided the audience step-by-step through the manufacturing process of what was, at the time, the largest television factory in the world. That same year, DuMont reported a 300% increase in revenue, and two of its affiliates, WABD in New York and WDTV in Pittsburgh, were turning a profit. DuMont was officially one of the big guys in the business.

CHAPTER SIX
ALL THAT GLITTERS, AND OLD GOLD

DENNIS' CAREER WAS thriving as he entered the 1950s, but personally, he still felt a sense of emptiness. He was a father-by-phone for most of the year, living alone in an apartment right in the middle of the biggest of the big cities. He tried to keep himself occupied, yet he really didn't like being in his apartment for much more than sleep.

Dennis got a boat to keep himself entertained on his days off, a 41-foot twin screw four-cabin Chris Craft flying bridge cruiser, with a $19,850 price tag. As a completely unexpected bonus, the boat came with a commercial endorsement deal. Chase and Sanborn learned that percolators were being included as amenities on the more extravagant watercraft on the market. The company struck a deal with the boat's manufacturer to include cases of Chase and Sanborn coffee in the galleys. When word spread to Chase and Sanborn that a popular broadcaster had purchased one of those boats, they immediately made a deal with Dennis, who would serve as their spokesman for a series of ads specifically made for boating magazines.

Dennis sailed often and became fond of Long Island Sound, habitually anchoring in Echo Bay and wandering around New Rochelle for a little bit before hopping back on the boat and calling it a day. He was especially fond of the houses surrounding the bay. Asbestos magnate Tommy Manville had a 32-room mansion that Dennis found amazing, but there was another house that Dennis became particularly fixated on. He watched as it was being built on the side of a hill, with the backyard sloping straight into the water. As quirky as it sounded, Dennis repeatedly stopped at that spot on Echo Bay and just gazed at that house.

Occasionally, he entertained the thought of buying a house in New Rochelle. He absolutely had the money in the bank to do so, but he lacked a reason.

What's the point? he thought to himself. He lived alone, and his apartment was located fairly close to work. It was functional, and Dennis couldn't see a reason to move out, as much as he might have liked one. Ever restless with his home life, or what passed for his home life, Dennis was perfectly happy when he found out that Old Gold was dispatching him to yet another show during the week to keep him busy. It was another game, one called *Stop the Music*. *Stop the Music* was a significant title in the history of game shows; not many game shows can say they were the subject of a hearing in the Supreme Court.

Mark Goodson and Louis Cowan co-created the program, which premiered on ABC Radio in 1948. Bert Parks served as master of ceremonies. The band and vocalists onstage performed a song, while a team of telephone operators offstage began telephoning people across the country at random. When somebody answered the phone, the announcer cried out, "STOP THE MUSIC!" and Parks asked the person who answered the phone to name the song. Anybody who did so was given a chance to identify a "Mystery Melody" for a jackpot of cash and prizes that swelled with every wrong guess. Jackpots routinely went north of $25,000, and the show quickly became a national phenomenon. *The Fred Allen Show*, in the same time slot, was abruptly run off the air, with Allen furiously venting about what a sick and greedy show the more popular *Stop the Music* was.

Dennis chatted with host Bert Parks backstage before a *Stop the Music* broadcast.

The Federal Communications Commission (FCC) ruled that the program constituted an illegal lottery and, as such, it couldn't legally air. ABC fought the ruling, while the FCC made a sweeping declaration that there were too many "giveaway shows" (the popular term for game shows at that point) and prepared to outlaw the genre altogether. Even people in the entertainment business who despised giveaway shows were quietly alarmed by that declaration by the FCC; the notion that an entire category of programs could be outlawed simply because there were too many of them seemed to be a dangerous precedent.

ABC disputed the ruling, and game shows continued to thrive on radio and television as the battle crawled through various courts until the Supreme Court finally agreed to hear arguments. In 1955, the Supreme Court unanimously ruled that there was nothing illegal about *Stop the Music* or any other game show.

ABC, undaunted in 1949, introduced a TV version of *Stop the Music*. Old Gold cigarettes sponsored the TV version, just as they had sponsored the original radio version, which meant that Dennis would turn up on the TV incarnation, along with the famous dancing cigarette packs.

The Old Gold cigarette commercials stood out not just because of Dennis' pitch but because of the larger-than-life cigarette packs featured in the campaign: the packs were actually costumes fully covering the heads and torsos of three immensely gifted dancers, who flawlessly tapped out a synchronized soft-shoe performance for every ad without being able to see each other. Long-legged Gloria Vestoff was inside the King-Size pack; petite Dixie Dunbar was in the regular pack; and a child, Terry Corin, was in the matchbook. The three of them strut their stuff while Dennis made his pitch:

"Ah...a box of matches and a pack of Old Gold cigarettes and a box of matches. That's all you need, my friend! And you're enjoying the smoothest, mildest, tastiest cigarette ever created. A treat instead of a treatment; that's Old Gold cigarettes, made by tobacco men, not medicine men."

That final line was indicative of an awful truth, one that even Dennis was being carefully shielded from at the time. General perception today was that nobody knew that tobacco was harmful until the late 1960s, when a series of studies confirmed the facts. In the 1940s and 1950s, tobacco companies

Chapter Six: All That Glitters, and Old Gold

certainly knew what was wrong with their products.

A generation of scriptwriters and producers from the golden age of radio and the early days of television were possibly the first "outsiders" to figure out something was wrong, primarily from the bizarre rules that they had to follow if the show was sponsored by a tobacco company. If you were writing for a detective show, the villain couldn't be a physician. Physicians could only be portrayed in a heroic light. When Camel sponsored NBC's evening news telecasts, the news writers were prohibited from using the word "cancer" in stories. If a newsworthy person died from cancer, they could only report that the person died after a "long illness."

Dennis showed TV viewers the way to a "treat": Old Gold cigarettes. Controversy was starting to swirl as Dennis continued doing commercials.

Dennis worked on unscripted programs, and as such, he was nicely cocooned from the eyebrow-raising orders that writing staffs had to endure from tobacco sponsors. At the same time, he had developed a positive relationship with his bosses at Old Gold, who were paying him handsomely and complimenting him profusely for keeping Old Gold rolling in green.

For the moment, Old Gold continued to print advertisements with copy that seemingly doth protest too much:

"We say it again: we're tobacco men, not medicine men . . . Old Gold cures just one thing—the world's best tobacco. Now, doesn't it stand to reason that a company with nearly 200 years of know-how in selecting, curing, and blending the world's choice tobaccos *must* produce a *better* cigarette? Isn't it only natural that a better cigarette is *better for you*? We believe honest facts will win Old Gold more friends than will "medical claims" based on fanciful evidence. With every modern safeguard, to eliminate harsh tobacco stems, to remove irritating dust, Old Gold offers you a cleaner, smoother, mellower smoke. In every way, it is better *for* you because *in every way Old Gold is a better cigarette.*

> "TO THE MEDICAL PROFESSION we leave—as is right and proper—all discussion as to treatment of your nose, throat, and respiratory tract, if any is needed. To you we say only: Old Gold is as fine a smoke-treat as nearly 200 years' tobacco-experience can produce. And doesn't it seem to you that a real treat like this will treat you right *in every way*?"

There you have it. If your cigarette was causing you coughing fits and respiratory problems, it must have been because you were smoking a poor quality brand of cigarettes.

While continuing to make that assertion, virtually every tobacco company was trying to stay ahead of whatever dangers were reported by the next medical study. A few companies introduced lines of "light cigarettes" as a way of trying to placate the experts who were voicing their concerns. Camel began mailing free cartons of cigarettes every week to doctors across the country. Camel then conducted a national survey to ask doctors if they smoked, and if so, what brand they were smoking. After collecting the results of the survey, Camel proudly boasted in ads that "More doctors smoke Camels than any other brand!" It was true, but not for the reason Camel was expecting you to think.

Dennis' face was attached to some of the print ads extolling the healthful benefits of smoking Old Golds. Next to Dennis' smiling face was this testimonial:

"Take it from me . . . If you want a treat instead of a treatment, smoke Old Golds! What's more friends: No other leading cigarette is less irritating, or easier on the throat, or contains less nicotine than Old Gold. Who says so? Not me, Dennis James. Not Old Gold. This conclusion was established on evidence by the United States Government."

What that statement meant, strictly, was that it was the dose that made the poison, so if a cigarette had nicotine, but not as much nicotine, it must have be safe, right?

Dennis and some other on-air talents from P. Lorillard-sponsored programs entertained the audience at a company luncheon. Dennis played the wash tub. The trombonist was *Queen for a Day* host Jack Bailey.

Dennis continued to endorse Old Gold cigarettes. He continued depositing checks from Old Gold, and he continued smoking the cartons of cigarettes delivered daily to his home by Old Gold.

To Dennis' ever-lasting credit, his legacy as a broadcaster would ultimately be the contributions he made to philanthropy in the name of public health. Dennis' knack for fundraising made itself known in 1948, when radio and television networks joined forces for a mass donation drive on behalf of March of Dimes.

The March of Dimes began life as the Georgia Warm Springs Foundation when Franklin Roosevelt, a polio survivor, established it in 1927. In 1938, Roosevelt, by then the President of the United States, organized a fundraising drive that involved selling lapel pins for 10¢ apiece. Radio, film, and stage star Eddie Cantor jokingly referred to the drive as a "march of dimes," as a pun on *The March of Time*, a popular newsreel series. Roosevelt liked the wordplay so much that he changed the name of his organization.

In 1948, during the week leading up to Roosevelt's birthday (he had since died in office and had now replaced the Roman god Mercury on the front of the dime), various efforts for fundraising were put together by the mass media. By far, the most effective of the fundraisers were the ones featuring Dennis James. He spent two weeks imploring his regular viewers to make donations, and the final tally determined that Dennis alone had been responsible for $7,000 pledged, $3,000 of which came from a single Sunday night special that he hosted on WABD. It was a particularly stunning total, given that Dennis hadn't been involved in any of the organization's preparations for the efforts. He truly had done it purely voluntarily. Grantland Rice of the March of Dimes sports committee was so dazzled by the effort that he bestowed upon Dennis the honorary title of Television Chairman of Sports Division of the March of Dimes Campaign.

The Heart Fund also benefited from Dennis' benevolent inclinations, via a special night of television on February 7, 1950. *Ted Mack's Original Amateur Hour* organized an entire episode designed to celebrate the American Heart Fund. Billed as "V.I.P. Night," a gallimaufry of unlikely contestants performed that night. Among them:

- The Navy Trio, with Admiral DeWitt Ramsey and Captain John A. Waters on piano, and Captain W. Gordon Beecher on guitar.

- Beverly Farrington, daughter of the Hawaiian delegate to Congress, performing an Island dance.

- Rep. Frank Chelf (D-KY) playing harmonica.

- Rep. Frances Bolton (R-OH) singing soprano.

- A group with the self-explanatory name The Square Dancing Congressional Couples of Texas.

- A surprise guest appearance by comedian/cellist Morey Amsterdam.

Dennis opened the show by announcing that the Old Gold dancing cigarette packs were taking the night off, and instead, Dennis spent the time between acts urging the home audience to support the Heart Fund and give all they could. As a surprise toward the end of the show, Dennis revealed what would later prove to be a darkly ironic special presentation to round out the night.

Dennis, clad in a tuxedo befitting the distinct atmosphere of the evening, announced, "Ladies and gentlemen, you know, every week on this show, our little girlfriends, the Old Gold dancing cigarette packs and the little matchbox, come out here and do a dance dedicated to Old Gold cigarettes. We explained to them that this week, after all, we were dispensing with commercial announcements. So both of them very cutely wiggled their boxes a little bit and asked 'Well, can't we dance for the New York Heart Campaign? So I asked Ted, and Ted said 'I think they should.'"

Radio Daily columnist Pinky Herman had unfettered words of acclaim for the presentation. "Tuesday nite [sic], we enjoyed what can easily be termed one of the best television programs ever produced . . . such an undertaking by its very nature might have resulted in an understandably uncoordinated hodgepodge production, yet so sincere were the principals, so unusual their respective talents and so apt the producers and assistance that the show glistened for sheer spontaneity and color. The Human side of our lawmakers also was refreshingly presented, and if Congressmen are as smart as they want us to believe, they'll pledge a vote of thanks to NBT, Old Gold execs, Ted Mack, Dennis James, and the Heart Fund executives for having been given the opportunity to prove that they are real, live, talented, and gracious citizens."

Dennis was proving to be real, live, and talented, but the depths of his gracious nature were just starting to come to the surface. As it turned out, there'd be plenty more where that came from.

CHAPTER SEVEN
LOOK AT US, WE'RE WALKING

IN LATE 1949, The *New York Times* reported that Dennis was preparing to host a new TV game for DuMont, to be titled *Lady Luck and the Tiger*. Dennis would show a contestant a pair of doors, and the contestant would choose one. One door was hiding a prize, and the other was hiding a penalty of some sort. The program never went on the air, but it is worth noting that, among the litany of firsts that Dennis accumulated over the years, he very nearly made a deal for a door fourteen years before Monty Hall turned the concept into a cultural icon.

Picking a door for a chance at a prize or a penalty was a bit of a metaphor for a business deal that Dennis struck at the same time. Dennis wanted to try his hand at being a sports mogul. Dennis, his business manager Vincent Andrews, and Ed Franco, a former All-American from Fordham, pooled their money together and bought a football team, the Jersey City Giants of the American Football League (formerly the American Association, and having no connection to the organization that eventually became the American Football Conference). They purchased the team for a rather low asking price, and pretty much got their money's worth. By the end of the season, there were only three teams remaining in the league. The Jersey City Giants were soundly defeated by both opponents, and Dennis cut his losses and folded the team. The league itself folded at the end of the season, after a championship game contested between the sole survivors.

Dennis could look back at the end of 1950 and smile proudly, though, because of a far more meaningful effort that prospered. It was the brainchild of two married couples, the Hausmans and the Goldensons.

Jack Hausman was the son in M. Hausman and Son, a textile manufacturer, and by the mid-1940s, he was helping run the entire operation. Leonard H. Goldenson, a Harvard-educated lawyer, had the bragging right of having helped build a television network from the ground up. He became an attorney for Paramount Pictures, but soon found himself put in charge of reorganizing Paramount's movie theater chain and rescuing it from bankruptcy. In time, he rescued the nearly-bankrupt ABC with a $25 million bailout, building the barely-there fourth television network into a viable entity.

Needless to say, neither Jack Hausman nor Leonard H. Goldenson could imagine that any child of theirs could be regarded as a second-class citizen. But at the time, that appeared to be the road that they were destined for.

The Hausmans' son, Peter, was born with cerebral palsy, a condition marked by a wide variety of symptoms: poor coordination, stiff or weakened muscles, tremors, sensory difficulties, and difficulties with speaking or swallowing, all caused by damage to the areas of the brain controlling move-

Chapter Seven: Look At Us, We're Walking

ment, balance, or posture. The ailment had been known for centuries; Hippocrates documented it in his writings during the fifth century, B.C.E. Some anthropological findings indicate that people recognized it a thousand years before that.

Dennis (standing, far left), during his sole season as a team owner; he invested in the Jersey City Giants of the American Football League.

Despite plenty of time to become acquainted with cerebral palsy, by the 1940s A.D., medical science seemingly just threw its collective arms in the air and gave up. Parents were encouraged to put the child in an institution to live their entire life in isolation from infancy until death. Such children were called "closet cases" because that was approximately the fate that awaited them. If parents elected to bring their children home, they were more or less on their own. There was minimal research, and no assistance made available. Government grants were non-existent, and no corporation was stepping forward to offer funding because, again, cerebral palsy wasn't a widely-known condition.

Jack Hausman and his wife, Ethel, came into contact with Leonard Goldenson and his wife, Isabelle, themselves the parents of a daughter with cerebral palsy. The couples commiserated and realized that other parents of children with cerebral palsy would appreciate an outlet to discuss their situation, preferably with others who related to it. They put an ad in the newspaper recruiting parents to join them for meetings. They initially called the group the Cerebral Palsy Society. It grew faster than anybody involved could have imagined. By 1948, it was called the National Cerebral Palsy Foundation (NCPF), and it now had a specific goal in mind: raising money for medical care for children with the disorder, and researching causes to initiate preventive care.

One of the first major efforts by the NCPF was a May 1949 fundraiser at Larchmont Shore Club, a private beach lodge. Goldenson, who, like anybody else in the entertainment industry, was more than familiar with Dennis, asked him to serve as Master of Ceremonies. Dennis sailed directly there in his cabin cruiser for a grand entrance, then oversaw a dinner and a benefit auction.

That same year, NBC television put together an unprecedented event, a 16-hour-long fundraiser for the Damon Runyan Memorial Cancer Fund. Milton Berle was Master of Ceremonies. A stage jam-packed with telephone operators had just enough space at the center for live performances from guest stars representing stage, screen, and television, concluding each performance with a sincere plea for donations. Jerry Lewis was one of the performers on-board for the event. The following day, a number of newspapers reported on the spectacular (which raised $1,100,000), and one writer coined the term "telethon" to describe the program.

NCPF, which changed its name to United Cerebral Palsy (UCP) shortly after the Larchmont fundraiser, set about to produce such an event for their own benefit. Ed Sullivan's *Toast of the Town* on CBS was only about two years old at this point, and he was the one who approached Dennis about co-hosting a 15-hour program emanating from New York, called *Celebrity Parade*. Goldenson used his connections at ABC and Paramount to put together a blockbuster line-up of guest stars. Ed Sullivan, Bob Hope, Jackie Gleason, and a host of prime time TV stars, including Dennis, took turns

Chapter Seven: Look At Us, We're Walking

hosting for an hour at a time, asking viewers for contributions. By the end of the show, Dennis and his cohorts had raised $972,106.

It wasn't the first telethon, but it would certainly be the first one to become a television mainstay. Only four were held for Damon Runyan. (The Jerry Lewis MDA Labor Day Telethon wouldn't come along until 1966.) Dennis James' annual effort on behalf of UCP would become a television tradition.

Dennis (standing, second from left) and some all-star help raising funds for UCP. Among those joining him: Art Carney (far right) and Gene Rayburn (kneeling).

Dennis contributed two distinctive trademarks to each telethon. The first was his recital of *Heaven's Very Special Child*, a poem by Edna Massionilla, the mother of a disabled daughter.

"A meeting was held quite far from Earth!
It's time again for another birth.
Said the Angels to the LORD above,
This Special Child will need much love.

His progress may be very slow,
Accomplishments he may not show.
And he'll require extra care
From the folks he meets down there.

He may not run or laugh or play,
His thoughts may seem quite far away,
In many ways he won't adapt,
And he'll be known as handicapped.

So let's be careful where he's sent,
We want his life to be content.
Please LORD, find the parents who
Will do a special job for you.

They will not realize right away
The leading role they're asked to play,
But with this child sent from above
Comes stronger faith and richer love.

And soon they'll know the privilege given
In caring for their gift from Heaven.
Their precious charge, so meek and mild,
Is HEAVEN'S VERY SPECIAL CHILD."

The second was a song, one of few that Dennis would venture to sing publicly, called "Look at Us, We're Walking." The rendition was always accompanied by a group of children, all with some form of cerebral palsy, joining Dennis on the stage.

Chapter Seven: Look At Us, We're Walking

"Look at us, we're walking,
Look at us, we're talking,
We who never walked or talked before.
Look at us, we're laughing,
We're happy and we're laughing,
Thank you from our hearts forevermore.
But there are so many other children
Who only speak with a silent prayer
For those of us who haven't been so lucky
We hope and pray you will always care.
And someday they'll be walking
Someday they'll be talking.
Imagine walking to the candy store!
But the fight has just begun
Get behind us everyone
The hope will make our dreams come true-
Thanks to you, thanks to you."

The following year, Dennis was invited back for *Celebrity Parade*, but he was surprised to learn that he was the only co-host being invited to return. UCP had assessed the phone calls and pledges that came in minute-by-minute during the first telethon and determined that Dennis' hour had been the hour that raised the most money. UCP reasoned, therefore, that every hour should have the power of the host that raised the most money, so Dennis hosted the whole show. He raised $200,000 on the 1951 *Celebrity Parade*.

With more attention being drawn to the cause, and more information becoming available, UCP began raising additional funds through corporate support. The Hausmans and Goldensons were very social couples, and counted among their friends many executives at major businesses. Charles Revson of Revlon began providing sizable annual donations on behalf of his company. Fred Trump (father of Donald) donated an entire apartment complex designated for occupancy by people with cerebral palsy. Dennis himself had struck up a personal friendship with a few of the higher-ups at Warner-Lambert Drug Company, and they began making regular donations, too.

Backstage at a UCP telethon. Hal March, later known as host of *The $64,000 Question*, stood next to Dennis. Directly behind them, face obscured in this photo, was Nat King Cole.

As more sponsors jumped on board, Dennis took the initiative to offer them something extra as a show of gratitude for participating. If a telethon sponsor was having any sort of function—a banquet, a ceremony, anything—Dennis was just a phone call away to serve as Master of Ceremonies, no questions asked. Because they were sponsoring the telethon, Dennis even hosted those corporate functions for free.

The 1951 telethon went so well that, in turned, Dennis found himself in high demand for hosting telethons. UCP was expanding and Dennis trav-

Chapter Seven: Look At Us, We're Walking

eled from city to city hosting telethons for the local branches of UCP. The San Francisco *Celebrity Parade* that year raised $162,000. Philadelphia raised $85,000. At the end of 1951, New York City's telethon raised $185,000.

Non-profit organizations across the country recruited him to host fundraisers for their causes. Others would have strongly preferred to use their weekends for sleeping in. Dennis, on the other hand, began an entire second career for himself going without sleep on the weekends, staying on the air for twelve to twenty-four hours for a broadcast. He was happy to take on the work as often as his schedule would permit it. Telethons brought him a sense of satisfaction that couldn't be matched by his other work, and it showed in the results. He went to San Antonio one weekend for a 16 ½-hour telethon, live from the city's Municipal Auditorium. For a telethon emanating from a single station doing a local broadcast, he helped bring in $130,000 for a local cerebral palsy organization. He also did telethons in Denver, Colorado and Ottumwa, Iowa, all for cerebral palsy organizations.

Dennis did all this while he was continuing his work with the March of Dimes. He still bore the title "Television Chairman of the Sports Division of the March of Dimes Campaign," and still did what he could to earn that title. For the 1951 March of Dimes fundraising drive, he built a full episode of *Okay Mother* around the cause. He welcomed Lydia Clark, a polio survivor and daughter of a DuMont employee, to talk about her experience with the ailment. It put a face on the problem, something that the people organizing the campaign felt was important.

On April 7, 1951, Dennis was part of an unusual presentation by Ringling Brothers and Barnum and Bailey Circus at Madison Square Garden. It was an All-Star circus with Arthur Godfrey as ringmaster, raising funds for the Heart Association. A variety of circus acts were presented, all performed with celebrities who were very much out of their element. Among the clowns were Bert Lahr, Red Skelton, Don Ameche, and Dennis James. Together, they laughed up $190,000 from delighted audience members.

This was the work that Dennis did for which he was proudest. He had used his talents to get people to buy televisions and buy cigarettes, and he had made a productive living for himself, but the notion that he could use exactly the same skills to do something truly good for other people gave him a feeling like no other.

CHAPTER EIGHT
HEY MICKI!

IN 1950, DENNIS James was busy during the day with five episodes a week of *Okay Mother.* His nights were booked solid with *Ted Mack's Original Amateur Hour, Stop the Music* (which won a Billboard Radio Editors' Award for Favorite Audience Participation Program), pro wrestling (for which Dennis won a Billboard Radio Editors' Award for Best Television Announcer), pro boxing, the movie premieres in New York, and narrating newsreels for Paramount and the United States Marine Corps. Considering what his work schedule looked like, perhaps his most amazing accomplishment of 1950 was that he had time to meet a woman named Micki.

Marjorie Crawford—Micki to her friends—was born and raised in Newcastle, Pennsylvania. She attended the Art Institute of Pittsburgh, with designs on becoming an illustrator. She was forced to drop out when her father became ill with cancer and died within a year, at only fifty years of age. Micki and her mother decided to take a road trip to recover from the rough spell that they had just endured, but found that they both liked Miami so much, they never went back to Pennsylvania. Micki's mother found a job, while Micki, a former beauty pageant winner—Miss Press Photographer of Pittsburgh—signed on with a modeling agency.

Micki modeled bathing suits at Saks Fifth Avenue, and sought a second job working as a Girl Friday to a radio station owner in Fort Lauderdale. The station owner was interested in meeting with her about the job, but pressed for time, he told her to drop by his house for a discussion about the work on a Saturday night, while he was holding a party for Dennis James. Micki, who hadn't seen television yet, didn't know who Dennis James was yet. She accepted the invitation to go to the man's house, but being a sensible young lady, she brought her mother along.

Dennis was taking some time off from all of his broadcasting duties for the moment. A routine visit to the doctor uncovered some polyps on his throat. The surgery was a success, but Dennis had been warned beforehand that, at least temporarily, he'd lose his ability to speak. Dennis and his manager, Vincent Andrews, made the best of a bad situation. They went to Florida, partly to go house-hunting because Dennis wanted to buy one for his parents, and partly decided to turn his recuperation into an extended vacation.

Word got out in the local press that TV star Dennis James was in Florida for a long visit, so Micki's boss-to-be, Jimmy Shearer, formerly of WAAT, who told Dennis while he was known as Demie Sposa to change to change his name, reached out to Dennis and told him to come on over.

Dennis was dismayed when he arrived. As he told *TV-Radio Mirror*

Chapter Eight: Hey Micki!

later, "I did not know he had planned a party for me. If I had known, I would sure as the dickens have objected, for I couldn't speak a word! I had to carry a pad and write everything out!"

Dennis and Micki found themselves side-by-side early in the evening. It was one of the more awkward how-we-met stories in the history of modern romance. Dennis, who made his living talking and talking well, couldn't do the one thing that he did better than anybody, while Micki, a "new girl in town," who really just wanted to be there to discuss the details of her new job with somebody else, found herself forced to hold up more than her fair share of this conversation.

"I don't know who this party is for," she told the quiet stranger next to her. "I think it's for some guitar player named Dennis James?"

Something wonderful managed to emerge from the awkward outer layer of the moment. Dennis wrote little notes to communicate. Micki replied by drawing some quick sketches. There was music playing, and Dennis pantomimed raising his arms and wrapping them around someone; he was asking Micki for a dance. Afterward, Dennis mimed turning a steering wheel. He was offering a ride home. Micki accepted.

His intentions were good, but this led to a rather cumbersome arrangement later in the evening. Micki warned Dennis that she lived in Miami and getting her home would be a twenty-five-mile ride, and to her surprise, Dennis seemed delighted to hear that. She accepted his offer of a ride home even though she had come with her mother, and Dennis was offering a ride home even though he had come with Vincent.

So Micki told her mother what had just transpired. She explained that she had been mistaken. This Dennis James fellow wasn't a guitar player like she thought. She had overheard somebody mention Old Gold, so she explained to Mom, "I think he has something to do with cigarettes."

The four of them met up at the parking lot of a church just off the highway, and arranged a passenger swap. Micki got out of her mother's car and walked to Dennis' car.

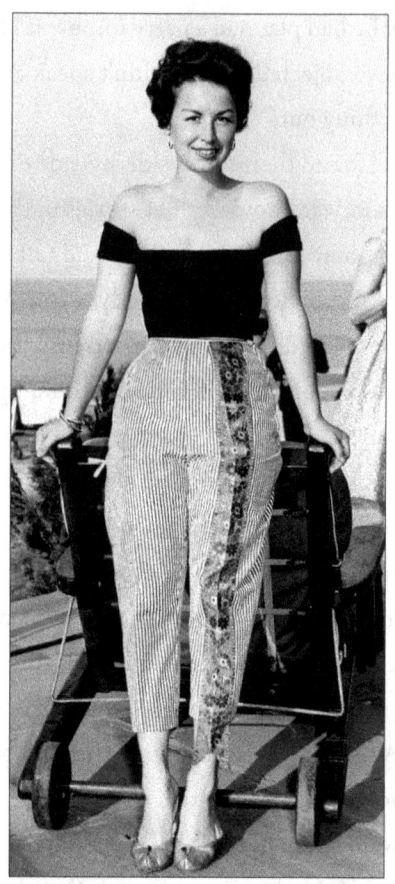

**Dennis flipped for Micki, and
who can blame him?**

That was the first time Micki heard Dennis speak. He turned to Vincent and said, "Get out."

Vincent left with Micki's mother, and Dennis left with Micki. Dennis explained, through a thick and not-fully-recovered voice, that he wasn't a guitar player. He was a television performer who appeared on many programs. He gave Micki a list of all the times during the week that he could be seen on TV, and promised that when he returned to New York, he'd have a TV sent to her apartment.

Dennis returned to New York, and for the next week, Micki made her

Chapter Eight: Hey Micki!

way to department stores throughout town at the different times that Dennis had mentioned to her. As it turned out, she realized that he wasn't kidding; he really was a star on this new thing called television, and he really was on it quite a bit. After about a week, a new television arrived for Micki and her mother. He really hadn't been kidding about that, either.

Romeo and Juliet? Not quite; Dennis and Micki didn't have a balcony, and it certainly wasn't a tragedy.

Not that she was completely won over by that. She was a small-town girl who was accustomed to small-town people. Dennis was from a big city, and he was in big-time show business. As *Radio-TV Mirror* later explained it, she was a little skeptical of Dennis.

Micki told the magazine, "Oh, Dennis overwhelmed me all right. But I thought, this man is too sophisticated for me; we live in different worlds."

She kept seeing him. Dennis had no problem with buying plane ticket after plane ticket to make his way to Florida on the weekends to see her. She got to know him more and found that this big-city show business fellow was more than slick hair and 32 pearly whites.

Micki elaborated, "Actually, I lost my first fear of Dennis early. I found that he was quite unaffected. He had good common sense, and he was sweet and considerate. When I was beginning to feel he was 'my kind of people,' I was started to pick up a magazine one day and see a picture of Dennis describing him as one of the ten best-dressed men in the country. Oh, I was impressed by it. Maybe too impressed! Because I was indecisive again—and that, I think, was because I wasn't quite sure of myself."

Micki continued modeling in Florida and found her way into the Orange Bowl Parade as one of the Orange Bowl Princesses. A week before the game, she and the other princesses were put up in a hotel for a busy week of photo ops and publicity appearances. Walking through the hotel lobby on her way to another in an endless string of appointments, she saw Dennis on TV and came to a sudden halt to watch him.

A chaperone came over to nudge her along. "Come on, Micki, we have to go."

Micki pointed to the screen and said, "My boyfriend is on TV."

The chaperone looked at Dennis on TV, rolled her eyes, and said, "I know. I like him, too. Let's go."

As busy as Dennis' workload was, he still had his weekends wide open, and he made the best of it. He began flying to Florida every weekend just to go on a date with Micki. He left late on Sunday evening and made it back to New York on Monday morning, just in time for *Okay Mother*.

Except once. Micki explains, "One night, he missed the flight going back to New York because we were sitting in the airport together, smooching, and we just both lost track of time. Dennis missed *Okay Mother* the next day. He was devastated when he realized he didn't get back on time. Dennis hated being late and he hated being thought of as unprofessional, so missing that flight and missing the show really upset him."

Chapter Eight: Hey Micki!

This was true. Dennis prided himself on punctuality. One day a few months earlier, he was driving to DuMont, when he and his brother, Lou, saw a man jump into the Hudson River. Dennis and Lou pulled the man out of the river, and then made it to DuMont in time to start the show, yet now, he had missed *Okay Mother* because a kiss distracted him.

The way Dennis saw things, there was only one solution to this problem. As soon as he finally did make it back to New York, he got on the phone and called Micki. "How soon can you and your mother be in New York? The way we're doing this isn't working out."

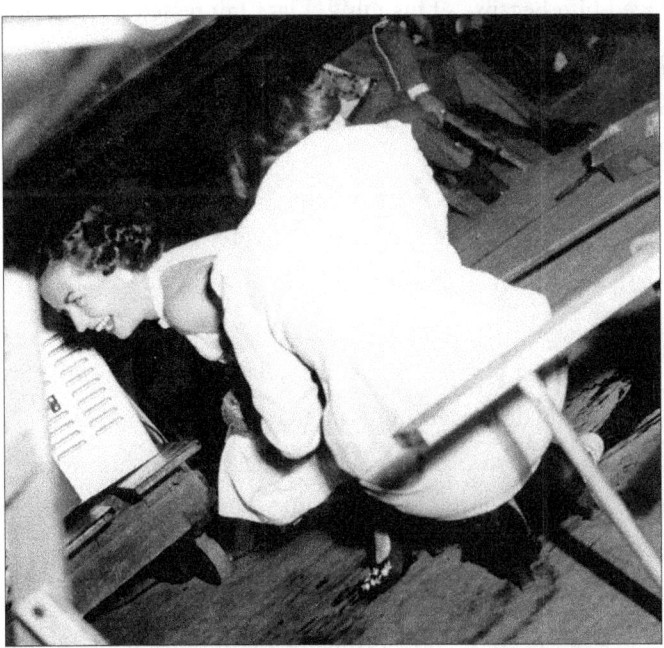

"This isn't what I signed up for!" Micki crawled under the ring during a wrestling match, an eventful introduction to her fiancé's night job.

Dennis bought Micki a plane ticket and waited for her visit to New York. The plane landed and Dennis didn't waste any time. As soon as she got off the plane, he blurted out, "Let's get married."

Micki fired back, "Yes! I've been wondering when you were going to ask me!"

Micki and her mother officially arrived in New York in May 1951 and rented a small studio apartment. Micki visited Dennis' bachelor pad, the walls covered with photos of boxers. She found work as an artist, while her mother began working as an interior decorator.

Micki remembers, "I was excited to move to New York. When I was growing up in Pennsylvania, moving to New York had been a dream of mine. And I got to move there and be with a man that I was in love with, so of course I was happy about that. I don't know what Dennis liked about me... He liked my size, at least, I know that. He used to say I was his fighting weight.

"I loved him because of his mind. I was impressed with his mind, and the way he processed things. He was interested in psychology, and what makes people tick. He was different from anybody I had met before. He had more experience in life."

Micki was still learning about what life with Dennis would be. He had to officially file for divorce from his first wife; they had only separated. With marriage to Micki on the horizon, he finally had to settle unfinished business.

Micki also got a glimpse of Dennis' relationship with his six-year-old son. "Dennis really did not like the fact that he couldn't see Dennis Jr. more often. He missed his son, and I could see that. It hurt him when he mentioned that. And he really did his best to maintain a bond from far away. They spoke on the phone often. Dennis always saw him for holidays and in the summertime. He really worked hard at being a father from far away. And I think he did as well as he could. Personally, Dennis Jr. and I have a wonderful relationship, and we always have."

Micki also discovered that she was in for a few adventures, just from being married to a professional wrestling commentator. "Dennis was always right at ringside when he called the matches. They had him at a table that was flush against the ring, with his microphone and all of his equipment and his sound effect props on there. One night, he's calling the action, and one wrestler flings his opponent through the ropes and he crashes right onto

Chapter Eight: Hey Micki!

Dennis and the table, which knocked Dennis out of his chair and flattened him on the floor.

"Dennis goes back to the locker room after the show and he tells all the wrestlers, 'Fellows, honestly, it doesn't bother me if you do that. It really doesn't. But in the future, can you give me a signal so I can be ready for it?' And the wrestlers talked it over for a minute and then they showed Dennis some kind of signal that they all agreed on.

"Dennis brought me along to the arena one night to watch the matches with him. I didn't talk on the air, but I sat next to him during the show. And right before the show starts, Dennis says to me, 'Now, at some point during the show, I might tell you to get under the ring. Just promise me that you'll get under the ring if I do that.' I had no idea what he meant by that, but I agreed.

"Later in the night, there's a match going on, and Dennis sees something happen that catches his eye. I don't know what he saw, but he covers his microphone and says 'Get under the ring!' So, I crawl underneath the ring, and as soon as I'm down there, I see this man's body fly out of the ring and crash on Dennis, and Dennis is flattened out on the floor. He kept me out of harm's way. And the best part is, there was a photographer there. I have this photo of myself underneath the ring after Dennis got his signal."

Gino Garabaldi surprised Dennis one night before the matches by approaching him and telling him, "I'm going to land right in your lap and break the chair you're sitting in."

Dennis tried to talk him out of it, fearing more for his own safety than Gino's, but Gino had his mind made up that he was going to do it, and Dennis' concern only seemed to strengthen his resolve. He was adamant that he could break the chair without hurting Dennis. When the match finally happened, Gino got flung out of the ring and crashed into Dennis. Gino landed with so much thrust that the chair collapsed underneath Dennis, who amazingly didn't feel a thing. Gino had protected him.

Micki met Dennis' friends in the next few months. "He was friends with a lot of comedians. I remember meeting Paul Winchell and Herb Shriner.

And I also remember him being extremely close to the people from P. Lorillard Tobacco, the makers of Old Gold. Mrs. Kent, who was the namesake of Kent cigarettes, gave us our wedding shower. He had absolutely formed a true friendship with most of them. You could tell they liked each other a lot. Dennis' friends were all much older than I was, I remember that. And I missed my own friends. By my second visit to New York, I decided to be very honest with Dennis. I told him, 'I don't know if this is going to work out.' I was a small town girl, and New York could be overwhelming. After I had been in New York for a while, it got to a point where I didn't feel uncomfortable anymore, but I still had my reservations, and I was always truthful about that when Dennis and I discussed what we were planning to do."

Dennis and Micki on December 5, 1951.

Chapter Eight: Hey Micki!

Dennis and Micki were married on December 5, 1951. Vincent Andrews, accidental matchmaker, served as Best Man. Aaron Steiner, Dennis' manager, gave away the bride. Micki managed to cast aside her reservations about packing up her life to move to New York with Dennis for a little while ... only about forty-six years or so.

CHAPTER NINE
A LIFETIME OF WORK

WORK KEPT DENNIS firmly glued to New York for the first two months of matrimony, but in February 1952, he and Micki embarked on a honeymoon in Rio De Janiero, compliments of Ted Mack, before returning to the United States and a big cozy apartment in the middle of the hustle and bustle of New York. He kept working, and Micki learned to adjust to life as the wife of a TV star.

She told *Radio-TV Mirror*, "It bothered me a little the first time people moved in on us when we were out to dinner, but I learned... I was reconciled to having a million mothers-in-law. But I didn't quite expect the taxi driver."

Dennis explained that remark. "Micki and I had the darndest things happen. The newspapers published pictures when we were married, but no one bothered us at the plush hotel to which we went. Then, next morning, as we got into a cab, the driver turned around and leered, 'Did you have a good time?' Well, Micki blushed and I all but socked him. My disposition was not improved by the fact that we hadn't slept a wink. Right beneath our windows, every restaurant and hotel in the block was loading its garbage. The clatter of cans and the grinding of trucks went on all night long."

Dennis went back to work after the honeymoon... truly right after the honeymoon. He had to do *Okay Mother* the day that he and Micki returned. Before long, he had a frightening moment that he considered to be the very end of his career. It wasn't until years later that he was able to laugh at it.

Dennis, who was still making a princely sum as the spokesman for Old Gold cigarettes, was backstage at *Stop the Music* one night, waiting for the program to go on the air, and to do his thing, extolling the virtues of the sponsor, "For a treat instead of a treatment, Old Gold cigarettes." As Dennis waited, he thumbed through a months-old magazine and glanced at an ad for Lucky Strike cigarettes. The ad, with some kind of old-fashioned Christmas theme to it, referred to the brand as "Ye Olde Lucky Strikes."

Dennis strolled out onstage to deliver his commercial, which touted the recent uptick in sales that Old Gold had enjoyed. He beamed, smiled, and told the television audience, "All over America, they're switching to Ye Olde Lucky Strike cigarettes."

Dennis finished his commercial, walked offstage, and encountered an aghast ad agency representative, with a face as white as a sheet.

"Why did you say that?!" the ad man asked.

"Say what?" Dennis replied.

"You said 'Lucky Strike'!"

"No I didn't!" Dennis hadn't heard the words coming out of his own mouth.

Chapter Nine: A Lifetime of Work

Dennis thought he'd be out of a job after a gaffe during a commercial, but as he found over the years, the folks at Old Gold had a sense of humor.

"Yes you did! You just said people are switching to Ye Olde Lucky Strike cigarettes!"

The argument went back and forth for a few moments. Dennis insisted that he had said Old Gold, as he was supposed to, asking he would say any other brand, since Old Gold was the only cigarette he had ever done commercials for. Fed up, he tried to close the subject by saying, "Here, I'll prove I said Old Gold."

Dennis picked up the phone. Micki, his #1 fan, of course, was tuned in at home, and he knew it. Micki answered the phone, and she was sobbing. "*Why did you say that?!*"

Dennis stayed on the telephone with Micki until she calmed down, assuring her—and really, trying to assure himself—that it was going to be okay. He seemed to put that fire out, and together they made plans to go to the movies after *Stop the Music* was over.

Dennis left the studio, put work behind him for the day, and headed off to the theater for a night at the movies with his wife. Micki remembers, "We were seated in the theater, and they brought the lights down. It was totally dark. And then the movie starts and the movie is giving off that glow that lights everyone's faces just a little bit. And I look over and tears are running down my husband's face. That's how he felt in that moment. 'I'm never going to work again. That's it. I'm done.'"

He wasn't done. To his surprise, the chairman of the board of Lorillard Tobacco sent him a message the next day, invoking the name of the ball player currently adorning every Wheaties advertisement on the market, simply saying "If Stan Musial can make a mistake once in a while, so can Dennis James."

Dennis happily, gratefully put the incident behind him and was able to almost forget about it, except for one night when he and Micki were at a fine restaurant and they were approached by a man neither of them recognized.

"Mr. James, I'm from Lucky Strike," the man said as he handed Dennis a phony check.

It wasn't the only time Dennis feared for his Old Gold contract. He once observed that there was an odd lot of fans out there who were determined to trip up TV spokespeople by tricking them into using a competing product. He was a victim of one of them.

As he recalled, "It was successful only once, and this guy must really have been plotting it. We were at a big party, there was a lot going on, it was getting late, and like everyone else, I ran out of cigarettes. This fellow offered me one, and automatically, I took it. You'd have thought I tripped the burglar alarm of the United States Mint. All of a sudden there were flash bulbs popping, people shouting, and this guy laughing like a hyena. He really figured he had put one over on me."

Dennis was quite happily still doing commercials for Old Gold, though he hardly had to worry if he had lost the gig. Even without those commercials, he couldn't have been busier. He also had commercial endorsement deals with General Electric, Ford Motor Company, United States Rubber, and Kaiser-Frazer Autos.

Chapter Nine: A Lifetime of Work

Dennis chatted with a referee between the matches on Dumont. Professional wrestling kept him tied to the network, but he was beginning to see signs that his fortune might be elsewhere.

Dennis even got to do a little TV acting. He played himself in a comedy sketch for *Texaco Star Theater*, calling the commentary for a bit in which Milton Berle became a professional wrestler. He also got glowing reviews for his performance in an NBC teleplay called *Pardon My Prisoner*. It was a surreal spot for Dennis, an announcer for so many years, to stand backstage just before the performance started, and hear the NBC announcer declare, "... Starring tonight: Dennis James!"

Critic C. E. Butterfield wrote the following week, "Most viewers who have watched Dennis James as a wrestling announcer, as an MC, or as a TV cigarette salesman don't know he also is an actor. Well he is, and he showed what he could do . . . He carried off the assignment without a bit of trouble."

In addition, Dennis, who had been a stalwart for Dr. DuMont over the years, was beginning to explore his options at other networks. It was, unfortunately for Dr. DuMont, a necessary career move for his faithful stars.

NBC and CBS were flourishing in the early 1950s, but DuMont had always had a few basic problems that kept it from growing as quickly as its competitors. NBC and CBS both previously had enormously successful radio networks, which meant that they had big-name stars from the radio that could transition to television and draw in viewers. They had networks of radio affiliates that could give them footholds in hundreds of cities for TV stations. They also could use the profits that radio was still drawing to fund the television programming until the television programming became popular enough to sustain itself. DuMont only had homegrown, new talent, and no big stars to attract loyal radio audiences. They also didn't have any established relationships that would help them establish new stations.

Also working against DuMont's favor was an FCC freeze on television license applications. The freeze was instituted in 1948 in response to the thousands of applications for licenses that the FCC was having trouble sorting through. The freeze was only supposed to last for six months, but instead, it remained in place until 1952. When the freeze was finally lifted, NBC, CBS, and newcomer ABC swept up most of the Very High Frequency (VHF) channels 2-13 on the television dial. This meant DuMont could only make use of Ultra High Frequency (UHF) channels 14-83. The problem with this was that most televisions in 1952 didn't have dials that tuned to UHF channels. An expensive converter was required. DuMont staff began quietly worrying that their days were numbered. These problems didn't pop up overnight, but when it was apparent that DuMont was off to a much slower start than its competitors (in 1951, it had less than half the affiliates of either CBS or NBC), Dennis was probably darn happy that he had begun making himself available to the other guys.

Chapter Nine: A Lifetime of Work

Just the three of us. Dennis and Micki would grow their family later, but for now, it was only the newlyweds and their dog.

Dennis' Old Gold commercials allowed him to get familiar with the other networks. Ted Mack had taken *Ted Mack's Original Amateur Hour* from DuMont to NBC in 1949. Dennis had also supplied commentary for ABC's coverage of Macy's Thanksgiving Day Parade in 1951, just twelve days before getting married. Also, when Sterling Drug Company broke their deal to sponsor *Okay Mother*, Dennis uprooted the show and took it to ABC, where it was retitled *The Dennis James Show* and held on for only another six months before expiring in February 1952. ABC, with a weak line-up of affiliates—even weaker during daytime hours—was struggling to establish a daytime line-up at that point. After *The Dennis James Show* was cancelled, it was replaced in the 11:30 a.m. timeslot by *The Paul Dixon Show*, which only aired every other day. After only a month, Dixon was moved out of the time slot to an afternoon spot, and ABC didn't air another show in a morning time slot for two years.

Dennis and ABC could still build a successful show at night. With ABC off to a slow start, with a low number of affiliates and limited cash flow, programming that network in 1952 worked very much the same way as programming for DuMont; the cheaper, the better.

With *Ted Mack's Original Amateur Hour* still drawing an audience after years on radio and television, ABC figured that the audience would be drawn to another talent show, and Dennis even put up a shingle for a production company, Jade Productions, to produce it. Finding a sponsor was easy. Dennis was naturally able to take care of that detail.

P. Lorillard Tobacco Co. proudly announced: "The *Chance of a Lifetime* is what professional entertainers strive for on our television show of the same name. It stars Old Gold's famous—and persuasive—Dennis James, popular with millions of viewers everywhere."

Chance of a Lifetime debuted on ABC on May 8, 1952, as a replacement for the TV version of *Stop the Music*. Although the radio version for which Dennis did the commercials and occasionally guest-hosted had always been a major hit, the TV incarnation was surprisingly never well-received. At the time that ABC cancelled it, the TV show had never aired one episode with a commercial because sponsors just didn't think it was worth their dollars.

Chance of a Lifetime welcomed contestants who were aspiring entertainers, unlike *Ted Mack's Amateur Hour*. They were acts that had at least a little professional experience but were on the hunt for more exposure. The acts were judged and scored. The winning act got $1,000, an invitation to perform the following week, and a guaranteed one-week booking at a New York City nightclub, such as The Latin Quarter.

Chapter Nine: A Lifetime of Work

Chance of a Lifetime was low-cost, but it generated high interest. The cash was nice, but the guaranteed nightclub engagement for a full week was even better, in light of the number of doors it could open for a winning act. Case in point, one of the show's early winners was a duo called the Impressionaires, a pair of singers, who did celebrity impersonations between their songs. They earned one week at The Palace. That, in turn, led to bookings at The Waldorf Astoria and The Meadow Brook, two appearances on *The Ed Sullivan Show,* then a record-setting run of performances at The New York Hippodrome, followed by a year on tour with one of the first ice skating variety shows, and then a long stretch as an opening act for Alan King, Red Buttons, and Buddy Hackett. *Chance of a Lifetime* wasn't just a catchy title; it was an accurate description of what was at stake.

Dennis searches for new talent on *Chance of a Lifetime*. Where could those new stars be?

Plenty of performers took full advantage of that chance. One was a pretty eighteen-year-old gal from the Bronx. By her own admission, she was shy, but young Diahann Carroll worked up the nerve to go to an audition and got on *Chance of a Lifetime*. Her rendition of "Stormy Weather" earned $1,000 plus a full week at The Latin Quarter. The following week, she returned to the show, sang "Can't Help Lovin' That Man of Mine," and wound up with another $1,000 and another week at The Latin Quarter. She came back for a third week, pocketed a third check, and did another week of shows at The Latin Quarter. That she lost on week four was irrelevant. She was already a celebrity by that point. Diahann Carroll walked away a "loser" that fourth week, went straight to another nightclub downtown, easily snapped up another week's engagement just by asking for it, and then hopped on a plane for a coast-to-coast tour of all the nightclubs that had called her during the past month. She never looked back; she never had to.

Neither did Jonathan Winters, who made his television debut on the program. In 1954, Dick Van Dyke also made his network television debut on *Chance of a Lifetime*, too, and so did pianist Roger Williams.

Rather than hire a spokesman to do the commercial breaks on *Chance of a Lifetime*, as most shows would, Dennis went ahead and did the commercials himself; he had the experience, after all. So skillful was he in that capacity that he turned a catastrophe into a victory one night, when things went wrong during a commercial.

That show was partially sponsored by Lentheric, a line of perfume. Dennis held a perfume bottle in his hand, spoke glowingly of the lovely fragrance it gave off, and pressed down for a light spritz. The top of the perfume bottle stuck into place, and perfume sprayed and sprayed and sprayed from the bottle, like insect repellent. A cloud of perfume mist was forming all around Dennis.

Dennis, without missing a beat, waved the perfume bottle around and spoke about how he couldn't get enough of the smell, how he was trying to fill the whole stage with this enchanting perfume and how he liked to do the same thing around his house, trying to fill his house with this wonderful perfume. As Dennis continued talking, his arm movements became more

Chapter Nine: A Lifetime of Work

exaggerated. He had a sly tone of voice as he extolled the wonders of a house that smelled like perfume. He didn't really want the audience to believe him. He was letting a barrier down, in a way, revealing to the audience that this commercial was going wrong without actually saying it. The audience in the studio caught on and had a high time watching Dennis struggle with the perfume bottle as he finished his plug.

Sponsor magazine detailed what happened next: "By Saturday [at] noon, retailers in most of twenty-seven markets covered were sold out. Retailers, in reordering, said customers asked for 'perfume advertised on Dennis James' show last night.' Lentheric ad manager, William G. Ohme, said the show 'left us unable to cope with the immediate response.' Aim of TV commercials was 'hard sell,' he said, noting that this was radical change from most perfume advertising, which is based on prestige."

Dennis endorsed toothpastes, medicines, and perfumes, but the nation still associated his face with Old Gold cigarettes. Next to Dennis, a statuette of the iconic dancing cigarette pack that joined him in the ads.

Dennis was able to turn reality into an effective commercial on another evening. He opened the show by briefly touching on what a bad night it was in New York, and then seemed to realize, quite suddenly, that the bad night he was in the middle of made a perfect commercial for the sponsor.

Dennis walked onstage that night and acknowledged the audience's applause, as he sat at his desk. He said, "Thank you very much. What are you trying to do, Herb, pick up my spirits? Our producer, Herb Moss, knows at this point that I'm just about a little bit miserable. The weather in New York is just horrible, I want to tell you. I want to thank all of you for coming to the theater tonight, because our show is built upon an audience, and we have a full house in spite of the worst night I've ever seen in New York. I say that Herb is picking up my spirits because I just flew in on an airplane from down on the sunny shores of Florida, and right after the show tonight, I'll be on a midnight plane going out, *if* it goes out. So you can have New York this week, kids, that's all I can tell you. I want to get back to where that sun is shining and just lay down and rest. Tonight, before the night is over, I *will* take a Bromo-Seltzer. If you want to call all of your friends in and see this demonstration, call your neighbors, because tonight, I will need it."

Despite the occasional upset stomach, Dennis liked *Chance of a Lifetime* and gradually realized he liked it for a different reason than most of the other work he had done on radio and television. He felt the same sense of satisfaction doing *Chance of a Lifetime* that he felt doing a telethon. Dennis liked the idea that he was doing a show that helped people.

Dennis took stock of his own career, and yes, he absolutely had talent, but he recognized that in a volatile field like show business, a big part of success was luck. He had a brother who helped him break in the business at the very beginning of television. He wound up in a position where he could gain experience when nobody else really wanted that experience, and he was always in the right place at the right time when the earliest new opportunities presented themselves. Dennis realized that there were plenty of people with talent, often with talent to spare, who didn't have those opportunities.

He was now introducing those performers week after week on *Chance of a Lifetime*, and he realized that, after a decade and a half in broadcasting, doing the show gave him a feeling of "giving back."

Dennis greeted two contestants on *Turn to a Friend*, a feel-good game show that helped the down-on-their-luck.

"Giving back" was what enticed Dennis to take on his next assignment, an ABC radio quiz called *Turn to a Friend*. It was an entry into what was quickly becoming a much reviled concept among critics, but wildly popular among viewers, the sob-story-as-game-show. The father of the genre was *Queen for a Day*, a controversial show in which women came onstage and related recent tragedies in their lives—the death of a loved one, a house in foreclosure, an extended stay in the hospital—and the audience voted on which contestant was "most deserving" of becoming *Queen for a Day,* in essence, voting on who had it the worst. *Strike It Rich* was another one. Having a sob story was merely a prerequisite for being allowed to play a Question and Answer game for cash and prizes. *Strike It Rich* also had a feature called the Heart Line, a phone number that viewers could call to pledge money directly to the contestant. The Heart Line blurred the line so badly between "game show" and "panhandling" that the state of New York conducted an investigation into the show.

For *Turn to a Friend*, Dennis introduced a person in need and then invited a friend of that person, or sometimes a random member of the audience, to come onstage and play a Question and Answer game on that person's behalf. A contestant's right answers earned money or a much-needed item for the friend in need, and as a reward for the good deed, a contestant received a little bit of money to put in his or her own pocket.

Radio listeners liked *Turn to a Friend* enough that ABC, struggling to build a daytime line-up (they didn't even start their broadcast day until 3:00 p.m.), put the show on their television line-up at 4:00 p.m.

At that time, an ABC statement said, "The secret of Dennis James' popularity with the housewife is his pleasant voice, cheerful manner, and his remarkable ability to be natural with women. He is neither coy nor condescending. His warmth and ability to project his personality comes from years of experience in TV."

ABC cut costs to the bone as a way to entice sponsors. At 4:30 p.m., it was followed by *The Ern Westmore Show*, which not only taped in the same studio but used the same set. At 4:29 p.m. each day, Dennis signed off and left the set, the audience remained in their seats, and then Ern Westmore walked out and did an entirely different type of program for them. Buzz Chapin, ABC's head of daytime programming, optimistically said that if viewers responded well to the concept, ABC may follow it by introducing a block of soap operas all making use of the same single set.

Part of the charm of *Turn to a Friend* was that it was a loosely run ship. All of the money given away was obviously going to a good cause, and the audience wanted the good feeling of someone in need receiving some much-

Chapter Nine: A Lifetime of Work

needed aid. Some minor cheating here and there was encouraged, and Dennis happily participated.

One day, a woman was playing to earn a new wheelchair for her father. Dennis asked, "Who was the author of the book, *The Good Earth*?"

The contestant stared back blankly. Dennis, in full view of the audience, opened up his own wallet, pulled out a $1 bill, and waved it in front of her face as a hint.

Dennis showed off his "Stick-to-It Award," given to him by the Minnesota Mining and Manufacturing Company (a/k/a 3M) as part of their celebration of the 25th anniversary of Scotch tape. The award commended Dennis for "perseverance, courage, and achievement."

"Dollar!" the contestant shouted.

"That's right! Pearl Buck!" Dennis excitedly replied. She got the wheelchair.

Perhaps the most unusual prize ever given away on *Turn to a Friend* was a cow. A fifteen-year-old named George Weaver wrote to the show about how his family had lost their possessions four years earlier, and times had been difficult for his father, an orchard worker, because the unusually cold winter looked like it would cost him some work in the near future. George was brought on the show to represent the family, and won a cow plus 200 chicks, allowing the Weavers to go into business for themselves as farmers.

Hosting *Turn to a Friend* could often be a tricky assignment for Dennis for the simple reason that he had to maintain a cheerful façade throughout the tales of woe. Even the contestants who were there for what seemed like joyful reasons couldn't hide their true feelings.

A woman was on the show in need of enough supplies to take care of her newborn triplets. Dennis couldn't help making note of her demeanor during the game, saying, "That's the quietest enthusiasm I've ever seen." The woman clearly did not see her three-for-one birth as a blessed event, and even when she won (with Dennis' help, of course), it went without saying that she still wasn't anywhere near the finish line for this challenge.

ABC's cost-cutting block of programming was a bust. *The Billboard* didn't really care for either show, but the paper was completely horrified by Ern Westmore's show, a real-life Pygmalion effort in which Westmore selected women from the audience, critiqued their hair, make-up and clothing, and then gave them a makeover. The problem was that these women didn't show up expecting or needing a makeover and thought they looked just fine, until Westmore had singled them out with a national audience looking in. *Turn to a Friend* and *The Ern Westmore Show* quietly disappeared, without ever obtaining a sponsor, after only a few weeks.

Dennis happily kept using his talents to give back, often for a more noble purpose than a career in show business. He rounded out 1952 with another telethon for United Cerebral Palsy, an eighteen-hour affair on the ABC Network. He was joined by President-Elect Dwight Eisenhower, Morey Amsterdam, Joey Bishop, Yul Brynner, Red Buttons, Jack Carter, Nat King Cole, Arlene Francis, Jackie Gleason, Gabby Hayes, Dorothy Lamour, Guy Lombardo and His Orchestra, Garry Moore, Johnny Olson, Les Paul

Chapter Nine: A Lifetime of Work

and Mary Ford, Jane Pickens, Martha Raye, Buddy Rich, Ceasar Romero, Herb Shriner, Ed Sullivan and more. Together, they raised $655,108.

Dennis did another Thanksgiving Day Parade in 1952, committing a mildly treasonous act in the year after covering Macy's Thanksgiving Parade by going to Philadelphia for Gimbel's Thanksgiving Parade. Dennis wasn't on commentary, but rather an active participant, riding in the WFIL convertible to represent the ABC affiliate in Philadelphia, as "Santa's Escort to Toyland."

Dennis and Micki were looking for something a bit finer than an apartment in the middle of the city ... and Dennis found it in New Rochelle.

Micki never had aspirations for show business. She actually looked at her husband in amazement, the way he could stare into a camera lens knowing that millions of eyes were staring back, or the way he could handle a crowd of thousands at an event like a parade without losing his composure or becoming claustrophobic. She did her best to stay out of the public eye, but Dennis wanted to share some of the fun. He talked her into riding with him and waving to the adoring public as the parade passed.

Micki remembers, "I was riding in the parade car with him when I suddenly had to go to the bathroom! I jumped out of the car and ran into the nearest department store as the parade moved on. Then I caught a cab back to the railway station and I waited for the parade to come that way. As soon as Dennis' car made it there, I hopped back in and finished the parade with him. I was relieved—and so was he."

In December 1952, Dennis and Micki celebrated their first anniversary. It wasn't so long ago that Dennis was dreading losing every gig he had as a domino effect from the "Lucky Strike" gaffe. Now, not only was he working more than ever, he wasn't in that lonely, dull apartment in the middle of New York City anymore.

Dennis was still using his boat to drift around Echo Bay, and was still utterly engrossed by the massive house with the backyard that sloped into the water. He later said, "The house on the Sound had always stuck in my mind, but you just don't go around envying someone else's property."

It bothered him so much that he finally began making inquiries about the house and found, to his delight, that it was going on the market. He took another look and realized what his life had turned into. It used to be that he didn't even entertain the thought of moving there because he didn't see a reason to, but now he had a wife, and he knew she wanted to start a family some day. He finally had a reason to buy a house . . . his dream house, too!

"When you marry a girl like Micki," he said, "you just naturally think of a real home and the things that go with it."

He told Micki, and they went together to inspect it. She went straight to the kitchen, and Dennis checked the garage. He noticed an overhead door and decided to test it. The door worked, but Dennis was knocked unconscious when the door fell off the track.

Undeterred by the knockout blow, they bought the house. Two weeks after moving in, Micki walked into the garage and found Dennis' blood on the ground. He drove himself to the emergency room, got himself stitched up, and came right home, to the consternation of Micki, who couldn't believe that he drove himself to the hospital after a blow to the head. He promptly replaced the overhead door with a remote control door opening system.

Dennis gave his father a tour of the new house.

Together, Dennis and Micki turned the four-level, ten-room house into a home. The curved living room, which Micki called the Cinerama, was surrounded by floor-to-ceiling windows that spanned nearly the entire width of the room. The chairs and couches faced the window. Dennis kept a telescope and binoculars in there, too. The opposite wall was filled with built-in book cases, but with the view they had, Micki admitted that she found it difficult to concentrate on a book after they had moved in.

Micki decorated the living room with white carpeting, offset by a variety of colors in the decorations. Clutter was minimal; Micki wanted enough space to accommodate the occasional party.

Dennis' contribution to the living room was a paneled fireplace that he custom-built so that some of the panels encased a television set. During the boring parts of a show, he could just cast his eyes a little bit to the left and watch the log burn. On the mantel, he kept a gift from ventriloquist Paul Winchell, a Swiss clock that was powered by barometric pressure changes, and a few mahogany figures that he had picked up during a trip to Haiti.

Beneath the living room was Dennis' game room, decorated by the various awards and photos that he had collected during his career. He kept a microphone and a reel-to-reel audio recording machine, in case he wanted to record a demo tape for a new gig or make note of a new idea. Near a large sit-down bar were another fireplace and another TV, plus a set of tables and chairs made from repurposed barrels. On the walls were all of Dennis' boxer photos, a dartboard, and a couple of antique musket. He and Micki had a couple of rifles; neither of them hunted but they took up skeet shooting together. Near the game room was the laundry room, which had a deep freezer; Dennis' mother lovingly made her son several gallons of her spaghetti sauce, and he thawed it out as needed when Micki made pasta for dinner.

There were indoor and outdoor dining areas. Near the outdoor dining terrace, Dennis kept a telescope for water-gazing. Upstairs was the temporary sewing room (Dennis and Micki always made it a point to use the word "temporary" when referring to it, because they both anticipated that at some point it would be a nursery) and the workroom, an all-purpose project space with desks, a film projector, a film cutting table, a phonograph and record albums, and an artists' space with a unique easel built for two.

Dennis explained, "I designed the easel and had it made after Micki taught me to paint. I learned on a dare. She was taking forever to complete a portrait. I got tired of seeing it around, so I said if she didn't finish it, I would! She replied, 'Start one yourself, smarty.' So I did."

In time, Dennis became pretty good at it. The dining room was adorned with a landscape by him. In the foyer entering the house was a portrait of Dennis' father, Demitrio.

Scattered throughout the house were plenty of modern appliances and gadgets, including a complicated tape-recording system that Dennis could set up to record radio and television programs if he wasn't going to be home to tune in as they aired; state-of-the-art stuff for the 1950s.

What's up, dock? Dennis' new house had a backyard that was just perfect for an avid boater.

Micki had a gadget that she was crazy about, too. When she and Dennis traveled to Italy, she became enamored with an unusual coffee maker, so Dennis went ahead and bought it for her. Even though it was just the two of them in the house, she returned from Italy with her very own fourteen-cup coffee maker. There were so many gizmos in the house that, to be on the safe side, Dennis kept a 5,000-watt generator hooked up to the house to keep everything up and running just in case there was a storm. There was a particularly bad storm shortly after they moved in, which destroyed the pier that led into the bay. It was the first major repair that Dennis had to make. After a lifetime of renting property, he suddenly became a handyman by necessity. He was surprised at how quickly he mastered plumbing.

Outside, there was a private swimming pool, even though the home was right on the water. The property came with a private dock and pier at the edge of the massive backyard. For a time, while Johnny Carson lived in New Rochelle, he'd use the dock for his own boat and go swimming in the James' pool, always leaving a note on the door for Dennis and Micki when he did so. There was so much space to dock a boat that a few of Dennis' friends who owned seaplanes flew over to Dennis' place for a visit and left their craft floating as they went inside.

It was the most perfectly designed home one could fathom for the purpose of throwing a party, and that's exactly what Dennis and Micki did.

Dennis once beamed, "You can see that here's where we work, play, and live. When I'm through with a show, I come home and relax, or take the boat out across the Sound, or pick up a brush and start to paint. When I must go out of town, Micki goes with me and we have a good time. Sure, television can get tough, but what other business would give me time and daylight hours to enjoy the things I like best?"

Dennis enjoyed boating quite often, befriending two kindred spirits on the water with similar careers. Garry Moore was a popular jack-of-all-trades, hosting a number of game and variety shows over his long career. Herb Shriner was an Indiana native with an unconventional path to stardom: he had started off as harmonica virtuoso who occasionally told jokes between tunes. He was so good at telling jokes and spinning long yarns about his hometown that the act eventually flipped. He became a comedian who played the harmonica between jokes. He and Dennis often struck out on the water together, although if Dennis wasn't out on the water during a given day, he

Chapter Nine: A Lifetime of Work

could still chat with his friends via the battery-powered portable speaker on the pier that he could use to contact the boaters in the Sound.

As much as Dennis and Micki liked the house, Demitrio loved it. He hoped his little boy would become a doctor, not so much for the prestige but for the knowledge that it would ensure him a comfortable life. Dennis, in turn, offered his father a share of that comfort. He bought his dad a house in Fort Lauderdale, Florida, and took care of all the utilities, to boot. It was truly Dennis' gift to his father.

Dennis and Micki thumbed through a magazine, even though the view made it a little difficult to concentrate on reading material sometimes.

Demitrio saw the way his son's life turned out—not a doctor, but a comfortable living owing to a well-developed set of skills. He received a healthy paycheck that afforded a house, a car, and a boat, and he had the beginnings of a new family. Demitrio was somewhat amused to admit to himself that Dennis' life looked exactly like a successful doctor's life.

The house and the career were nice, but Dennis told a reporter, "As wonderful as the house is, it would be nothing without Micki. I wouldn't want it without her."

Micki got to know many of Dennis' friends at the clambakes, but there was one friend in particular that she hadn't crossed paths with just yet. It ended up being the friend who left the strongest impression. Dennis and Micki had gone to see Nat King Cole, and as they made their way past one alley, they happened to spot Frank Sinatra standing alone at a door near the club. Sinatra had some well-publicized troubles recently. His marriage to Ava Gardner had gone sour and had caused him a great deal of public embarrassment. A hemorrhage of the throat required him to take time off and cancel a number of bookings. Columbia Records had to loan him $200,000 to help him pay off his back taxes.

For all of that, Sinatra was still a major star, but definitely a major star in a turbulent time. Micki, a former bobbysoxer, watched in astonishment as her fiancé walked up to Sinatra and said, "Hey Frank, if you ever want to get out of the city and just be quiet, we have a really nice place in New Rochelle."

Frank looked at him, nodded, and said, "Thanks, Dennis."

Dennis was genuinely trying to do something kind for an old friend, but the sight of it left Micki agog. Not only was Dennis a nice guy, he was a nice guy who kept high-ranking company. He was genuine . . . and genuinely impressive.

Frank's career would recover in time. A few months later, Dennis and Micki attended a party at the home of one of the east coast-based executives for Columbia Pictures. Columbia was in the process of casting a film that they had high hopes for, *From Here to Eternity*. Dennis and Micki sat and ate with the executive's wife and actress Gene Tierney, when the executive walked over to his wife. He was fuming. "They just gave the part of Maggio to Frank Sinatra. That will ruin the whole goddamn picture!"

Far from it. Dennis' friend and ex-co-worker, Frank Sinatra, won the Oscar for Best Supporting Actor.

CHAPTER TEN
DON'T JUDGE ME

Dennis' endorsements of Old Gold caused him to drift back toward the field of game shows in late 1952, and to his delight, he'd be working with some people he liked an awful lot.

By 1952, Mark Goodson and Bill Todman, known by that point as the "Gold Dust Twins" in television for the wide swath of game shows they had created so far, and for the fact that nearly all of them had been hits, came up with a worthy competitor for *You Bet Your Life*.

You Bet Your Life had become one of radio and television's preferred templates for duplicates since it premiered in 1949. Legendary comedian Groucho Marx hosted the program, ostensibly a game show, but the game show existed merely as an excuse to put people in close proximity with Groucho Marx. The game itself was intentionally dirt-simple to explain and not particularly time-consuming. All that extra time was devoted to Groucho's extended interviews with contestants, in which he'd fire off a mix of ad-libs and pre-scripted quips. It was Groucho's personality and his knack for extracting humor out of every tête-à-tête that drew audiences to the show, not so much the game.

Goodson-Todman whipped up their own version of *You Bet Your Life*. They called it *Two for the Money*. Hosting the show would be Dennis' boating buddy, Herb Shriner. Shriner would engage in lengthy interviews with the contestants and then play a short Question and Answer game for some cash. Dennis was there on behalf of Old Gold for the commercial breaks.

"Herb and his wife lived in Larchmont," Micki remembers, "And at that time, they were our best friends. They would come over almost every Sunday by sailboat and show up at our dock around dinner time with their three kids. Herb was really something special; I've never met anyone else quite like him. He was funny when he wasn't trying to be funny; he was funny without knowing he was being funny. And he collected so many things. Cars, helmets, grenades and other war memorabilia—I could probably write a book myself about Herb Shriner."

Herb could be wonderfully spontaneous away from the spotlight. He always maintained a very laid-back persona on television, but in person, he could hardly sit still. He called Dennis one day and said "Let's go horseback riding!"

"We don't ride, Herb," Dennis answered.

Herb, anticipating the line, said, "Neither do we!"

Herb wanted to go horseback riding, found a place that offered lessons, and talked Dennis and Micki into coming along.

On one Sunday, he again called up and suggested, "Let's take our boats out!"

Chapter Ten: Don't Judge Me

Herb identified a buoy out on the Sound that he and Dennis could use as a rendezvous point. Dennis and Micki arrived at the buoy. A few minutes later, Herb and Pixie Shriner arrived, along with a guest they weren't anticipating, Pixie's visiting sister, who was very pregnant, had just gone into labor. Herb had taken a slow sailboat over to the buoy, Dennis and Micki were using a speedy motorboat. Everybody carefully helped Pixie's sister into the motorboat, Dennis made a hasty u-turn, headed back to New Rochelle, and got Pixie's sister to the hospital in time.

Dennis and his pal Herb Shriner. Their shared passion for the water would take them on some strange adventures.

Eventually, it was the James' turn to take Herb on an adventure. The James had a friend in the Florida Keys, who converted old Navy PT boats into deep sea diving boats. The James had a standing invitation to use a boat staffed by a private chef and a professional diver. Dennis and Micki invited Herb and Pixie to come along, so everyone headed for Florida.

As Micki remembered, "We soon realized that we really didn't want to learn to dive."

Dennis and Micki looked on in awe as Herb tried repeatedly, determinedly, to go deeper, but every time he made it to about the ten-foot mark, he'd throw up in his mask. The diving expedition was a flop, but Herb, with a "never give up" spirit, came over to the James' house in New Rochelle, with his diving equipment, to practice in their pool.

Goodson and Todman had actually created *Two for the Money* with a different host in mind. Fred Allen, whose radio show had been run off the air by a game show just a few years earlier, had decided that if he couldn't beat 'em, he'd join 'em. Mark Goodson and Bill Todman intended *Two for the Money* to be a vehicle for Allen, but when Allen was sidelined by illness just a few weeks before premiere date, Herb Shriner was abruptly pushed into the role.

When Allen recovered, Goodson and Todman gave him a different series, *Judge for Yourself* on NBC. It was an oddly complicated game show/talent show in which three amateur acts performed for two panels of judges; one panel consisted of show business professionals and the other panel consisted of people chosen from members of the audience. An audience member could win $1,000 if they scored the acts the same way that the judges scored them.

Old Gold sponsored *Judge for Yourself*, too, so there was Dennis. Fred frequently led into commercials by saying "Dennis, anyone?"

Fred Allen spoke glowingly of Dennis' talents as a pitchman, too. When a newspaper writer was working on a profile for Dennis and asked Allen for a quote, Allen said, "Dennis is such a good salesman, one time he sold me some tires before I realized I didn't own a car."

The general public, on the other hand, didn't really have any glowing words for *Judge for Yourself*. TV critics generally never cared for game shows anyway, but syndicated columnist John Crosby actually summed up all of the problems with the show rather well in his blistering review:

Chapter Ten: Don't Judge Me

Dennis with the hosts of Old Gold's two game shows: Fred Allen of *Judge For Yourself* and Herb Shriner of *Two for the Money*.

"To those of us who admire him, it's always nice to have Fred Allen on view some place but... *Judge for Yourself* has eight wheels in place of the usual four, which seems a little excessive. Goodson and Todman, those intrepid pioneers of television, have loaded this one with gimmicks, just about every gimmick. There's a panel of experts. (An expert is anyone invited on the program as opposed to those who wrote in for tickets.) Then there are studio contestants or non-experts. (You might define a non-expert as anyone who comes from out of town.)

"... When all the talent has sung and tap danced or played the marimba, the non-experts vie at picking the most talented, the second most talented, and so forth, and comparing their choices with those of the experts... How you compare a marimba player with a tap dancer is beyond my non-expert comprehension...

"When you add it all up, you have a contest, prize money, talent, studio contestants, experts, jokes (Mr. Allen) and even Dennis James. What more can you ask? . . . No review of the Allen show would be complete without some mention of those Old Gold girls who tap dance about covered from thigh up in outsize Old Gold packages. There is Regular and there is King Size. Well sire, King Size needs practice. She keeps bumping into Regular. Pick on someone your own size, King Size."

Broadcasting Magazine chimed in, "Dennis James was on hand to deliver commercials for Old Gold, the show's sponsor. Even his perennial high spirits and ear-to-ear smile showed signs of strain."

That observation seemed to be the beginning of a trend. Micki remembers, "Dennis didn't really enjoy working for Goodson-Todman. He liked Fred Allen a lot, and Fred liked him, but even early on, Dennis said there was always something about the mood in the room that he didn't like when he worked for Goodson-Todman. He had trouble putting his finger on it early on, though."

The death blow for *Judge For Yourself*, however, came from the agent of Georgie Tapps, a dancer who appeared as a contestant on the show. The audience members chosen for the panel cast their votes and Tapps came in third. Tapps' agent publicly griped about how "some banana picker rated [my] boy third" and other agents were now strongly discouraging their clients from performing on *Judge for Yourself*. On May 11, 1954, *Judge For Yourself* was cancelled after only nine months.

In the fall of 1954, Dennis took on a couple of TV game shows. Both were jobs that he landed somewhat by accident; in both cases, he was replacing a host who had departed.

On Your Account premiered on NBC in 1953 with host Win Elliott. A year later, the show jumped to CBS, and only three months later, Win Elliott was out and Dennis was in.

Chapter Ten: Don't Judge Me

All the contestants on the show played on behalf of people who deserved it. The show encouraged people to write in nominations for deserving recipients, who were then brought to the studio and watched on while a contestant played to win money for them, with correct answers paying $25-$100, plus a chance to win a $1,500 bonus along with some extra prizes. A four-year-old boy had fallen ten stories and miraculously survived with injuries to his knee, leg, and wrist. A contestant collected $3,200 in cash and prizes to help pay off the boy's medical expenses. A seven-year-old Pittsburgh girl was nominated because she had turned over all of the money in her piggy bank, which totaled a rather impressive $118.60, to the Old Newsboys Fund, which helped care for elderly men who had spent their childhoods as newsies. A contestant helped refill the piggy bank and then some—the girl got $125 in cash, plus $1,500 in savings bonds, a puppy, and some ice cream bars.

Dennis with some contestants lent a helping hand for *On Your Account*.

The show also encouraged representatives of charities to appear on the show to play on behalf of their own causes. Milton J. Huber was the headmaster of The Boys and Girls Republic, a home for neglected and delinquent children in Farmington Hills, Michigan. Huber appeared on the show in March 1955 and won $300 for the Boys and Girls Republic. He happened to learn during an exchange backstage that Dennis was an avid boater and that he had just purchased a new motorboat from Chrysler and that Dennis wasn't expecting the boat to arrive until July. He was so grateful for the airtime that he returned to Michigan, contacted some friends at Chrysler, and got the boat delivered before the end of March.

Then, there was the other game show that Dennis commandeered in fall 1954. *The Name's the Same* on ABC was a bit of a variation on *What's My Line?* from Mark Goodson-Bill Todman Productions (the people that oversaw *Judge for Yourself* and *Two for the Money*) that specialized in odd names instead of odd jobs. The celebrity panel asked yes-or-no questions, and then tried to guess unusual names, often the names of the contestants (a six-year-old girl named Yvonne DeCarlo) or sometimes the name of their hometown (Tightwad, Missouri). Robert Q. Lewis had been the program's original host when it debuted in 1951, but in 1954, he departed from the program and Dennis stepped in to take over the show.

Panelist Gene Rayburn tried to guess the name of the town of Tightwad, Missouri:

GENE: This is a type of person? Would it be possible that one or more members of the panel is this type of person?

CONTESTANT: No.

DENNIS: It's not possible? I don't want to contradict you, but I would say *yes*!

GENE: You would say yes, Dennis, but what about you, dear?

DENNIS: She doesn't know in this particular case.

GENE: Could you tell just by looking at us which one of us might fit into this category?

CONTESTANT: Probably you!

DENNIS: No comment.

GENE: Let's explore this a little further.

Chapter Ten: Don't Judge Me

DENNIS: If you want to take my advice, you should let it lay right where she left it.

GENE: Is this type of person found elsewhere in the television industry?

CONTESTANT: Yes sir.

DENNIS: Yes.

GENE: Might he be the producer of a television program?

DENNIS: Oh, sure!

GENE: What about our bosses, Goodson and Todman? Are they this type of person?

DENNIS: No, Gene, positively not!

Dennis and the panel of *The Name's the Same*: Arnold Stang, Bess Myerson, Joan Alexander, and Gene Rayburn, all proudly represented sponsor Ralston-Purina. After a few months, Gene Rayburn was cast out, a slight that he'd unfairly hold against Dennis for years to come.

Micki said, "We once invited Gene and his wife, Helen, to our home in New Rochelle for dinner. We had a new boxer puppy and Helen asked if she could see it. I handed it to her, and the moment the puppy was in her hands, it peed all over her lap."

The Name's the Same proved to be an unhappy experience for Dennis because of an intense personality clash with boss Mark Goodson. Goodson was an avowed perfectionist, who famously nitpicked the production of any show down to the bones. He fretted about the light not being angled exactly right, about set pieces that needed light retouching with paint, and about minor words in the announcer's script. Goodson-Todman's track record spoke for itself, so Goodson felt fairly justified in his never-ending quest to make sure that every show went precisely according to his own vision.

On the other hand, there was Dennis, who had been in television for fifteen years. In television's infancy, he was the only one who had any boast to make about longevity, and he had a track record of success to go with it. Sponsors' products always sold well, and audiences always tuned in. When Goodson began critiquing Dennis' performance week after week, the input wasn't particularly well-received. The concept of "Irresistible Force vs. Immovable Object" had nothing on the clash between the producer who wanted it done his way and the host whose own way had always worked. The conflict came to a head one night when Goodson stationed himself just offstage, out of view of the cameras, to give Dennis signals through the entire show. For the entire half-hour broadcast, Dennis tried to host *The Name's the Same* with the corner of his eye catching glimpses of a finger twirling, a hand waving, an arm stretching, as if Goodson was the third base coach trying to wave Dennis in for a full half-hour.

For fifteen years, Dennis had operated with, at most, minimal instruction. After getting nothing *but* instructions from Goodson, his boss struck entirely the wrong cord, and it triggered something unpleasant in Dennis.

After the program concluded, Goodson waited for his host backstage. Dennis saw him, grabbed him by the neck, ripped the lapel of his coat, and shoved him against a wall.

"Don't ever tell me how to do my job again!" Dennis shouted.

Chapter Ten: Don't Judge Me

Dennis with the new panelists of *The Name's the Same*. Little did they realize that Dennis was on his way out.

Dennis stormed out of the theater in a rage. Goodson and the staff surrounding him could only stare in disbelief. When Dennis finally calmed down later in the evening, he was so shaken by what Goodson's hand signals brought out in him that he felt unable to continue working for m. He went to ABC executives and requested his release from *The Name's the Same*. Request granted. Dennis only hosted the show for eighteen weeks.

The whole fiasco also caused some animosity between Dennis and Gene Rayburn, who had been one of the regular panelists on *The Name's the Same* since before Dennis had been there. Casting a game show panel, as Mark Goodson and his staff would explain many times over the years, was like casting a play. You needed people who meshed well with each other and with the host. Thirteen weeks into Dennis' tenure, it was determined that Gene and Dennis didn't have great chemistry, and Gene was off the show. Five weeks later, it was a moot point. Gene had been booted from the show because he didn't have the right chemistry with Dennis, and now Dennis wasn't even there. Gene didn't let on to very many people that he had animosity toward Dennis about the situation. When asked about it later, Gene's daughter didn't know about the issue, and neither did Dennis' family, but Gene certainly didn't forget about that unfortunate turn of events. Three decades later, when Gene and Dennis were booked as guests on a talk show, they got into a shouting match backstage. After all those years, Gene was still irritated with Dennis about losing that weekly gig.

During the fall of 1954, Dennis' work had at least one positive outcome. On October 23 and 24, he devoted seventeen hours of airtime to the *Celebrity Parade for Cerebral Palsy*, and it was quite a parade, too. Singers Lena Horne, Steve Lawrence and Eydie Gorme, Patti Page, Janis Paige, Jerry Vale, and Bobby Van performed during the program. Former Miss America Bess Myerson was there, as was Mike Wallace. There were plenty of laughs to be had while raising funds for a serious cause. Ernie Kovacs, Henny Youngman, Garry Morton, Herb Shriner, Dick Shawn, Roger Price (creator of Mad Libs) and Jean Shepherd (*A Christmas Story*) provided the amusement. When all was said and done, they had helped Dennis raise $511,369. It was the second year in a row that the telethon raised more than $500,000, a figure that many involved would have considered extremely optimistic at best when the telethons began a few years earlier.

United Cerebral Palsy was getting its message and its cause out there, occasionally getting creative with its fundraisers. The same year, UCP even held a beauty pageant for women afflicted by cerebral palsy. The winner, Mary Sue Sherman, worked as a typist who taught children to swim in her spare time. Only a few years after "closet cases" represented the typical fate of a person with cerebral palsy, Sherman's day-to-day life demonstrated what people with the ailment were actually capable of: she was holding down a job and teaching a skill. A cynic could easily deride a beauty pageant as schmaltzy or exploitative, but the true intention was showcasing how normal these people truly were, and that they could live as such.

CHAPTER ELEVEN
CLEARING THE AIR

THE 1953 CELEBRITY *Parade* raised $550,000, and the 1954 *Celebrity Parade* raised $511,369 for UCP, so Dennis knew he'd be working with the organization plenty more in the future. It was never a paying job; that wasn't why Dennis did it. As much as Dennis did for UCP and for other charities over the year, he never collected a dime. If travel was required, the charity paid for his plane ticket or his hotel, but that was the only form of compensation he ever received. He never received any money for the time he devoted or the performances that he gave over and over again, across the country.

The incident at *The Name's the Same* with Mark Goodson almost seemed to be an omen for Dennis. He always had as much work as he could handle, and he had certainly never walked away from a job before. He departed from *The Name's the Same* in early 1955, a year when he would see quite a bit of his work disappear little by little.

The DuMont Network was still crumbling, and crumbling, and crumbling, and in 1955, "crumbling" had turned into "collapsing." Their revenue in 1954 was less than half of what it had been in 1953. By February 1955, DuMont executives determined that the company could no longer function as a full-fledged network. Their two most prized affiliates, WABD and WTTG, continued operating as independent stations, and DuMont, knowing that they were reaching the end anyway, dropped nearly all of their shows. By May 1955, only eight DuMont shows remained in production. Pro wrestling and boxing matches announced by Dennis James were not among them. Dennis had helped popularize and nationalize the spectacle over the past decade, but his association with professional wrestling ended with something of a thud. Dozens of wrestling promoters divided up the business into a "territory" system, with each promoter agreeing only to syndicate television programs and present live events within set boundaries. Dennis would not be associated with any of them.

"Dennis was quite sad to see Dumont come to an end," Micki remembers. "It had been the very beginning for everything—for television and for Dennis personally. So, when Dumont went away, so did this big piece of Dennis' life."

Perhaps most amazingly in 1955, Dennis' wildly successful run as a spokesman for Old Gold cigarettes came to an end.

"Here's the crowning treat of them all! A taste treat so different that it has made OLD GOLD the fastest growing of all leading "regular" cigarettes . . . last year and every year for the past five years . . . now yours for extra cool-

Chapter Eleven: Clearing the Air

ness, extra mildness in King Size. And it's a common-sense treat that simply offers you this assurance: No other leading cigarette is less irritating, or easier on the throat, or contains less nicotine than OLD GOLD. You can count on that, because this conclusion was established on evidence by the U.S. Government. So... smoke OLD GOLD for a treat instead of a treatment."

Once again, Dennis' face was emblazoned across the ad, assuring readers as always, that there was no health risk at all for Old Gold cigarettes. Those weren't really Dennis' words they used for the print ads. He simply lent his face to the print campaign and Old Gold printed whatever they wanted, but he was quickly finding himself one of a growing number of people who didn't completely believe what Old Gold had to say about the safety of cigarette smoking. Unlike the vast majority, he had to stare at his own face when he saw claims that he no longer believed.

Dennis and Herb Shriner represented the sponsor with pride in this print ad, but Dennis found some emerging information in medical studies a bit hard to ignore.

Okay? Okay! Dennis James' Lifetime of Firsts

Dennis had once entertained a generous offer from Philip Morris to switch allegiances, but he had a strong sense of loyalty to Old Gold and declined the Phillip Morris offer because he felt a stunning amount of pride in being a commercial pitchman—even though he was fully aware that it was a line of work that many in show business didn't respect.

Dennis felt that as a commercial pitchman, he had certain ethics and a reputation to uphold. He himself actually had a low opinion of actors and athletes who signed endorsement deals for products. They signed a contract, read a few prepared lines of somebody else's advertising copy from a cue card, smiled, and cashed their check. Dennis considered himself a *true* pitchman. He researched the product before signing his name on the dotted line. He used the product, whether that meant eating it, drinking it, wearing it, driving it, or smoking it. He not only used it, but used it forsaking all other brands. He got acclimated with it to the point that he could ad-lib a commercial from start to finish if he had to. He became familiar with that product to the point that if a fan on the street challenged him, he could give them every detail, inside and out.

One of the things that Dennis had always prided himself on as a pitchman was sincerity. He really used the products that he endorsed, and he was proud of that. When he told boaters that Chase and Sanborn was a great coffee to take along for sailing, he was telling them that from personal experience. When he told *Chance of a Lifetime* viewers about how well Bromo-Seltzer helped ease the physical effects of stress, it was because he had used it himself. Dennis was a good salesman because he had always believed in the products he sold.

Dennis declined the offer from Philip Morris, because after years of telling TV viewers that Old Gold cigarettes were the very best, he couldn't go out there with a straight face and tell them that Philip Morris was the best. The television audience quickly would have figured out that he was just saying it for a paycheck, and in an instant, all the merit that he had as a pitchman would disappear. Why would anyone listen to Dennis James when they know he's just endorsing the highest bidder?

On October 19, 1953, beloved daytime TV and radio staple Arthur

Chapter Eleven: Clearing the Air

Godfrey, known to millions for his folksy, friendly demeanor, fired singer Julius LaRosa on the air—not on his live television series, but a bit later on the longer CBS Network radio version. The move was so distasteful that in the blink of an eye, Godfrey's down-to-earth persona was shattered and the entire country discovered that Godfrey was a hardnosed egomaniac. When Godfrey tried to salvage things at a press conference by explaining that he felt LaRosa lacked "humility," the choice of words struck people as so ridiculous that Godfrey became a national punchline. He never recovered from the fiasco. Godfrey's fall from grace was legendary.

Dennis and Micki with Mrs. Kent, of Kent cigarettes. She paid for the wedding shower after Dennis and Micki announced their engagement, a personal connection that made Dennis' next career move particularly difficult.

Dennis had a different perspective on Godfrey's crashing popularity. If it had just been the incident with LaRosa and nothing else, Dennis opined, that would have been fine, but he believed the problem was that the LaRosa incident happened shortly after Godfrey did something that dropped a hint that he wasn't what he seemed. It was when his TV show underwent a change in sponsorship.

Dennis said, "I think Arthur Godfrey's demise as a TV star came about from suddenly switching to a pipe after all those years of selling cigarettes, then trying to tell his public that he'd always liked a pipe best anyway."

The lesson, according to Dennis: The audience didn't believe Godfrey's explanation of the LaRosa firing because they now knew that they couldn't believe Godfrey's commercials, either.

Dennis said "No thanks" to Philip Morris and continued singing the praises of Old Gold cigarettes.

Dennis had certainly won fans in high places during his tenure as a spokesman. *The Billboard*, covering the television broadcasts of the 1952 Democratic and Republican National Conventions, made it a point to acknowledge him for the delicate task of doing live commercials in the midst of a major news event, calling his pitches for Old Gold that night "dignified."

Norman Barasch, a writer for *Two for the Money*, said in his memoirs, "Dennis James... projected an image of total sincerity and dedication when extolling the deep-down pleasure of smoking an Old Gold cigarette. The way Dennis smiled, the way he held the cigarette, and the genuine satisfaction when he inhaled made him the consummate tobacco salesman. No one, but no one, could sell a cigarette like Dennis James."

NBC executive Grant Tinker told the A&E cable channel in 1992, "If you bought a show, or even half of a show, frequently the talent or some part of the show would be devoted to the product so that there was a very direct association. If somebody has a lot of acceptance or credibility in the home, then getting that somebody to sell the product really works... Dennis James is one that I obviously remember. People liked him. Dennis James could sell a cigarette the same way that Sinatra could sell a song."

Old Gold's advertising agency once released a statement acknowledging Dennis' "conscientious efforts and intelligent manner in representing our

Chapter Eleven: Clearing the Air

product to the public." Alden James, director of advertising for P. Lorillard, once said, "We are very proud of the outstanding job he has done for us," and clearly he meant it. Dennis had signed a staggering ten-year deal with Old Gold in 1948, but in 1955, with three years left on his deal, Dennis and Old Gold parted ways. He asked for it.

Dennis proudly displayed a cigarette box given to him by his bosses. To put a happy face on his departure, they surprised him with one made of solid gold.

In 1954, physiologist Richard Doll announced the earliest results of the British Doctors' Study, a comprehensive research effort searching for a link between tobacco use and lung cancer. The study began in 1951 and concluded in 2001. By 1954, there was enough information gathered that Doll confidently declared a twentyfold increase in the likelihood of cancer among tobacco smokers. At the same time, Dr. Ernst Wynder of the Sloan-Kettering Institute for Cancer Research revealed that tobacco tar applied to the skin of lab mice had proved carcinogenic. All of these discoveries were documented in a scathing *Readers' Digest* article called "Cancer by the Carton."

Fourteen major tobacco companies, including Dennis' bosses at P. Lorillard Company, jointly released an advertisement bearing the title "A Frank Statement to Cigarette Smokers." The advertisement gave a list of four major arguments against the recent research: studies had shown that there were many other possible causes of lung cancer; there was no unanimous agreement among experts about what those causes may be; there was no concrete proof that cigarettes were a cause; and there were many aspects of modern life that, combined, were capable of causing lung cancer, and it was an invalid argument to point out one single element and say it caused cancer. The ad went on to note that tobacco had been accused of causing multiple diseases in the past 300 years, and that all accusations were gradually abandoned due to lack of evidence. The tobacco companies maintained that they did not believe their products were harmful and even pledged to establish what they called the Tobacco Industry Research Committee, pledging that they would conduct their own investigation as to the causes of lung cancer.

Dennis continued coming to the set and filming commercials, posing for photos with a lit cigarette between his fingers and smiling for the magazine ads. The studies were something of a faint noise that Dennis couldn't place. They were off in the distance, and he was able to ignore it. By 1955, he found that the faint noise of those studies seemed to be getting louder and louder, and he couldn't shut it out, ignore it, or pretend it wasn't there.

The straw that broke Dennis' back was Old Gold's announcement of a new line of Old Gold Filter-Tip cigarettes. Filter tips were a new addition that many cigarette manufacturers added to their products during the 1950s in response to the inquiries that the public was now making about the safety of smoking. Supposedly, the filter would take out some of the harmful elements in a cigarette as it was being inhaled.

Dennis, much later, said to one reporter, "How could I start telling the TV audience about the safety factor in filters after saying for years that those of us at Old Gold 'aren't medicine men, we're tobacco men?!'"

Dennis also decided that he no longer believed in Old Gold. As much as

Chapter Eleven: Clearing the Air

he liked P. Lorillard chairman Herbert Kent, and as much as he adored Mrs. Kent, who hosted Micki's wedding shower, and as much as he had forged many positive relationships with the higher-ups in the company, Dennis saw a cloud of suspicion over all of them now, and he couldn't be a pitchman if that cloud was hanging over him, too. He requested and received his release from his contract.

He told the A&E cable channel in 1992, "[The public was] starting to say 'Hey, cigarettes cause cancer, and doctors are saying that cigarettes cause cancer, and [Old Gold] said, 'We'd better change our attack and we'd better say, 'Here's a cigarette you can trust.' And I said 'That's silly. Remember what I said about integrity.' Somebody else would have to say that. It would not be right for me, all those years on the air saying 'We're tobacco men, not medicine men,' and all of a sudden, what, I got a Ph.D. in psychology or something? I'm going to be a medical man? I said 'No, now look, I got two years left on my contract. I'll step aside without any remuneration of any kind, and if this cancer scare goes away, I'll come back. Well, it never went away."

This put Old Gold in a delicate position. Dennis had been there so long that most customers, and most potential customers, couldn't separate him from the company. Many of them had never seen or heard an Old Gold commercial without Dennis. When the fast-approaching day arrived when viewers saw someone else on TV with an Old Gold clasped between their fingers, they were going to ask, "Where's Dennis?"

Since announcing the true reason for Dennis' departure was the last thing the company wanted, he and Old Gold made one final deal with each other, to put as pleasant a face on things as possible. Old Gold announced that his many television commitments, like *On Your Account* and *Chance of a Lifetime*, were keeping him so busy that he felt the need to lighten his workload, so Old Gold was graciously releasing him from his contract, allowing him to focus his energies on his other obligations.

On the last night that Dennis appeared as a spokesman for Old Gold, Bert Kent, the CEO of P. Lorillard, made an appearance on the program and gave a grateful testimonial to Dennis' relationship with the company. He finished by presenting him with a gold cigarette box. No commercial pitchman had ever been given such an affectionate send-off.

Puffing a cigarette so that the cloud looked juuuuuust right on camera was a skill that Dennis mastered during his years with Old Gold. To his own chagrin, it caused him to form a habit that he couldn't break.

Micki admitted that, despite all the money Dennis had made from the deal, she wasn't exactly sad to see that her husband was no longer endorsing Old Gold. To her chagrin, he continued to smoke two packs a day for years to come—regular Old Golds, not filter-tipped, because he didn't believe that the filter actually did anything. Old Gold lost a spokesman, but those commercials had created at least one customer-for-life.

CHAPTER TWELVE
THE NEW ARRIVAL

As QUICKLY AS Dennis said goodbye to some work, new opportunities seemingly appeared out of thin air. It was just the way his career always seemed to work out. The United States Marine Corps was overseeing the production of a syndicated television series, *America's Newsreel Album,* a low-budget program that assembled a variety of newsreels from the past and present (although newsreels were a rapidly disappearing part of the movie-going experience) with Dennis supplying new narration. Interspersed throughout the program were recruitment ads for the Marine Corps, and Dennis always made a point of drawing attention to newsreel footage of disasters, like floods or massive fires, and acknowledging the Marine Corps' role in the aid and rescue efforts during the aftermath.

There were two big parties that Dennis and Micki looked forward to every year. At Christmas, they welcomed twenty-five underprivileged children to the house for lunch. Micki always noticed how attentive Dennis was with the kids, waiting on them and giving his undivided attention the entire time they were there. It was one of Micki's favorite traits of her husband. He really loved kids, and in the back of her mind, she was looking forward to seeing him as a father. She knew he'd be great at it.

The other big party happened every summer, when Dennis celebrated his anniversary in the television business with an all-out feast. In the summer of 1955, he celebrated sixteen years in broadcasting, and celebrated his professional anniversary the same way he always did with a lavish backyard clambake.

Micki remembers, "The clambakes were truly old-fashioned New England parties catered by a man called the Clambake King. He was based in Connecticut, and he'd come over to our house with a crew who dug a hole in the backyard and filled it with seaweed, then layers of chicken, corn, potatoes, lobsters, and clams. Lots of beer, lots of raw clams on the half shell. So good!"

Dennis and Micki invited all of their friends and acquaintances—*all* of them, the whole rolodex of about 300 in total. They attended each year. Some drove, some boated over, and a few who flew as a hobby and even landed their seaplanes near the dock in Dennis' backyard. By virtue of his career, every clambake was a television Who's Who. Bert Parks was always there. So were Herb and Pixie Shriner, and Herb brought his harmonica to help provide some entertainment. Boxing referee Artie Aidala was an unexpected source of amusement at some of the get-togethers. One year, he disguised himself and spent the evening hassling Garry Moore about the improper way that Moore was eating his clams. Aidala used double-talk in a thick Italian dialect to teach him "the right way" until Moore finally figured out who he was. Jack Carter and Red Buttons tended to crack up the guests sitting around them. Sam Levenson, the comedian/teacher who replaced Herb as host of *Two for the Money,* dropped by. So did ventriloquist Paul Winchell. Peter Lind Hayes and his wife Mary Healy attended, too.

Scenes from a New Rochelle clambake. Among the guests were Herb Shriner's wife Pixie (in the background) and Bert Parks (wearing the patterned shirt). They were waiting to be served Carvel ice cream from Tom Carvel, another guest at the party, who always brought along one of his own company trucks to serve everyone.

Dennis ordered a few dozen baskets of clams, on the half-shell and steamed. Steak was also served, and to make things easy on everybody, Dennis marked the tables in the backyard with signs reading "RARE," "MEDIUM," AND "WELL DONE." Rather than ask around, guests were simply expected to sit at the table that met their liking.

Micki remembers, "Zsa Zsa Gabor came to our parties if there was steak. But only if there was steak. She didn't come if it was just a clambake because that was too messy for her."

Dennis also ordered a supply of lobster, shrimp, chicken, corn, pie, watermelon, and draft beer. For dessert, Dennis and Micki's friend, Tom Carvel, would loan out one of his Carvel ice cream trucks to park there for the evening. If you were a friend of Dennis and Micki, the backyard clambake was the social event of the summer in New Rochelle, a true can't-miss spectacular.

Elsewhere in the summer of 1955, the rest of America was focused on another can't-miss spectacular in New York. Beginning on June 7, 1955, the eyes of the nation were focused squarely on a tiny soundproof booth in the center of CBS Studio 52, on every Tuesday night. *The $64,000 Question* had arrived, and so had the era of the big-money quiz show.

Dennis had actually been offered the opportunity to host *The $64,000 Question* by Charles Revson, the big boss at Revlon, the cosmetics firm that would be sponsoring the new series, but there was a catch: he would have to give up *Chance of a Lifetime*, and his opening contract for *The $64,000 Question* would be only six weeks long. The offer carried so much risk that Dennis instantly lost interest and said no. Hal March got *The $64,000 Question*, which became the #1 series on all of television.

Many big money quizzes would follow in the upcoming television season. *Stop the Music* returned for another brief run, although Dennis wouldn't be there. *Name That Tune* introduced a $25,000 top prize. *The Big Surprise* offered a $100,000 payday. *Break the $250,000 Bank* pulled out all the stops. Jan Murray created a big money game of his own, *Treasure Hunt*, with $25,000 up for grabs. The most popular competition in the wake of *The $64,000 Question* was NBC's *Twenty One*, which offered the allure of unlimited money.

Dennis was a businessman, and specifically, he was in the business of giving television viewers what they wanted. A $1,000 talent show just wouldn't get the job done anymore. He and ABC agreed to bring *Chance of a Lifetime* to an end in the summer of 1956. Dennis got right to work brainstorming something a little more in tune with current trends in television. During the spring of 1956, he showed his own idea for a big money quiz show to the major networks, and he had more reason than ever to hope that he could get his idea on the air. He was awaiting an addition to the family.

The secret's out! Waves of gifts began coming in after word of Micki's pregnancy spilled.

Dennis and Micki had always been ready for a baby and had seriously discussed how to handle it if and when the occasion finally happened. They agreed that they should keep it a secret for about four to five months. When it was impossible to keep Micki's physical condition from being noticeable, they let their friends know. Dennis, being in the public eye, had to consider how to handle that, and they decided that they absolutely would not tell the press.

Around October 1955, Micki began to detect signs that she might be pregnant, so she went to a laboratory and had her blood tested. She got the results while Dennis was at the studio preparing for *Chance of a Lifetime*.

Dennis told the story of what happened next. "I picked up the phone and got the news . . . and my face must have been a picture, because someone asked, 'What's happened, Dennis?' And I just answered, 'We're going to have a baby.'

"Afterwards, I felt like a fool. Here, I'd let it slip out, and Micki still had nearly eight months to go. And, of course, it leaked to the papers and we had to explain to relatives and friends why we hadn't told them first."

At the end of 1955, when Dennis wasn't having meetings with network executives about a new prime time quiz show, or raising $550,000 for United Cerebral Palsy in that year's *Celebrity Parade*, or recording a Christmas album for Kapp Records, or doing commercials for his new bosses at Kellogg's, he was joining Micki for a seemingly endless list of chores and preparations. They did indeed convert their guest bedroom into a nursery, complete with her hand-painted murals on the walls. They bought a baby doll and used it to train their boxer dog, Candy, for how to behave around an infant. When they had a spare moment, they sat down together and opened all the packages that had piled up. Word got out that Dennis James was going to be a father, and TV viewers eagerly mailed in gifts. Micki's mother, Mildred, stayed busy, too, sewing a full wardrobe, both for the baby and for Micki.

Micki told a writer, "Mother went shopping with me for maternity clothes, and we were disappointed with many of the things. Nearly all of the dressy clothes were in black, and Dennis hates black."

At the time, Mildred elaborated, "Black has come to look like a uniform on pregnant women, and the color doesn't have anything to do with camouflage. A pregnant woman looks pregnant in any color, so we decided to buy some fabrics that were cheerful and make the clothes ourselves."

Mildred came up with some ingenious designs, using seams and pleats, plus adjustable waistbands, so after Micki gave birth, all of her maternity clothes easily converted into regular outfits. Micki also received the delightful task of being ordered by her doctor to gain weight. She always had impressive metabolism, and Dennis was always stymied by the way she could eat second and third helpings of anything and not gain a pound. With a baby on the way, a doctor was concerned that Micki was underweight and ordered her to gain twenty pounds, a chore Dennis happily assisted her with.

Dennis and Micki weren't the only ones who had to prepare for a new baby. The expectant parents used a baby doll to train the dog for how to behave around the impending arrival.

The hard part was "first baby jitters." When Dennis, Jr. was born, Dennis was 3,000 miles away for military service, so this was all a new experience for him. He worried constantly about Micki climbing stairs or driving, until a doctor finally told him that she could still function the way that she did before.

For the time being, the staff of *On Your Account*, which was starting to wind down its run (its final show was March 30, 1956), began having some fun with Dennis during the later weeks of the show. They became fond of showcasing female contestants with stories about unusual labor. Among the contestants were women who had given birth in trucks, treehouses, and a department store. Dennis kept his game face during the show but later he admitted he found the contestants' stories perfectly terrifying.

One contestant's story rattled him so much that he made some new plans for the baby's arrival. She talked about her husband driving eighty miles per hour to get to the maternity ward in time, and it still wasn't fast enough. She gave birth in the car. Once the baby was out, she told her husband he could drive a little slower to the hospital. By the time they pulled into the parking lot, the twin had arrived, too.

Dennis listened to the story, and all he could think about was the forty-five minute drive from New Rochelle to midtown Manhattan, where he had made the hospital reservation for Micki. The baby was due on June 13, so Dennis decided that at the end of May, he and Micki would move into Manhattan and stay there until the baby arrived.

Dennis, who had initially tried to keep the big news a secret, was now chatting with interviewers about impending fatherhood. He gazed at the backyard, where he had seen his friends land their seaplanes, and joked with one writer about the impending arrival of a wing-propelled single-passenger stork.

"Well, it figures to be single-passenger," Micki told writer Martin Cohen. "There are no twins on either side. We don't expect them. But on the other hand, we can't predict. We have a pretty good idea of what the baby will look like, though."

Dennis and Micki were both hoping for a girl, but he admitted that his genetics probably meant they'd be getting a boy. His brother, Lou, had a daughter, who was absolutely the only girl in the Sposa family bloodline. Dennis was one of three sons. The child he already had was a boy. His brother Frank had two boys, and Dennis' father had only brothers.

On June 21, 1956, just a *little* behind schedule, Dennis and Micki welcomed the expected boy, Randy James. The timing on it seemed to be just perfect. Two days later, the final *Chance of a Lifetime* aired, and by that point, Dennis had sold his big money quiz show.

CBS, the network of *The $64,000 Question*, was the one that bit, and two

Chapter Twelve: The New Arrival

sponsors, Mennen and Bulova, quickly signed up to bankroll the effort. On July 7, 1956, exactly two weeks after the final *Chance of a Lifetime*, Dennis was back on TV with yet another show of his own creation, *High Finance*.

Dennis demonstrated a new idea for a big money quiz show at a meeting with CBS executives. The network liked what it saw.

High Finance was a current events quiz. A contestant was given three recent newspapers to study and told that all of the questions would be taken from those newspapers. The game itself was an unusual one, based on the concept of investing. The first time a contestant appeared on the show, he or she were asked five questions worth $300 apiece. As long as at least three were answered correctly, the contestant could return. Each time the contestant won money, some prizes would be awarded along with the cash. The contestant could choose to forfeit some of the prizes in exchange for questions that offered more cash. Continuing success meant more cash, as well as more valuable prizes, which in turn could be forfeited again for questions worth even more money. Over the span of five weeks, it would be mathematically possible for a single contestant to accumulate as much as $75,000 in cash.

As an added perk, every contestant was asked to share a wish. Regardless of how much money the contestant won, if he or she could last for five weeks without coming up short in the Question and Answer portion, the show would grant that wish. A young girl appeared on the show hoping to win her own nursery school. A man dreamed of getting his own stable of racehorses. Neither of them lasted the necessary five weeks, but the possibility of getting a heart's most unusual desire was a neat little gimmick that gave the show a handy boost with publicity.

Among the *High Finance* contestants who charmed audiences: Pat McMurray, a ten-year-old girl, who said her secret wish was "an office." What kind of office? Why, a law office, of course. In the span of five weeks, young Pat fired off answers about the Russian discoverer of electricity and Operation: Deep Freeze, with a manner that amused viewers. Whereas the other big money quiz shows featured adults agonizing, biting their lips, and sweating in extreme close-up, Dennis and the viewers chuckled as Pat answered question after question indifferently and without much thought. She knew the information, so agonizing wasn't necessary. She lasted the full five weeks and racked up $40,650 in cash. She also held back some of the prizes she was offered, so she also walked away with two horses and $4,000 worth of stocks. For her secret wish, *High Finance* gave her a $35,000 fund to cover her tuition for college plus law school.

Andrew Taylor of Silver Spring, Maryland, made a wish for his own miniature golf course in Florida. Taylor made it through five weeks, took his money, and relocated to a new home in Daytona Beach. Awaiting him when

Chapter Twelve: The New Arrival

he arrived was Dennis James, presenting him with the deed to a nearby miniature golf course. That night, the Daytona Beach Chamber of Commerce held a dinner in Taylor's honor, congratulating him on his new status as a self-employed business owner. The entire weekend was filmed and photographed, with highlights shown on *High Finance*.

No reason to be teed off. Andrew Taylor christened his *High Finance* prize, a miniature golf course, with the ceremonial first swing. Dennis helped in an unusual way.

Also giving the show a minor boost in publicity was the policy Dennis instituted regarding payoffs. Contestants who won exceptionally large amounts of money were paid with a series of annuities. When the big money quiz craze struck, the shows got some backlash in various publications for pointing out that big money meant big taxes, and that a $64,000 payday would be significantly reduced after the IRS claimed their share. By paying the contestants in annuities, they would, in the long run, be able to keep more of their winnings.

By far the most interesting contestant on *High Finance* was Joe Louis. No, the name wasn't a coincidence. He was *that* Joe Louis, the former Heavyweight Boxing Champion of the World from 1937-1949. Joe had accumulated more than $4.6 million during his boxing career. After paying off his handlers, he was left with about $800,000, most of which went into bad business ventures (The Joe Louis Restaurant and Joe Louis Milk among them). By 1956, Joe owed the IRS more than $1 million.

During that year, he tried to supplement his income by becoming a professional wrestler, a career move that devastated his wife, Rose, who told the press that watching her husband become a professional wrestler was "like making an ex-President wash dishes for a living."

After only a few matches, doctors found a previously undiagnosed heart ailment (a fractured rib had caused scar tissue to form on his heart), and Joe was told not to wrestle. He needed a lot of money, and the sooner the better. A big money quiz show was perfect for him, and Rose thought so, too. Despite a career full of blows to the head, she noticed that Joe had an unusually good memory and a knack for retaining anything he was given to read. She wrote to *High Finance*, offering herself and her legendary husband as contestants. Joe dove into the opportunity with gusto, fervently studying each week's supply of newspapers and taking detailed notes

Since the money was clearly more enticing than any prize that Dennis could offer, Joe and Rose forfeited almost every prize offered along the way, racked up $60,000 in cash, and split the money 50/50, a clever arrangement that helped them live somewhat comfortably in trying circumstances. The IRS immediately seized Joe's $30,000 cut, obviously, but they legally couldn't touch Rose's take, except for when she declared it for income taxes, so they had $30,000 to live on for a little while.

High Finance lasted only five months, meeting its demise just before Christmas 1956. In the years to follow, a wave of accusations led to investigations, and one by one, the big money quiz shows were struck down once it was discovered that the fix was in. *High Finance,* during its time on the air, had been lambasted by critics for having questions that were "too easy." Shows such as *Twenty One* and *The $64,000 Question*, where the fix was quite provably in, had thrived on contestants solving seemingly impossible esoterica. Dennis escaped from the quiz show scandals with his reputation intact; not one accusation made, not one finger pointed to the game where contestants won fortunes by answering "too-easy" questions. The flaw that critics had detested had proven to be its saving grace.

The most famous contestant on *High Finance*, former boxing champion Joe Louis, accompanied by his wife.

Around the same time that *High Finance* met its demise, another game show went on the air to considerably greater success. It was a daytime game that Mark Goodson-Bill Todman Productions had approached Dennis about earlier in the year. He was always happy to pick up a good gig, and he was doubtlessly happy that Goodson-Todman was extending an olive branch after the ugly incident that led to his departing *The Name's the Same*, but Goodson-Todman only extended that olive branch so far. The contract they offered Dennis guaranteed him only a week as host of the new game with a salary of $500 for that week, a preposterously low salary for a master of ceremonies, particularly one with Dennis' resume.

Given Dennis' past with the company, the lowballing made sense from Goodson-Todman's perspective. One week would be long enough to see if they could co-exist with Dennis this time, and if they saw any red flags, they didn't have to worry about tying themselves down for too long. That didn't seem worth the trouble to Dennis. He declined. Goodson-Todman subsequently offered the show to Dick Van Dyke, who also said no, and then to Bill Cullen, who finally said "yes" and became host of their new game, *The Price is Right*.

CHAPTER THIRTEEN
JOIN THE CLUB

THE JAMES' BABY, Randy, didn't have much time to settle into the crib at New Rochelle. As it turned out, the temporary guest room had converted into a temporary nursery, because they were moving to Chicago.

Chicago had been an emerging center for broadcast television early on. Many Dumont shows emanated from the Windy City. By the mid-1950s, television was migrating away from the town, but some NBC executives were still clinging to the city and wanted to use it as the location for a new daytime series.

The Tonight Show, starring Steve Allen, had premiered in 1954 and set the template for late night television. It was a talk show, with low frills and minimal structure, freewheeling in nature, and spontaneous in content. The format worked so well that by 1957, NBC wanted to adapt the same format for daytime television.

The new show was called *Club 60*, and it would be, in essence, a late night talk show in a daytime slot. There would even be a live band, and the show would air in full color—part of the reason the show was being done in Chicago. The NBC Chicago affiliate was one of the first local television stations to become fully-equipped for color broadcasting. The network was quite ambitious about the new series, which they advertised in the weeks leading up to the premiere with the slogan "Big Time in the Daytime."

The host was to be Don Sherwood, a successful disc jockey in San Francisco, who agreed to move to Chicago for the new series. Sherwood arrived for the rehearsals smack in the middle of winter, and the California man experienced a real live Chicago blizzard. He showed up for rehearsal already rattled by weather unlike anything he had ever experienced.

The rehearsal got underway. Although *The Tonight Show* at that time, was airing for 105 minutes every night, *Club 60* only had an hour a day to work with, so NBC executives were pushing for the show to be fast-paced, in essence, to cram 105 minutes worth of content into 60. The rehearsal seemed to go fine, but the following day, Sherwood surprised NBC executives by calling them on the phone from Phoenix, Arizona. He was going back to his disk jockey gig in San Francisco. The weather and the show's pace were too much for him.

"I can't stand the brown snow and the gray people," he said.

Club 60 debuted on February 18, 1957, with comic Mort Sahl as host. Sahl was a dressed down satirist, who walked onstage with a newspaper for his stand-up act and just did freeform jokes from the newspaper, tossing in his opinions about the events of the world. Consensus was that Sahl was funny on *Club 60*, but a bad fit for what was supposed to be a crowd-pleasing for-the-housewives hour of fun. Even Sahl himself used to joke with the crew off-camera about how wrong he was for a show like *Club 60*, so he wasn't terribly surprised or angry at all when he was fired after only three weeks.

Dennis and Sammy Davis Jr. discussed photography during a segment of *Club 60*.

NBC explored options for replacements, someone who could talk without a script, and someone with a track record of appealing to female viewers. They knew exactly who to call; Dennis and the family were on their way to Chicago.

Club 60 had one of the most hectic schedules Dennis had ever experienced. Everyone had to be at the studio by 7:30 a.m. Make-up and wardrobe went until 9:00, and then a one-hour camera rehearsal, followed by a one-hour music rehearsal. At 11:00 a.m., everybody got to take a one-hour break, and at the stroke of noon, the show went on the air live.

Club 60 had comedy sketches and jokes. Dennis was never much of a comedian, but he had a solid team preparing the material for him. One of his writers was Bill Daily, who had such a natural knack for performing—in his off-hours, he had founded an improvisational comedy group—that Dennis began putting him on the show to perform the comedy pieces himself.

Some of the humor on the show wasn't really a sketch or a joke; it was just a funny idea. Dennis and a few of the men on the staff decided to go on diets together, so a scale was prominently displayed onstage, along with a chart of each man's weight. Dennis regularly weighed himself and updated the chart as a regular feature.

The show's director, Dave Barnhizer, compared Dennis' style of hosting to Arthur Godfrey's, the former daytime mainstay of that era. Like Godfrey, Dennis tried to expand the program to have something of a "family" feel. The show had a troupe of regular performers: the thirty-piece Joseph Gallichio Orchestra, Art Van Damme and His Band, Nancy Wright and the Mello-Larks, and Mike Douglas—who got along just fine with Dennis—even though, behind the scenes, he had been strongly lobbying for a chance to host the show himself. He thought he might be good at that.

During spare moments on the program, Dennis had extended chats with the orchestra members and the singers. Home viewers got to know them all very well, and *Club 60* felt more and more like a home for Dennis as he got settled in. (Behind the scenes, it turned out that a few people on the show were getting to know each other too well. A trumpeter in Joseph Gallichio's orchestra was fired for having an affair with the wife of a Mello-Lark.)

Even though the bulk of big-time celebrity guests were based in Los Angeles and Chicago, an impressive roster of stars still managed to pop in for *Club 60*. Because Chicago was a major stop for any touring production, the show was able to attract any stars who happened to be passing through town. Dennis' personal photo mementos from the program alone provide a glimpse of a star-studded daily hour: Sammy Davis, Jr., Jerry Lewis, Jack Paar, Andy Griffith, Jim Backus, Milton Berle, Jack Webb, Nat King Cole, Francis X. Bushman, Red Skelton, and even Lassie visited.

Dennis and Micki liked Chicago personally, but not professionally.

Chapter Thirteen: Join the Club

Dennis had a saying about his career in television: "I live my life in thirteen-week cycles." Every three months, your show's ratings were evaluated, and the network and producers decided if it was worth keeping things going for another three months. If not, the show was off the air and it was time for the air talent to move on and look for other gigs.

Dennis, joined by the Mellow-Larks and Mike Douglas on *Club 60*.

NBC was keenly aware that their host wasn't happy in Chicago, but there appeared to be a serendipitous solution on the horizon. Steve Allen had departed his late night show to focus his energies on his Sunday night prime time extravaganza. *The Tonight Show* needed a new host, and Dennis, who had dazzled everybody with the loose, freewheeling, ad-lib heavy performance he was delivering on *Club 60*, seemed to be their man. NBC offered *The Tonight Show* to Dennis.

Dennis said no. He later elaborated, "It was live [at that time], and at that stage of the game, I just didn't want to be in there every single night doing a live show from 11:15 p.m. to 1:00 a.m. You just don't go in and do the show. You have to prepare for it every stinking night."

The Tonight Show went to Jack Paar, who served as host for a stormy, controversy-laden five years, punctuated by public walk-offs and censorship battles. James later said he didn't regret saying no. "I would not have been as controversial as Jack Paar to begin with. It's easy to say I could have done that... but I don't think I would have done for *The Tonight Show* what Jack Paar did. He was so controversial and that's what it needed."

Dennis also maintained a somewhat healthy pessimism about future employment. Eighteen years in television didn't guarantee that *anybody* would still be working in television tomorrow, and Dennis always reacted to every cancellation as though it would be his last show ever. That might sound like a grim way of living, but for Dennis, that attitude ensured financial stability—save for the occasional boat or dream house. He was actually extremely conservative with his money, and he possessed a varied skillset as a sportscaster, commercial pitchman, or game show host.

Even though *Club 60* had been an ambitious effort to revitalize Chicago, the writing was on the wall: to work in national TV, he had to be in Los Angeles or New York. If Dennis committed himself to Chicago, the next show might actually be his last. He was so cautious about moving to Chicago that he hadn't even sold their house in New Rochelle. It was still there and still fully furnished. Dennis gave his notice to NBC after only four months of *Club 60* and went back to New York. A local Chicago personality, Howard Miller, took over on August 19, but the show was cancelled just after the New Year. Singer Mike Douglas got his wish, hosting a talk show of his own, and taking Bill Daily with him to serve as a writer. Steve Allen appeared as a guest and hired Bill Daily for himself, setting Daily on his path to stardom.

Dennis returned to New York as if he had never left. He went right back to work for United Cerebral Palsy, and the *Celebrity Parade* that year raised $440,124. His telethon gigs became more frequent. He was turning in such positive results for United Cerebral Palsy that he became in demand for regional telethons across the country, and by the time his son, Randy, had learned to speak, Dennis was travelling about every other weekend, and during some parts of the year, every weekend, to host one telethon or another, an invitation that he rarely turned down, even though he was never paid for it.

It became a long-standing joke in the family that on a weekend when Dennis miraculously didn't have any charity obligations, Micki told Randy, "Daddy's going to be home this weekend."

Randy answered, "Daddy who?"

Dennis got a little corny during a commercial for Kellogg's.

True to Dennis' hopes and expectations, the moment he was back in New York, he had new gigs lined up as a commercial pitchman. Bulova Watches, the company behind the first television commercial ever (a simple shot of a watch, an announcement of the time, and the announcer concluding by spelling the name "B-U-L-O-V-A") had signed to become the primary sponsor for *The Jackie Gleason Show* on CBS. A 1955 independent survey by A.C. Neilsen Company found that more Americans saw national advertising for Bulova than for any other brand name, or category of product, in the entire world. He signed on to endorse Kellogg's breakfast cereals. Gleason's show was a weekly event, featuring the legendary "Honeymooners" sketches with Art Carney, Audrey Meadows, and Joyce Randolph, plus performances by the June Taylor Dancers. Its popularity commanded a colossal price tag, and the deal Bulova made in 1956 to sponsor *The Jackie Gleason Show* was, at the time, the most expensive advertising commitment ever made by a jewelry company. Wanting every penny to count, Bulova hired Dennis James.

Dennis' commercials for Bulova were always as creative as they were basic. The ads consisted of little more than Dennis holding up a watch and doing something odd to it to demonstrate some feature. For one spot, he slammed the watch against the corner of a table repeatedly to show that it was "shock-proof." He dropped it in a glass of water to prove that it was waterproof, too. He passed it back and forth between the tines of a fork to demonstrate thinness, and he put the works on a balancing scale, with a dime that sank on the opposite side.

Elsewhere during the week, Dennis was on *The Patti Page Show* to say a few words about Kellogg's of Battle Creek.

DENNIS: Well, tomorrow is Thanksgiving. I don't have to tell you that. And that gives me a chance to say that, uh, maybe you ought to take this Kellogg's Special K and use it in your turkey stuffing. I ain't gonna do it, but don't get the idea that it's not a good idea. What I really want to talk to you about tonight is just tell you that all of us folks around Kellogg wish you and your families a very, very happy, pleasant Thanksgiving. And speaking of families, well . . . Kellogg's has always had your family in mind and that's precisely why Kellogg's came out with this Special K. Now this is a cereal that's just loaded with protein. More protein than any other leading cereal hot or cold. I told you before and I think you'll agree, every one of us every

Chapter Thirteen: Join the Club

day needs protein. It repairs and sustains all body tissue. And Special K here gives you protein in a very tempting way. Now . . . it's not a puff and it's not a flake. It's more than both of those. But I can tell you this, here's a cereal whose flavor you going to love. Special K with the big red K on the front and all that wonderful protein inside, so try it tomorrow for breakfast, will you? Or if you want to stuff the turkey with it, that's fine with me . . . Okay? Okay.

A still from a kinescope of one of Dennis' Kellogg's commercials. Note the busy background of a fruit stand was relevant to the offer being made in the ad. Dennis was adamant that his commercials contained no more content than was necessary, wary of anything that would distract viewers from his message.

The "Okay? Okay" at the end became a signature line for Dennis in the ads. It was redundant, but it was a very human touch, something you say to a friend after relaying some instructions. Dennis had an ear for language like that and he used it to great effect when adding his own touches to the scripts that advertisers had given him.

Micki remembered, "Dennis always prided himself on performing his scripts so it didn't sound like a script. He really got to know the product well and read up on it, and he had things he needed to say in every commercial, but he really tried to make it sound like a conversation."

Son Randy told Stu Shostak in 2014, "I think that one of his hallmarks was that at a time where there was a certain cadence and a certain type of delivery, back in those days—back in the fifties—that seemed a little rehearsed and seemed a little bit scripted, he decided early on that when he was going to do a commercial, he was going to do it just as if he was talking to a friend ... Back in those days, the pitches were very quick. He slowed it down, and that became his style."

He was enthusiastic, but not excited. He spoke clearly but he didn't shout. He urged, but didn't demand. Yes, he was a salesman, but he didn't want to be a phony about it.

Not being a phony was paramount to Dennis as a commercial pitchman. The entire reason he left Old Gold was because he felt he could no longer speak honestly about a product, and if he couldn't be an honest pitchman, he just didn't want to do it.

He signed on to do a series of commercials for a line of blankets. The commercials involved a balancing scale. He was to put a wool blanket on one side, and the sponsor's blanket on the other side. The main talking point of each ad was that the sponsor's blanket was lighter than wool but just as warm. Whatever else Dennis said, the ads always involved him placing the blankets on opposite sides of the scale to show that the sponsor's blanket was lighter than wool.

After a few months of these ads, Dennis was in the studio preparing for the next commercial in the campaign. During rehearsal, he was abruptly told to take a dinner break. "They're having some trouble with the scale."

Dennis and Micki headed to dinner with his manager, Aaron Steiner, and his wife. Dennis curiously asked, "What was wrong with the scale?"

Steiner told him, "The sponsor's blanket isn't lighter than the wool blanket."

Dennis was perplexed, given that this was the entire point of the commercial he was about to shoot. "What do you mean it isn't lighter?"

Steiner clarified, "The sponsor's blanket isn't lighter than the wool blanket. They're going to put a weight on the scale so that the wool blanket looks heavier."

In an instant, Dennis was seething. "You knew this?"

Chapter Thirteen: Join the Club

Steiner answered, "Yes."

Dennis fired Aaron on the spot and terminated his contract with the blanket company. Dennis was an honest salesman. He continued doing honest pitches for Kellogg's, and they appreciated Dennis as much as Old Gold did.

As an honest salesman, Dennis did his best to present his honest self. He was by no means egocentric, but after so many years of building and maintaining an image, he recognized a certain truth. Kellogg's could have signed literally anybody to appear in their commercials. If they went with Dennis James, it must mean that they wanted Dennis James, and that's why he resented it so much when he was given certain directions. He did what he wanted to do, because, to his way of thinking, that was the whole reason that he was there.

A director was filming a Kellogg's commercial with Dennis once. Dennis wrapped up the ad by winking at the camera, smiling, and saying "Okay? Okay."

The director looked up at him and said "Let's do one more take, this time without the wink."

With a stern countenance, Dennis responded, "The wink stays."

Kellogg's wanted Dennis James, and Dennis James winked.

With so many television firsts already happening, and Dennis already claiming so many of them, it's somewhat remarkable that his Kellogg's endorsement deal afforded him an opportunity to claim another first. Shortly after he joined the company, Ampex introduced the first line of practical videotape machines, capable of recording broadcast quality tapes. Kellogg's advertising department saw potential and a need for videotape before even some entertainment programming recognized it, and quickly declared that going forward, all of Kellogg's commercials should be recorded on videotape. Dennis would be the first person to appear on a videotaped commercial.

Dennis took such a liking to his bosses at Kellogg's that he opened his home when one campaign called for it. Kellogg's was promoting a new line of single-serving cereal boxes, intended for use when traveling; the small boxes all had seams down the middle that could be torn so that box unfolded into a bowl.

When Kellogg's wanted to do some commercials depicting Dennis using the single-serve boxes on a camping trip, he told the crew to come to his backyard in New Rochelle. The sprawling grass and trees, with a body of water behind it, looked exactly like a campground. He donned a flannel coat, built a campfire, and extolled the goodness of Kellogg's cereals from his backyard "camp site."

Dennis' backyard provided the setting for a Kellogg's ad.

For the spot that Kellogg's people devised, Dennis and four-year-old son Randy were camping together. Randy watched attentively, as the director made his final announcement before taping started.

"Cameras rolling!" shouted the director. "Five! Four! Three! Two! One!"

The director pointed to Dennis and Randy. Randy shouted "BLAST OFF!"

Kellogg's long had a standard procedure to keep their advertising spokesman well-stocked with their product, and every month, a truck arrived in New Rochelle with fresh boxes of Kellogg's cereals. The entire family happily welcomed a month's supply of breakfast. Micki, looking back, remembered that the sight of a delivery truck dropping off boxes of cereal made her much happier than the delivery truck that dropped off the cartons of cigarettes.

CHAPTER FOURTEEN
WAY OUT WEST

DENNIS PRIMARILY WORKED for Kellogg's for the next few years, a perfectly innocuous assignment, while scandal erupted elsewhere. Quiz shows, primarily the prime time shows of the previous four years, were now the subject of Congressional hearings. Dennis and his creation, *High Finance*, escaped scrutiny, but many of his peers weren't so lucky . . . or innocent, for that matter. In almost a single sweep, all of the big money quiz shows were knocked off the air. Producers were blackballed, and some contestants went into hiding.

With all that was going on, it was actually somewhat courageous of Dennis to accept a new game show (a term that became popular in the wake of the scandals, as a way of distancing the surviving shows from those that were implicated) in early 1959. Scrutiny and cynicism toward the genre were at an all-time high.

Haggis Baggis had debuted in prime-time on June 20, 1958, with host Jack Linkletter. Jack, son of Art Linkletter of *People are Funny* and *House Party* fame, had drummed up some publicity for the show due to the unusual fact that he was hosting it during summer vacation. A mere twenty years old at the time, Jack was wrapping up his sophomore year at USC, where he was majoring in English, just before starting work on the show. A daytime version premiered ten days after the prime-time version, but because it aired in direct competition with *House Party*, Jack declined to host the daytime version, which was hosted by Fred Robbins.

Dennis replaced Fred Robbins on February 9, 1959, and it was apparently quite an abrupt switch. One of the few surviving remnants today from *Haggis Baggis* is a kinescope of the February 18, 1959 broadcast. This was how Dennis opened that episode:

"We're in the middle of the week now . . . of my second week here on *Haggis Baggis*. And again, I want to say thanks, not only to you folks for being so nice with your letters welcoming us aboard, but also to our crew who have been so patient with me. I didn't know myself that I was going to be doing this show until the day before I came in to do it. When you get a new master of ceremonies stumbling through the show, it makes it tough on the cameramen, directors, and everybody else, and I just want to openly say thanks to a wonderfully cooperative bunch of guys for making my job a lot easier."

Dennis was abruptly thrust into the show because of market research. *Haggis Baggis* had no sponsors as of yet, and obviously, that just wouldn't do. *Haggis Baggis* producer Joe Cates and NBC's advertising sales department conducted some research. They delivered their conclusion to the network:

"The emcee accounts for seventy percent of the game show's success.

Chapter Fourteen: Way Out West

Audiences . . . go for performers who make them sit up and listen. And by the same token, sponsors go for performers who talk convincingly about their products."

Emcees accounted for seventy percent of a game show's success, according to an NBC study.

NBC took this to mean that Fred Robbins had to go. Cates was tasked with finding a new host, and the network suggested that they literally meant a fresh face in television. Cates reasoned that the logical candidate was a forty-two-year-old veteran with 10,000 hours of television on his resume, plus a couple of long-running and wildly successful advertising campaigns that seemed to speak to his ability to get a viewer's attention and point them to the sponsor. Cates argued, and NBC quickly agreed, that Dennis James was the right man.

On *Haggis Baggis,* two contestants faced a grid of twenty-five boxes. The Y-axis displayed five letters of the alphabet; the X-axis displayed five categories; the contestants were given a letter and a category and had to give a word starting with that letter, fitting the category. An acceptable answer lit up the box corresponding to the two points. The grid was hiding a photo of a famous celebrity. The first contestant to identify the star won the game.

The winner and loser were both shown two prize packages; one was called HAGGIS and the other was called BAGGIS. Each contestant secretly chose a prize package. The winning contestant got whichever one he or she selected. If the loser managed to select the opposite prize package, the loser got those prizes; otherwise, bupkis.

Reporter Marie Torre played Devil's advocate while talking to Dennis, reasoning that *Haggis Baggis* couldn't possibly be a desirable gig in February 1959. *The $64,000 Question* and *Twenty One* had both gone off the air within the past five months. Wasn't Dennis a little wary?

Dennis replied, "I don't regard this as typical of the shows that fall into the category of 'fix.' It is purely and simply a game show that offers the housewife a pleasant respite from the housework routine. In other words, we're not as interested in handing out prizes as we are in spreading a little enjoyment. And if we accomplish that, I really couldn't ask for anything more."

The show did accomplish that, but ultimately, the game was pretty thin soup. In the surviving kinescope, three full games are played in the half-hour. A game could be completed in only about four minutes.

Dennis didn't worry about having to sit around the house with nothing to do. He was with Kellogg's and continued with them for some time, and of course, there was still his volunteer work with United Cerebral Palsy. The 1960 *Celebrity Parade* brought in $413,265.

January 20, 1961 was a historic date for America, and it would prove to

Chapter Fourteen: Way Out West

be an infamous date for American television. On that night, Dennis got to make a rather dubious addition to his resume: he was the commercial announcer for possibly the worst game show in American television history.

Some guys have all the luck. Dennis rehearsed a scene in *Two for the Seesaw*.

You're in the Picture, created by Don Lipp and Bob Synes, and produced by Steve Carlin of *The $64,000 Question*, was a CBS prime-time panel show inspired by a popular carnival activity: paintings with the faces removed, so that people could stick their heads in and pretend they were in the scene. The four celebrity panelists—Pat Harrington, Jr., Pat Carroll, Jan Sterling, and Arthur Treacher—had their peripheral vision blocked and were unable to see what they were sticking their heads into. They asked questions to host

Jackie Gleason in an attempt to figure out the subject of the picture, and Gleason could only answer with a yes or a no.

Kellogg's agreed to sponsor the show on an alternating basis with L&M Cigarettes. Kellogg's would have the premiere broadcast, L&M would have the second episode, and they would trade off sponsoring from there. For that premiere broadcast, there was Dennis to say a few nice words on behalf of Kellogg's.

To say that *You're in the Picture* wasn't a good game was putting it mildly. Jackie Gleason, a legendary comic with a famously blunt way of expressing himself, concluded the premiere broadcast with a much better summarization, telling the studio audience, "You have braved a blizzard."

The following week's episode was one of the legendary broadcasts in television history. Jackie Gleason walked onto an empty stage, sat down, and declared that last week's game "laid, without a doubt, the biggest bomb in history." The full half-hour consisted of Jackie Gleason apologizing for how bad the show was.

In the span of that thirty minutes, though, Kellogg's felt that Jackie Gleason had committed an unpardonable sin. He made it clear that, for the remainder of the show's thirteen week contract, whatever the show would be, it wasn't going to be a game show (ultimately, Gleason settled for a talk show format to run out the show's commitment). Kellogg's contract made it clear that they had signed up for a game show. Kellogg's was so irritated by Gleason's apology that they pulled sponsorship, but Kellogg's had sponsored the show just long enough for Dennis James to have a role on one of television's most notorious flops.

Dennis pursued a new challenge in the summer of 1961. Over two decades after taking acting classes by night, he put them to good use by starring in *Two for the Seesaw*, a summer stock production of a popular Broadway play. He played lawyer Jerry Ryan, a divorcee, who begins a relationship with a dancer. It was a rare opportunity for him to try something aside from being Dennis James. His schedule usually precluded that, but he enjoyed the experience and hoped he could do more acting in the future.

Meanwhile, his good friend of Dennis, Monty Hall, was hard at work

Chapter Fourteen: Way Out West

trying to sell networks and game show packagers on a format he had conjured up for a new game called *First Impressions*.

First Impressions was a word association game that Monty had been showing Goodson-Todman for months. The company suggested changes, Monty modified the format, returned for another meeting, made more changes, and eventually, Goodson-Todman launched a word association game of their own, *Password*, in 1961. *Password*, in its finished form, was really not very similar to *First Impression*, and Monty even admitted as such, but privately he was annoyed that he had at least planted the seed for Goodson-Todman to explore word association tests as a game show concept, and he was hurt when he wasn't given a cut of the new show's profits or even consideration for hosting. Allen Ludden had a long, successful run as host of *Password*.

Dennis sat on the panel with the quintessential
game show panelist on *Your First Impression*.

Monty took the unusual step of coming up with a new format to suit the title, and at about the same time that *Password* was making its debut on CBS, the NBC network bought *First Impressions* from him. Because "First Impressions" was a subtitle of the book, *Little Women*, Monty agreed to retitle the show *Your First Impression*.

Okay? Okay! Dennis James' Lifetime of Firsts

Your First Impression was a guessing game. A celebrity guest was asked a series of personal questions or blanks to fill in. A panel, which hadn't seen the celebrity guest, then tried to guess the guest's identity based on the answers given to the personal questions. Monty asked Dennis to be a regular panelist on the new show.

Monty explains, "Dennis and I knew each other back in New Rochelle. We lived near each other, and our birthdays were only one day apart so we celebrated our birthdays together every year. He had a nickname for me; he was only three years older than me but he always called me 'Junior.' But I liked him as a friend and I was impressed with him as a talent, so I always told him that if I ever sold a series to one of the networks, I would hire him. I sold *Your First Impression* to NBC and I kept my word, I hired him."

Dennis agreed, the contracts were signed, and then NBC blindsided Monty and Dennis both with an edict that the show had to be taped out of the NBC Studios in Burbank, California, not at 30 Rockefeller Plaza in New York, as both men were initially expecting. All of a sudden, the James family was packing up Dennis' dream house in New Rochelle and heading for the west coast.

Their move was different from going to Chicago for *Club 60*. In Chicago, Dennis could see television drifting away from the city. In Los Angeles, he could see television drifting toward the city. Leaving New York was an easier decision when he followed Monty out there.

Micki remembers, "At the beginning, the only thing about Los Angeles that made Dennis unhappy was that he pretty much had to give up boating. We figured, 'Oh, Los Angeles, southern California, that's close to the water.' But Dennis quickly figured out what the living situation was going to be. You have to arrange for your boat to be kept somewhere in Los Angeles, and Dennis didn't like that as much as he liked what he had, which was a house on the water where he could literally keep the boat in the backyard. So not being able to go boating on a whim was a bit of a disappointment to him, but he wanted to keep working."

Your First Impression launched on NBC on January 2, 1962. Host Bill

Chapter Fourteen: Way Out West

Leyden kept things running as the celebrity panel played. To start each game, Dennis and the other panelists were shown photos of five celebrities and told that one of them was the celebrity who was about to join them. The celebrity sat behind the panel in a soundproof room and relayed answers to the panel's questions through Leyden. It was an unusual game show in one regard—there was absolutely no reward involved. No cash, no prizes, there wasn't even a point score in the game. It was an unheard-of game show that truly was "just" a game, no stakes.

Dennis had a good time with a new challenge, asking
questions as a panelist on *Your First Impression*.

Monty Hall said at the time, "I didn't explain the show to NBC. I demonstrated it and sold it immediately. It's literally an analysis game. It uses psychology and doesn't give away a thing. It calls for mental agility and the ability to associate and to literally give your first impression. I think NBC should be congratulated for taking a chance on the show."

Your First Impression was marred by growing pains behind the scenes. Monty, who had set up an office inside the Burbank complex, found himself on the telephone almost every day with NBC executives, who had suggestions about how to improve the flaws that they saw in the show. Particularly irksome to him was that it was the executives at NBC in New York, where he was expecting to do the show originally, and he could have met personally with them.

Monty lamented in one interview, "When you're a producer, you have all the headaches. When your show is on the air and something goes wrong, you're powerless. On *Video Village* [the game show Monty was hosting at the same time, for Merrill Heatter-Bob Quigley Productions], I'm on top of the show constantly, and I have a good working relationship with my producers. Yes, I tell you, a producer is a worrisome thing."

When the show's first thirteen-week commitment ended and Monty learned, to his own surprise, that NBC was picking up the series, he flew to New York, met with all of the executives he had been speaking with, and laid down the law: he wasn't talking to them anymore. He was hiring a new producer to oversee *Your First Impression*, and, if the executives wanted to keep nitpicking, they could call the new guy.

The "new guy" was Stefan Hatos, a former oboist for the Detroit Civic Symphony. He joined NBC as an announcer and part-time writer, penning episodes of *The Lone Ranger* and *The Green Hornet*. Early in his radio career, he worked for an audience participation program in which the emcee was fond of wandering into the audience and offering small awards for people who happened to have unusual items on their person—"If you have a postage stamp with a President on it in your purse, I'll give you $5!" He moved to Los Angeles in 1951 and produced some of Bob Hope's early television efforts before accepting a job with Ralph Edwards Productions as producer of *It Could Be You!*, a daytime game show that had actually been cancelled and replaced by *Your First Impression*. Monty credited Stefan Hatos with whipping *Your First Impression* into shape. He recalled in his autobiography that for the initial three months of the series, notes for the staff, panelists, and host were usually scrawled in pencil on the back of used envelopes. The first noticeable change once Hatos took over was that all of the notes were suddenly organized into typewritten scripts. Monty was happy with his new business partner, and he and Hatos began collaborating on an idea for another game show.

Meanwhile, Dennis was front and center on the panel of *Your First Impression*, along with the other regular panelist on the series, George Kirgo,

Chapter Fourteen: Way Out West

a prolific writer of books, films, and television shows, who had made himself known in front of the camera as a frequent guest of Jack Paar. Much as the Goodson-Todman staff maintained that casting a game show panel was like casting a play, the regular panelists, TV critic Fred Danzig noted, were clearly playing roles in their questioning. It was a good cop-bad cop approach. Kirgo took something of a dim view of any answer given to the questions, while Dennis approached it more optimistically and built up whatever guests Kirgo had just torn down.

The show actually got some thumbs up from critics, who typically didn't have nice words for game shows. Danzig, who called Dennis "a quick-thinking pro" in his review, said, "It's almost refreshing to see actors exploiting each other for the edification of the star-struck viewers among us instead of exploiting the unfortunates who flocked to *It Could Be You*."

Dennis dealt with a puzzling group of Buster Keaton impersonators during a game of *Your First Impression*.

Case in point, Danzig cited a game on the premiere broadcast in which guest Walter Brennan was asked to complete the sentence, "My friends think I'm . . . ." Brennan candidly answered, "A tightwad."

There were other celebrities who provided blunt answers. Cathy Nolan of *The Real McCoys* completed "The problem with this country is . . . ." with "President Kennedy." 7,000 letters alone came in because of her game. Joannie Sommers threw everyone in a loop when she finished the simple, vague statement "I won't . . . ." by saying "Go to bed with every Tom, Dick, and Harry."

Dennis himself could be surprisingly direct sometimes. While trying to figure out the identity of the guest, he muttered to himself (and into his microphone), "I don't know who she is, but she sounds over the hill." Nina Foch came out of the soundproof booth and threw a punch at him.

Monty Hall recalls, "Dennis was the very best panelist we had on that show. He could have been a fine host, but I remember from the beginning I sensed he'd be better on *Your First Impression* if he was playing the game instead of hosting it. Dennis could read people very well. He was a skilled amateur psychologist."

Frankness and self-deprecation wasn't common from celebrity guests appearing as themselves, and *Your First Impression* was sometimes a revealing program, allowing celebrity guests to show sides of themselves that they didn't reveal all that often.

Such was the case on a headline-making episode that aired July 19, 1962, with Dennis sitting on the panel, joined by Inger Stevens and Steve Dunne. The game started with Bill Leyden telling the panel that their guest was John Glenn, Robert F. Kennedy, Bing Crosby, James Stewart, or Richard Nixon.

Nixon, who had made his game show debut on *Masquerade Party* eight years earlier, took his seat in the soundproof room and began fielding questions. Having lost the Presidential election in a squeaker to John Kennedy less than two years earlier, Nixon was now in a hotly-contested race for the Governor's seat in California. The feeling from most political analysts was that if he lost, his career in politics was over for good.

"A woman past forty is . . . ." Nixon's answer: "Still beautiful."

"The one person in the world I'd like to meet is . . . ." Nixon's answer: "The President."

Chapter Fourteen: Way Out West

"If I could be at a moment in history, I would like to be . . . ." Nixon's answer: "The President."

"The one thing you could never get me to do is . . . ." Nixon's answer: "Quit."

At this point, the panel was pretty sure they had solved it, just from the one-track-mind nature of the answers being given, but Nixon had one dynamite line waiting, when he invoked President Kennedy's well-documented military service for an answer to his next question.

"My one regret is . . . ." Nixon's answer: "That I wasn't assigned to a PT boat."

NBC wasn't laughing. The network was already worried about having a candidate in an active campaign appearing on the show, but now, word from the taping was that the segment had gone so well, and Nixon came off so charming and good-humored, that it virtually made the show look like an endorsement. NBC handed down word that Nixon's episode wouldn't air.

Hatos and Monty acted quickly, calling Governor Pat Brown and extending an invitation to him to appear on the program. Brown accepted the offer, and NBC, satisfied that both candidates were given an opportunity to look good, allowed Nixon's appearance to air. Nixon lost the Governor's race four months later, and the press in California wouldn't have him to kick around anymore, for a while.

That Election Day, November 6, 1962, Dennis was part of a small bit of television history, filming an appearance on a variety special called *From This Moment On*. Filmed in Hollywood, the special, hosted by Jerry Lewis, featured performances by numerous guest stars, including Pat Harrington, Jr., Stubby Kaye, Troy Donahue, Caesar Romero, Ed Wynn, Bobby Darrin, Jim Backus, Betty White, Hugh Downs, Bobby Van, Rose Marie, and Henry Mancini and His Orchestra. The special was produced by the Muscular Dystrophy Association of America (MDA), and the response was so positive to the special that by 1966, *From This Moment On* was supplanted by an annual telethon on Labor Day weekend. The MDA Telethon, under several names, became a television institution, lasting until 2014.

CHAPTER FIFTEEN
IN THE GREEN

Your First Impression stayed on the NBC schedule, and with television slowly moving out there anyway, Dennis held a family meeting and got everyone's input. They all agreed it was time to move to California. He and Micki took Randy, of course, but they also brought along Micki's mother. She became enamored with California during a visit and moved in with her daughter's family.

For the time being, they still had the house back in New Rochelle, but during the family's first visit to the city of San Francisco—where Dennis considered driving along the hilly, winding streets so aggravating that he put the car in a garage and didn't drive for the rest of the trip—Micki discovered that not only had he put the house in New Rochelle on the market, but he seemed to be an extremely motivated seller. Too motivated, it turned out.

Dennis got a phone call one night, excitedly hung up the phone, and announced, "Well, I just sold our house!"

Micki, who didn't realize it was for sale, blurted out, "What?!"

Dennis answered, "Somebody wanted it in New Rochelle. He approached a real estate agent, real estate agent contacted my manager, and we closed the deal. We sold the house. And I sold it furnished, as is, so we don't have to go back for the furniture or anything. I just sold the whole thing."

Micki, growing incredulous, clarified, "You sold *all* of it? You sold the clothes we left there? You sold our wedding gifts? You sold *everything* we own?"

Dennis confidently replied, "Yeah, it's easy that way!"

Dennis returned to Los Angeles after that trip to get to work on *Your First Impression*. Micki and her mother booked a hasty flight back to New York and spent a week gathering up everything in the house before the new owner moved in.

The James family settled down in a nice house in Los Angeles. They also bought some property in Encino and rented it out, so that the family would always have steady income if employment turned lean for Dennis. While he may have given up boating, he quickly found that California was salubrious toward another activity for passing the time. He got hooked on golf.

He had certainly played the game before, but always as an ancillary part of another career; he golfed for *Sports Parade*, and when non-profit groups held fundraisers at country clubs, Dennis, there to serve as master of ceremonies, picked up a club and played the game just to be a part of the experience. In 1960, he trekked up to White Plains, New York, for a celebrity golf tournament, competing against show business legends Perry Como, Fred Waring, Joey Bishop, Ed Sullivan, and Benny Goodman. Dennis was part of

Chapter Fifteen: In the Green

the winning foursome, along with golf pro Betty Bush, amateur Jim Maver, and Paul Grossinger of Grossinger's Hotel. Dennis, with a handicap of fourteen, had a gross score of 79. On the eighteenth hole, he managed to land his second shot within five feet of the hole and then successfully putted for a birdie 3. His handicap made this an eagle 2 and allowed the team to finish eleven under par. For somebody who only played golf when a gig required it, he was quite good.

Dennis took a swing at a new hobby.

Once out in Los Angeles, he decided to give golf another shot. What kind of golfer was he in California?

Micki answers, "Passionate."

Dennis seemingly filled the boating void with golf, devoting the same time, energy, and enthusiasm to the new hobby. He joined Lakeside Country Club and struck up a new round of friendships over many games. He became close with game show hosting brothers Tom Kennedy and Jack Narz. Bob Hope was a member, too. Jack Clark and Peter Marshall played many games at Lakeside. Fitness gurus Jack and Elaine LaLanne golfed there, too.

Tom Kennedy remembers, "I met Dennis through my brother, Jack. They were friends from their time doing game shows in New York before the scandals. Dennis would come into Manhattan on his boat, and Jack would hitch a ride with him and come into New York City by boat to go to work. I got to know him better when he moved out to California. As soon as we met, we hit it off. Dennis was absolutely a live wire. He was aggressive, curious, and always wanting to move forward. Whatever he did, he thought about how to make it better. I admired him for his hustle. He was never out of a job, and for good reason."

Elaine LaLanne says, "My husband Jack was an amazing golfer. He didn't take up golf until his late forties and he was so dedicated to it that he worked his way up to a four handicap. He had a saying: 'When I play, I play for keeps; tear up the grass in great big heaps.' And that's exactly what he did out there."

Jack was so dedicated to golf that he became one of numerous celebrities to lend his name to a charity competition, the Jack LaLanne Golf Tournament. They were lavish, full-day events that gave dozens of celebrities a chance to indulge in their favorite sport while raising funds for a worthy cause. For a typical golf tournament, a large group of celebrities were divided into foursomes and played eighteen holes. With so many celebrities hamming it up for spectators and cameras, the tournament usually lasted well over five hours. Afterward, there was a cocktail party, a banquet, an award ceremony, and then live entertainment, with most of the golfers dancing, singing, performing stand-up, or whatever else brought them to fame. Hosting such a lengthy event was a herculean task, and Jack LaLanne recognized that there was only one man for the job. Despite the name, it was Dennis James who served as Master of Ceremonies for the Jack LaLanne Golf Tournament.

Elaine remembers, "Dennis would never say no to anything. He always wanted to do something, always offered to help. There was just no ego in that man."

Elaine's son, John LaLanne, adds, "My high school, Buckley School had a talent show every year and Dennis was actually master of ceremonies for the talent show. And Buckley School was heavily show business children. As an adult now, I appreciate the experience more. As a teenager, it never entered my head how strange it was to look in the audience and see Vincent Price watching me play the guitar. The Buckley School Talent Show was an annual event in the auditorium, and the people in the audience were exactly the same people you saw on the red carpet on TV; it looked like Oscar Night in there. Tony Griffin, Merv's son, actually did stand-up when he was a teenager, and he was hilarious. He did a perfect impression of Richard Nixon. And Dennis hosted it, and he hosted it exactly as if it was a major television event. He wasn't casual about it, he got everyone excited, welcomed the performers, congratulated them at the end."

Dennis also joined a group called the Hollywood Hackers, a golf club opened to anybody in show business, not just performers, but stagehands, writers, directors, and producers were welcome to join. Together, the Hackers would travel across California, competing against locals in tournaments to raise money for a variety of causes. Among the Hackers who hit the links with Dennis: Jack LaLanne, Clint Eastwood, Larry Fine of the Three Stooges, Alan Hale, and Max Baer. It was a way to put your off-hours to good use. Hackers, who were in the middle of shooting a film or singing in Las Vegas, weren't expected to appear at the tournaments, but any Hackers who weren't otherwise engaged travelled to and fro to hit the links and generate funds.

Elaine LaLanne says, "Dennis and Jack were both part of that group for years. If a charity reached out and asked for a fundraiser, the Hackers who were available that day would make the trip, play golf, and put on a show afterwards. Jack loved that because he had an operatic voice and he loved being able to sing, and Dennis loved it because he loved everything he did."

Fellow Hollywood Hacker Tom Kennedy says, "I was a lifelong member. Bill and Nancy Sims, who founded it, had a Rolodex of everybody in show business. They'd contact charities and offer them a celebrity golf tournament to raise funds, then call the members and see who didn't already have a commitment on a specific weekend. They kept stats on all of the celebrities who participated too. Strong players were always matched with strong players, weaker players competed against weaker players, so every game was competitive. The tournaments were so well organized, and we raised a lot of money for a lot of great causes.

"Two of our members were Alan Hale, Jr. He played Skipper on *Gilligan's Island*. He was a huge man. About six-foot-four and 300 pounds. And then we had Billy Barty, the dwarf actor. They had a bit they would do at every tournament. Alan would ask Billy to go get the golf cart. Billy would go right past the cart and go to Alan's golf bag, which was taller than Billy. And Billy would struggle with the bag and yell 'How do you start this damn thing?!'"

Dennis kept at it and kept at it, eventually working his way up to an 11 handicap (after all these years, everybody in the family effortlessly remembered that number when asked about it). His crowning achievement as a golfer happened in Puerto Rico.

Micki remembers, "There had been an incident a few years earlier, a shooting at a country club in Puerto Rico. And it was covered in the news and it did a lot of harm to Puerto Rico tourism for a while. So to boost the tourism industry, they organized a celebrity golf tournament and put it on television, so you could see how beautiful it looked as the stars played golf and had a good, relaxing time in Puerto Rico. So Dennis got invited and he happily accepted."

Dennis approached the tee, took his swing, and watched in amazement: the ball didn't even bounce. It went in the air, came down, and landed directly in the tin cup. Lest anyone doubt such a perfect shot, he made sure he had the videotape of the shot to prove it. It was the first hole in one he ever hit, and it happened to be on television.

Micki says, "He was in the tournament with host Carol Mann, who was a very successful pro golfer. On that tape, you can hear her screaming, 'IT'S IN THE HOLE! IT'S IN THE HOLE!' because she couldn't believe Dennis made that shot. She was so happy for him. Dennis used to joke about being cheated out of a car that day. Usually in these tournaments, there's some kind of prize awarded for hitting a hole in one, but I guess this place in Puerto Rico didn't expect anyone to actually hit one. Dennis got that hole in one and walked away empty-handed . . . except for a videotape of the tournament!

"Back in California, the way our house was set up, we had our bedroom, and next to the bedroom was Dennis' home office, and he had a tape deck for playing three-quarter-inch videotapes. And for months after we got back from Puerto Rico, I'd wake up in the morning and I'd hear Carol Mann in the next room screaming, 'IT'S IN THE HOLE! IT'S IN THE HOLE!' Dennis played that videotape over and over and over again. He was so proud of himself."

Elaine LaLanne offers some insight about Dennis' pride. "Golfers are very competitive, but when Jack and I started doing golf tournaments and I had a chance to really watch other players, I realized an interesting thing. Golfers are most competitive against themselves. They all want to win, of course, but the most important thing is they want to be better than they were the last time they played. You're your own biggest rival when you're a golfer."

Dennis had become so fervent about golf since moving to California that it caused him to develop some surprisingly passionate opinions about television coverage of the game. He griped that there were too many broadcasts devoted to golf, and that the tournament schedules were clumsily arranged for television purposes.

Dennis warned viewers to avoid the Whammy on *Beat the Odds*.

He told one reporter, "The networks always put the golf show on at the worst possible time. Just when the fan is out on the course. I'm usually out there playing and I'm not going to stop and run for the TV set. Run [the golf tournaments] against Johnny Carson... If the tournament is beamed live in the afternoon, give the average buff a break and do a taped repeat at night."

One of the things that helped Dennis get comfortable in California was that he instantly landed a second job. A popular local game show in Los Angeles, *Beat the Odds*, was in search of a new host to replace the departing Mike Stokey. It was at this point that Dennis came to realize that he had struck upon his favorite gig in television. He preferred game shows above all else. He had been in broadcasting so long that he commanded a sizable paycheck for it. He didn't offer specifics, but he told one reporter than unless you meant someone on Cary Grant's level, he was making better money than the average actor.

That observation seemed to validate something he had said some years earlier. In 1954, a reporter asked what he expected the long-term effects of television to be. He anticipated that "star power" wouldn't mean much. He told the reporter, "I think the day of idolizing the star has passed and that there will be no Garbos in television. The stars become human beings."

He was fine with being a human being. Having a passing motorist yell "Hey Dennis!" suited him better than being swarmed by photographers and autograph seekers, and the money wasn't bad for a human being. For that payday, he got to do a totally spontaneous, freewheeling gig hosting a game show.

Beat the Odds pitted two contestants against each other. A pair of wheels with letters of the alphabet printed on them would spin and spin until a contestant pressed a button, stopping the wheel on two letters as a light lit up, revealing a number. The contestant would have to give a word starting and ending with the selected letters, and containing at least that number of letters. For example, if the contestants spun C-E-5, some possible correct answers might include "chase," "cheese," or "caboodle."

Any word given was automatically ruled correct unless the opponent challenged, in which case the dictionary was checked. A contestant could keep spinning and giving words, accumulating points as long as they wanted. The title *Beat the Odds* came from "Sammy the Whammy," a villainous little cartoon character, who appeared in scattered spots throughout the wheels. Stopping the wheel on Sammy the Whammy cost a contestant all the money earned on their turn up to that point.

For many years on radio and television, the selection process for people wanting to appear on game shows was rather slipshod. The "warm-up man" came out before the show started, struck up a conversation with a few people in the audience, and picked the ones with the best personalities. Little or no regard was given to whether or not they were actually qualified to play the game.

Beat the Odds was one of the first game shows to pre-screen potential contestants by having people audition for the show and seeing how well they played test games. Dennis explained the need for it in one interview. "Who in the world knows the answer to everything? A certain man is an expert in a certain field. We must find out where the knowledge of our contestant is above average. If not, you could ask five people a two-letter word beginning with 'a' and ending with 't' and four would fail to answer."

After twenty-four years in television, Dennis had hardly grown jaded about the business. He was actually quite proud about his chosen profession. He was providing entertainment to, among other people, a demographic that needed cost-effective amusement.

He told Vernon Scott, "Television is the poor people's medium. They can buy a set and then have the world of entertainment brought right into their homes week after week, year after year without spending another cent. I've seen it change from an experimental gimmick into the huge entertainment medium it is today."

Your First Impression continued chugging along on NBC, and the probing questions that Dennis and the panel asked to the mystery visitors were gradually turning it into the most dangerous game on television. Certainly one of the most frequently edited. The panelists, Dennis included, could be stunningly blunt in their cross-examinations, and producer Monty Hall effortlessly rattled off to a reporter a string of incidents that NBC insisted on deleting before broadcasts.

Dinah Shore was sitting in the booth one day. After saying some sweet words about her spouse, she was aghast when George Kirgo pontificated, "It couldn't be Dinah Shore because this person loves her husband, and Dinah Shore couldn't care if her husband lived or died."

A fading movie star, who Monty graciously refused to identify, was the subject of discussion on another day when a panelist speculated, "This person is either very old or very dull."

On another day, another celebrity guest, also not identified by Monty, was offered the statement, "Fat men are . . . ." After some thought, the guest finished it with ". . . overbearing and pugnacious, like William Morris agents."

All deleted. Monty was fine with the content that made it on the air, because much of the edgier discussion stayed intact. Daytime TV could be awfully bland, and Monty rather liked that his show felt like a nighttime show. NBC executives even asked him to draw up a budget statement for a nighttime version if they ever decided to make it a weekly prime-time offering, but that plan fell through.

Despite the psychological wringer that the game put its guests through—an actress refused to be on the program, telling Monty, "I wouldn't put myself through that for all the money in the world." A well-known Western star panicked and cancelled at the last second. Plenty of celebrities were willing to come there and put the panel to the test.

Guest Jackie Cooper, married and divorced several times, heard "A man isn't ready for marriage if he . . . ." and added ". . . hasn't been married at least twice before."

Dennis, for his part on the panel, showed off how impressively perceptive he could be. While interrogating one mystery visitor, he pontificated, "She sounds to me like a woman who once knew a great love, lost it, and found it again." The guest was actress Ruth Warwick, who had divorced and re-married the same man.

California seemed to agree with Dennis. He even changed his look a little bit after his arrival. In search of a new barber, he crossed paths with a hairstylist who suggested one simple change: he stopped putting products in his hair. Throughout his entire career on the east coast, he always had a lustrous shine to his smoothed-down hair with a dollop of Brylcreem, or some other substance. In California, he adapted the dry look, which gave him a strong pompadour crowning his head.

Dennis rehearsed with Efram Zimbalist Jr. for his guest spot on *77 Sunset Strip*.

Dennis, whose interest in acting had been somewhat dormant ever since he finished his formal education back in New Jersey, suddenly felt a twinge again and got some chances to indulge it. He guest-starred on the detective series *77 Sunset Strip,* and appeared on two episodes of *The Dick Powell Show*, an anthology series.

Just in case *Your First Impression* and *Beat the Odds* weren't keeping Dennis busy enough, he picked up a third game show. NBC was buying a new game show from producers Merrill Heatter and Bob Quigley, the same men who created and produced *Video Village,* the show that Monty Hall had been hosting the past few years. Heatter and Quigley's new game was called *People Will Talk.* It premiered on July 1, 1963.

The game began with man-on-the-street interviews. A roving reporter asked people a yes-or-no question, like "Should wives allow their husbands to play golf on the weekends?" A person who said "yes" and a person who said "no" were both brought into the studio to be contestants, each representing the point-of-view expressed in the pre-recorded interview. The contestants faced a panel of fifteen people, a mix of ordinary people and occasional celebrity guests. The panelists secretly voted for the point of view they agreed with, and the contestants took turns picking panelists, trying to find people who agreed with them. A contestant won $25 for finding somebody who agreed, with $100 winning the game and a bonus prize.

Despite some impressive star power—in a single week, the panel included Gene Barry, Connie Stevens, Nick Adams, Gisele Mackenzie, Fernando Lamas, Gloria Swanson, Lee Marvin, Agnes Moorehead, and Michael Landon—the show lasted only six months, expiring on December 27, 1963. There was just no competing against *Password* on CBS.

The notion of a giant celebrity panel captured Heatter and Quigley's imagination. They tinkered with the format somewhat and sold the show to CBS the following summer as a prime-time game, *The Celebrity Game* with host Carl Reiner. The all-celebrity panel of nine heard a series of questions first and secretly voted "yes" or "no." The contestants won money by predicting how each individual celebrity answered.

It worked better, but not better enough, until Heatter struck upon the idea of arranging the nine celebrities into a grid of nine boxes, changed the personal opinion questions to trivia questions, and made the game a very slight re-work of tic-tac-toe. The game would run for fifteen years on NBC and in first-run syndication with host Peter Marshall.

**Dennis with some puzzled panelists
on the set of *People Will Talk*.**

Dennis woefully said in the following years, "I said yes when they asked me to host *People Will Talk*, but I said no to *Hollywood Squares*!"

Despite the move to Los Angeles, Dennis was able to keep some of his commitments from the east coast. He continued his commercials for Kellogg's. When Kellogg's became the main sponsor of the long-running CBS Sunday night panel game *What's My Line?*, the company paid for him to fly to New York to deliver the commercials live, or sometimes to film them in advance.

In his own right, he had such an established name that *What's My Line?* moderator John Charles Daly segued into commercials by announcing, "And now, a word from Dennis James."

Chapter Fifteen: In the Green

Dennis played off *What's My Line?'s* famous Mystery Guest segment, in which the panelists put on blindfolds and asked yes-or-no questions to guess the identity of the star seated across from them. Dennis, for his Kellogg's commercial one night, donned a blindfold, borrowed from one of the panelists, and demonstrated that "Getting your daily supply of protein is so simple, you can do it blindfolded." With the blindfold fully obscuring his eyes, he poured cereal, milk, and a spoonful of sugar into the bowl, without a drop spilled or a flake out of place. Smiling broadly at his own flawless effort, he removed the blindfold and told viewers, "See for yourself. Try Special K. Okay? Okay."

He also recorded two syndicated radio shows during his visits to New York, *Startime USA* and *Entertainment USA*. He remained as devoted as ever to the annual *Celebrity Parade for Cerebral Palsy*. The *Celebrity Parade* was about to take on a deeper meaning for Dennis and Micki than any viewer could ever imagine.

On August 20, 1963, Dennis and Micki arrived at the hospital for the birth of their second son, Brad. There was a big problem, though: Brad wasn't supposed to be here for another three months. Brad was born and doctors broke the news to Dennis and Micki that he was a candidate for cerebral palsy.

As Dennis and Micki watched and waited, doctors examined Brad's bilirubin count. A high count would indicate brain damage. Doctors performed a relatively new procedure on him called a blood exchange. Needles were inserted into him and slowly, all of the blood in Brad's body was removed while a fresh supply of donated blood was transfused. That still didn't bring the bilirubin count down to the doctors' liking, so Brad was subjected to a second exchange with more donated blood. That stabilized him. He had avoided cerebral palsy.

As Dennis sat in the hallway, collecting himself after such a traumatic day, a doctor who recognized him walked up and said, "You know, it's interesting that this happened to your baby. Blood exchanging for a cerebral palsy candidate is a relatively new development. We figured it out from a study that was conducted with a research grant from United Cerebral Palsy. So the money you raised was actually what saved your son."

United Cerebral Palsy suddenly took on a personal meaning for Dennis and for his entire family. The James family formed a commitment to the cause that would last Dennis' lifetime and onward.

CHAPTER SIXTEEN
BEATING THE ODDS

AFTER THE TERRIFYING near-miss involving Brad, Dennis threw himself into the 1964 *Celebrity Parade* with gusto. He was helping book the telethon in addition to hosting it, and calling up celebrities and asking them to appear. Rattled by the thought that a few donations here and there had made all the difference for his own son, he organized a whopper of a show for the 1964 telethon: Bettye Ackerman, Eddie Albert, Steve Allen, Ann

Blythe, Jimmy Boyd, Lloyd Bridges, Jackie Coogan, Richard Crenna, James Drury, Rhonda Fleming, Peter Fonda, James Franciscus, Bob Hope, Sam Jaffee, Rick Jason, June Lockhart, Marilyn Maxwell, Vera Miles, Ken Murray, Chris Noel, Allan Sherman, Phil Silvers, Guy Williams, and Keenan Wynn.

Brad could barely walk the first time that he followed in his father's footsteps. He was in a commercial for Kellogg's, along with big brother Randy. Dad did all the talking.

"Hi, I'm Dennis James. You know, we've got a fellow staying at our house and you would not believe it . . . he has never eaten Kellogg's Corn Flakes. Never in his life! Here's the most popular cereal in the whole world today, and this guy has never even given it a try. Is it crisp? Is it fresh? Is it good-tasting? Nourishing? He doesn't know, and what's more he doesn't care! But I'll tell you this . . . you never saw a healthier guy in your life. Lemme show you his picture . . . .

"There he is. Bradley James. One year old. I'll make you a promise. We'll turn him into a Corn Flaker real soon, because if I can't convince him, here's a man who can. His big brother, Randy. Now he knows what brings the best to you each morning! Well, how about your family?"

Dennis always enjoyed getting his boys involved in his work in the years to come. Both of them took very active roles in United Cerebral Palsy, including appearing with their father on the telethon.

Brad says, "I remember when I finally reached about age ten, my father pulls me in front of the camera during a telethon and introduces me, and suddenly he says, 'Brad, would you do me a favor? I need to go to the restroom, you stay right here and talk to the folks at home, I'll be right back.' And he hands me the microphone and walks off. He didn't tell me he was going to do that. And for a twenty-two hour show, you certainly don't have cue cards, so I didn't have anything that I could work from. And so I just looked into the camera and talked and talked. My dad did these telethons all the time, so I was pretty knowledgeable about the subject matter, and I had seen my dad host anyway, so I had a good idea of how to perform, I was sort of copying what I thought my dad would do. I never had any inclination to become a TV host like my dad but I do remember, in that moment, when I was ten years old and filling time on a telethon, I had this moment of clarity. I thought to myself, 'I can see why my dad likes this so much.' There actually is something kind of fun about talking just off the top of your head and making it something of value."

Dennis hovered over Peter Fonda's shoulders at the all-star operator bank answering the phones for United Cerebral Palsy's *Celebrity Parade*.

On June 26, 1964, *Your First Impression* came to an end on NBC. *Beat the Odds* had also concluded its time on KTLA, which meant that for the first time since Dennis had moved to California, he had no television shows on the air. He was still commuting to New York for his work with syndicated radio, Kellogg's, and United Cerebral Palsy. In 1965, a banquet was held in his honor, naming him Humanitarian of the Year for his efforts raising funds for United Cerebral Palsy. The award was presented to him by former President Dwight Eisenhower.

Monty Hall, who attended the ceremony, remembers, "Eisenhower pointed to Dennis and said 'We need more people like this.'"

Despite the accolades and the work available to him on the east coast, he never entertained any thoughts of returning permanently to New York. Los Angeles had been good to him so far, his boys had settled into their home nicely, and perhaps most importantly, New York couldn't offer the prospect of year-round golf. His only real problem at this point was that the commitments that he had took too much time for him to actively pursue dramatic performances. He had enjoyed his handful of experiences guest-starring on prime time shows, but most dramatic show acting roles required a full week's commitment, and Kellogg's combined with the radio shows took too much of his time.

Dennis along with executive producers Bob Quigley and Merrill Heatter, who were in charge of *People Will Talk*, and later *PDQ*.

Chapter Sixteen: Beating the Odds

Dennis' next career opportunity came courtesy of Merrill Heatter and Bob Quigley, the producers of *People Will Talk*. Dennis had struck up a good relationship with them. He and Micki were particularly close to Bob Quigley and his wife, Keith, while Merrill Heatter always spoke glowingly of Micki's gift for cooking Italian dinners.

Merrill Heatter and Bob Quigley came up with a new game show format in 1965 and tapped Dennis to host it. The game was called *PDQ*. Two celebrities played against another celebrity and a contestant. One member of each team was put in a soundproof booth, the other was shown a title or phrase, such as "Okay Mother." The player posted three letters from that phrase onto a sign in view of the player in the isolation booth. He couldn't post the first three consecutive letters, so in this example, the player might have posted "OKM." When a chime sounded, the player had to add one more letter, and continue adding letters until the partner in the isolation booth guessed the phrase. The opposing team played the same phrase. After both teams played, the team that used fewer letters earned one point per letter separating the teams' performance. (Example, the first team solves it with five letters; the second team solves it with seven letters; the first team scores two points for that round).

Four Star Television syndicated the show beginning in the fall of 1965. Only seventeen stations carried the program to start, but they were the right seventeen cities. A trade ad touted the fact that the seventeen stations carrying *PDQ* could be seen by 44% of the United States population, and they liked what they saw. Station WNBC in New York posted a 40% ratings boost for the time slot in which *PDQ* aired.

Dennis was paying close attention to the games on *PDQ* and, when reporter Charles Witbeck asked him to evaluate the stars he had seen playing up to that point, he immediately pegged Michael Landon as the strongest *PDQ* player around. "Mike's quick-witted, uninhibited and genuinely fond of playing games. I have to put him at the top."

Every performer's dream: your name in lights. Dennis' face loomed over the streets of New York City in an advertisement for his new game show, *PDQ*.

Close to the top of the list were actress Ruta Lee, actor Dick Patterson, and actress Rose Marie. A singer/actor named Peter Marshall played the game, too.

Peter Marshall remembers, "I had just been hired by Heatter-Quigley to host a new game show they were putting together, and they wanted the audience to get accustomed to seeing my face so I wouldn't seem like a stranger when the show got on the air. They had me appear as a guest on *PDQ* a few times. Dennis and I hit it off right away. I had watched Dennis do the commentary for professional wrestling years earlier, we were both members of the Hollywood Hackers, but we hadn't really spoken to each other. *PDQ* was how we really got to know each other. I really liked him a lot."

Dennis found that, after years of helming game shows, he had developed a sixth sense of what made a good contestant. "If a person is inflexible, he will turn out to be a poor contestant."

He generally believed that, oddly enough, brainiacs made for boring game shows. He found that, in the case of either celebrities or contestants, a smart player wouldn't really deliver any sort of "performance" while playing. It would just be straightforward correct answer after correct answer, with no trace of life or personality. Nothing against geniuses personally, they just made for uninteresting television.

"Of course, some fool you," he clarified. "Actress Dana Wynter appeared [to have] a restrained, controlled manner, [but] she's well-traveled, has a good mind, and she knows how to unbend. Phyllis Diller is another one who flies."

Any advice for people who wanted to appear on his game shows? "Don't listen to yourself, concentrate on listening to others, and stay loose."

What did it take to be a good emcee? "My job really centers on listening. It's hard since other things are going on in your mind but for an emcee, listening is the key."

Being a good emcee meant being able to bring your own personality front and center, and not playing a character. That was a part of the trade that Dennis took pretty darn seriously, to the point of avoiding anything that would remotely constitute research. According to his children, he never watched game shows. He recorded his own on a reel-to-reel recording machine, and later a Umatic video recorder, and then a Betamax, but he didn't watch other game shows or even other telethons. His friend, Monty Hall, hosted many for Variety Clubs, but even if it meant supporting a friend, Dennis wouldn't watch.

As Brad remembered it, Dennis once told him, "If I ever watch a telethon, I'll probably never host another one."

Ruta Lee, Dick Patterson, and their contestant partners, in the *PDQ* tournament of champions.

Dennis was worried that one of two things would happen: he'd watch the show with a much-too-critical eye, focusing on what he'd do if he was there, or focusing on things the host did that could be better, or worse yet, he might wind up focusing on things that the host did better than the way he did them, and the show would turn into a self-auditing exercise. For that reason, he strenuously avoided watching anybody do the same type of work that he was doing.

If he needed any criticism of his performance, though, he could count on friends. Tom Kennedy laughs, "I picked on Dennis sometimes. I would critique him when he was hosting *PDQ*. I'd tell him things like 'Why don't you be nice to your contestants? I caught your show a few nights ago. Some woman made a mistake and you gave her hell! You just crucified her there

Chapter Sixteen: Beating the Odds

on stage! Be nice to the contestants! They're the reason you have a job!' And Micki would stand next to him and she'd snap her head around and say 'Tom's right! You tell him, Tom!' And Dennis would pretend to get mad and say things like 'I was hosting game shows before you were born!'"

Besides, Dennis already knew what made a good emcee, and more importantly, what made a lousy one. He despised the term "traffic cop," a description that many writers, and even people inside the TV business, had used to describe game show hosts. Enforce the rules, recap the score, and that's it. He did *not* like the term "traffic cop" and politely corrected anybody who used it when talking to him about game shows. He felt that the ideal game show host had a loose approach, stayed out of the way of the game, but still had fun and let the audience know that fun was being had.

Part of that fun involved Randy, now ten years old, and a big fan of his dad. He frequently came to the studio on taping days and explored the set during break. One day, as a goof, Randy opened the show instead of Dennis, popping out from underneath the podium and reciting the lines that Dennis normally recited leading into the game.

Dennis brought that sense of fun to the game as much as he could. Among other things, a catch phrase/running joke. When a contestant on *PDQ* was an attractive young woman, he, without fail, asked, "Would you like to meet my son?"

Dennis Jr. had reached adulthood by this point, and Dennis indicated to one reporter that he was hoping to bring his son into the family business. Dennis, still interested in creating and producing his own formats, had come up with a game show format with a title that was just perfect for America in the 1960s. He called the game *Race for Space*. He told the reporter that he had his son in mind for hosting.

Dennis Jr. had grown up as close to his father as circumstances would allow. His mother, Marion, raised him in another part of the country, while Dennis maintained a relationship with him largely by telephone and the occasional extended visits. Every summer vacation from school growing up,

Dennis Jr. had come to New Rochelle to be with Dennis and Micki. Despite all that, he wasn't interested in his dad's line of work or his dad's wishes for him—which Dennis was fine with, because, after all, he himself hadn't become a doctor like his parents were expecting.

Dennis' pride and joy. From left to right: Randy, Dennis Jr., and Brad James.

Dennis Jr. did a tour of duty in Vietnam, including a frightening six weeks where his whereabouts were unknown. He was eventually found in a tent city in Guam. He eventually returned stateside and completed his education at Georgetown Law School. He moved to Washington, DC, with his wife, whom he met in Vietnam. As an attorney, he specialized in international trade law cases as part of the firm Davenport & James PLLC, representing clients from Israel, India, and Chile, who had business interests in America.

Chapter Sixteen: Beating the Odds

Back in the states, Dennis was still a full-time father to Brad and Randy. As Randy recalled for interviewer Stu Shostak, "He was a terrific father. He taught us great life lessons. A good father is a good role model, not just someone to tell you what to do, but walk the walk. And he definitely did that.

"And yes, he had a temper. He was Italian. But the thing about him was that we could be at the dinner table, and he could blow up and yell and scream at us, and then thirty seconds later, he'd say 'Pass the Parmesan' and it was like nothing happened. He was honest and he was a great role model."

More than a decade after his last commercial for Old Gold cigarettes, Dennis was still smoking two packs a day, but the habit came to a terrifying end one night after a taping of *PDQ*. He made his way to Abby Dalton's house for a small get-together with a few other television performers, a few cast members from *Petticoat Junction*, plus Foster Brooks, Richard Long, Jack Narz, and Tom Kennedy were there, too.

Tom remembered, "We got some scotch. We had a few and I said, 'We can't have a scotch party without candy!' Scotch and candy together taste amazing. So, I ran out and got a box of See's Chocolate, and we had that with the scotch. We were laughing, having a good time. It was a wonderful evening. And then we had some trouble."

Dennis got an uncomfortable feeling in his chest, but brushed it off for a time, thinking that the combination of chocolate and scotch had given him indigestion. As the night went along, he and Micki, sitting next to him, figured out that it was something worse. Dennis was having a heart attack. An ambulance rushed him to the hospital.

He was convalescing while Micki took care of Brad and Randy by herself for a while.

One night, while she was cooking dinner, gossip columnist Rona Barrett popped up on TV. Barrett reported, "All of Hollywood is saddened tonight by the passing of Dennis James."

Micki dropped her pan in shock, and called the hospital to confirm that, yes, her husband was still there. Dennis was talking with a doctor, who was trying to figure out the cause of his troubles and how to prevent a repeat. The doctor, trying to get a sense of what a typical day in Dennis' life was like, asked him, "What did you do last night?"

Dennis gave him an honest answer. "Last night, I drank a lot of scotch and ate some chocolate."

The doctor replied, "That's a good way to kill yourself."

Dennis, with an unbridled sense of humor even about a near-death experience, always later greeted Tom at social functions as "The man who almost killed me!"

He survived the ordeal, but the heart attack scared the addiction right out of him and he quit smoking. For a while.

CHAPTER SEVENTEEN
HERE WHEN YOU NEED HIM

DENNIS MADE A full recovery, and he owed it all to golf.

"It's a whole new thing now," he explained to writer Martin Hogan Jr. "They emphasize activity. The doctors get you back on your feet and right back into movement. I'm just as glad. Frankly, I'd go dingy if I had to sit around all day."

Aiding in the recovery was Jack LaLanne, who helped Dennis alter his diet a bit after the heart attack. The LaLannes and the Jameses were having dinner at Lakeside Country Club one night when Dennis began picking the LaLannes' brains about nutrition. "Do you usually eat dessert?" Jack asked.

Dennis nodded.

Jack enticed him, "I'm going to make a dessert that you can have any time you want. Guilt free." Jack disappeared for a few minutes, then returned with something behind his back. "Cover your eyes."

Dennis covered his eyes, Jack fed him a spoonful, and Dennis loved the sweet juicy taste of whatever it was. He uncovered his eyes and saw a champagne glass filled with a gooey red and yellow paste.

Jack told him, "I smashed a banana. When you mash up fruit, a lot of the natural juices and oils come out, so fruit's more flavorful when you eat it that way. And I mixed in some strawberries, too. If you want, you can mix some honey into it, too."

With Jack's advice and dessert, Dennis managed to drop about twenty pounds.

PDQ made a full recovery that year, too, after nearly being stricken down by a minor whiff of a scandal. Heatter-Quigley had sold *The Hollywood Squares* to NBC in 1966. Host Peter Marshall asked a trivia question to one of the celebrities in the giant tic-tac-toe grid. The stars usually fired off a snappy joke before giving their answer, a process that involved *Squares* staffers meeting with the stars before a taping and briefing them on the questions they'd be asked and some funny answers they could give. To a handful of people in the Federal Communications Commission, this sounded an awful lot like rigging the game.

The FCC conducted a thorough investigation of Heatter-Quigley operations, which meant that for a brief period, an FCC representative was keeping a close eye on everything happening backstage at *PDQ*. There wasn't anything going on at *PDQ*. *The Hollywood Squares* was mostly exonerated—the FCC concluded that giving the stars funny answers wasn't really rigging

Chapter Seventeen: Here When You Need Him

a game show, but the practice bothered them enough that *The Hollywood Squares* placated them by putting a disclaimer in the show's closing credits admitting to the practice.

By 1968, Dennis' tenure as Kellogg's spokesman came to an end. His game show creation, *Race for Space,* didn't get on the air, but even when those setbacks happened, Dennis didn't give in to the fear of unemployment. He cheerfully told his family, "I'll always have golf."

As it turned out, a close friend of Dennis, Wendell Niles, *did* want him to host a talent show, and that was all it took to get his attention. He had a good sense for what worked for him, and after all the hours he had logged at *Ted Mack's Original Amateur Hour* and *Chance of a Lifetime,* he knew that talent shows were a good fit.

Here come da judges! Dennis welcomed Paul Lynde, Della Reese, and Ken Berry to *Your All American College Show*.

The new show was titled *Your All-American College Show*. The proposal quickly secured a sponsor, Colgate-Palmolive, and a distributor to sell the show for first-run syndication. Wendell Niles, a longtime radio announcer, who had announced for George Burns and Gracie Allen and toured with

Bob Hope in World War II, canvassed college campuses across the country with his son, recruiting amateur performers to come to Los Angeles and perform for a panel of judges. Each season was structured as a tournament. An act received $1,000 for their initial winning performance, then $1,500 for their second win. The last act standing at the end of the tournament got $2,500, for a total of $5,000.

Dennis was optimistic about the talent he saw in the opening weeks, marveling, "They're good kids. They're talented youngsters. I don't want this to seem corny but, really, the real kick is watching them go on to other things . . . John Wayne saw a little girl and hired her to play his daughter in a movie."

John Wayne was only one of the A-listers to sit at the judges' table. *Your All American College Show* rounded up an impressive group of visiting superstars during its run: Milton Berle, Della Reese, Sid Caesar, Andy Griffith, Michael Landon, Ryan O'Neil, Caesar Romero, Michael Landon, Cliff Robertson, Dean Martin (who threw off the staff by saying he refused to wear make-up because "the sun does it for me"), and Eartha Kitt, who came to the studio in an eye-popping python skin dress and explained "It makes me feel well-protected."

After only a few months on the air, Dennis and his staff had zeroed in on what they felt was the most talented college in the country—Brigham Young University in Utah.

Dennis explained, "It's because they concentrate on music up there and sent their youngsters out on tour."

UCLA was a close second, but Dennis reluctantly acknowledged that the show wasn't in a hurry to send talent scouts to Berkeley or San Francisco State. Casting a college show in 1968 was a tricky proposition. The counterculture movement was in full swing with hippies, Yippies, and "Don't trust anybody over thirty" anti-authoritarian attitudes in full swing, and a lot of college students were then treating performance, particularly music, as an outlet for rebellion.

To be blunt, they weren't welcome on *Your All American College Show*. The show was going for a broad audience. *Your All American College Show*

Chapter Seventeen: Here When You Need Him

didn't want to alienate viewers. As Dennis told interviewer Vernon Scott, "We don't put any heavy rock groups on the show, because we don't want to go the hippie route, or with rioters. And we avoid the shaggy, bearded types."

The greatest success story of *Your All American College Show*;
Dennis congratulated Richard Carpenter.

Wendell Niles and his crew came to Long Beach to recruit contestants in the summer of 1968. A student named Richard Carpenter recruited his sister, Karen, a talented singer who also played the drums, to join him for the audition. He also recruited a bass player, Bill Sissyoev, to join them. Their performances of "Dancing in the Street" and "Shadow of Your Smile" won over Wendell Niles, and a few short weeks later, Dennis introduced America to The Carpenters.

They performed "Dancing in the Street" for their television debut. It was the easiest $1,000 they had ever made. They returned to the show a few short weeks later and collected another $1,500.

Your All American College Show stayed on the air for a while, but Dennis didn't. He was replaced by Arthur Godfrey when the show got picked up for a second season, The sponsor thought that *Your All American College Show* could become the faded Godfrey's big TV comeback. This left Dennis, for the first time in quite a long while, without a regular TV series or a commercial endorsement. Even his radio work for the military had come to an end.

He reacted to the sudden influx of free time quite optimistically: he bought a 29-foot-long motor home.

Micki jokingly says, "I blame Madman Muntz. Earl Muntz was this famous TV pitchman who wore costumes and used props and shouted and did all sorts of ridiculous things in his commercials. He was the opposite of Dennis, basically. But he was more than a pitchman; he had his hands in a lot of the products that he sold. He had helped invent the eight-track cassette, and he had marketed the first big-screen television. We actually had that, Dennis bought it. It was this device on a tray that you were supposed to pull out so that the image on the screen would be reflected onto a mirror and then another mirror, and that was the first big-screen TV."

"Dennis saw one of Madman Muntz' commercials for a motor home, and he said 'Gee, you know, the kids are getting older, I have a little more free time. We should go on family vacations." This was a man who was afraid of driving in San Francisco, keep in mind. We drove across Canada. We drove to Mexico. We drove from Los Angeles to Key West, Florida. We went to every national park in the country."

Oldest son Randy remembers, "The really fun part of those vacations was how we'd stop somewhere in Boise, Idaho to get dinner, and we'd walk into the restaurant, and you could see people in the restaurant staring at my dad like they thought they were in a *Candid Camera* stunt. 'What the hell is *he* doing here?' You could see it in their faces that they were thinking that."

Micki says, "It was a lot of fun going on those trips. It was a lot of work, too. Not for Brad and Randy, they'd just sit in the back of the motor home reading comic books for the whole drive. 'Look kids! Look at that mountain we're passing!' And they'd barely look up and then go back to the comic book."

Chapter Seventeen: Here When You Need Him

If I could be serious for a moment... Dennis and Brad, all dressed up, in the late 1960s.

They occasionally visited Dennis' father, Demetrio, in Fort Lauderdale, still living in the house that Dennis paid for.

Brad says, "It was summer. Blazing hot and humid. My grandfather would not turn on the air conditioner. My dad said 'Pop, we are dying. Turn on the air.' My grandfather said, 'That costs money.' My dad said, 'Fuck, Pop, I'm paying the bills, turn on the air!' It was the first time I heard my father use that word."

Dennis did some strategic planning with these vacation destinations. They always remained at their destination for an extended stay, but knowing that, he always picked destinations that had airports, so if some one-day job came up, he could fly out of town, take care of it, and fly back to be with his family in the motor home. He even interrupted his vacation time to spend a day in Ottumwa, Iowa, or some other spot in the United States offering his services, absolutely free as always, hosting a local telethon.

All the frequent traveling gave Dennis a chance to examine local television, and he found that wherever he went, most locally produced TV commercials were lacking. This was understandable, because they were shot on low budgets, sometimes by inexperienced crews, and often featured inexperienced talent, or worse, the owner of the business and his friends doing the best they could.

Dennis reasoned, he had experience, and he had access to Hollywood production facilities, with experienced editors, cameramen, directors, lighting crews. He started a national business for himself, producing local commercials. He made his services available to businesses anywhere in the country, charging a fee that varied depending on the size of their location. He agreed to do commercials only for that company and no competitors in that location, and the business, in turn, got a slickly-produced commercial, built with experience, complete with a well-known celebrity spokesman, himself. Once the contract was signed with a business, he recorded two radio commercials and two television commercials for that business every month. Because he was so skilled at doing commercial pitches (he had roughly thirty years of experience at this point), he could knock out most of the commercials in one take. He walked into a TV studio, and then a recording studio, and in the span of two hours, he fulfilled his monthly commitment for twenty clients.

"Lucrative" would be an understatement for Dennis' new business. He charged such a low price that he began filming thirty commercials a day. Because he was such a quick study, those thirty commercials only took a few

Chapter Seventeen: Here When You Need Him

hours in the studio for him to film, and then he was back in the studio later in the week to churn out more. It was a volume business. Some of those clients in smaller towns were only paying a few hundred dollars, but it added up quickly. A single day in the studio recording commercial after commercial earned him about $30,000. For at least one client, Dennis had a particularly profitable deal in which he did more than a 30-second ad; he hosted a late night movie show. *The Dennis James Theater* was actually an extremely long commercial presented along with a motion picture. Dennis broke into the film eleven times to deliver a 2-minute advertisement, each one different, each one almost entirely off the top of his head. He was good at the work, which was why the work was always good to him.

Son Brad remembers, "My dad had a saying. He used to say 'I live my life in 13-week cycles.' Year-by-year pick-ups weren't standard procedure for my dad. All of the shows he did, like daytime game shows, were done on thirteen week commitments. So, when the network delivered the news that they were picking up a show, it only meant 13 weeks of guaranteed employment. So, for much of my dad's career, years and years and years, his job was on the line every three months. Performers have so little control over their careers, when you think about it.

"So with that kind of insecurity, my father always resisted depending on single sources of income. He was always on the look-out for multiple jobs. That was his approach to self-preservation. So, the local commercials were a wonderful way for him to depend on income from multiple sources; he had dozens and dozens of clients. If he lost one or two, he still had dozens and dozens of clients and an opportunity to reach out toward other businesses. And because my father was running the operation, it gave him some control that most performers don't have. That business was good for him."

Dennis also began an association with Physicians Mutual Insurance. Initially, he started as a commercial spokesman, but it grew into something more.

Gary Lortz was the head of production for Physicians Mutual's television ads. "Our spokesman died suddenly in 1969, and that was when the company was really going to start diving into direct response commercials, which means the viewer is being asked to take action directly toward the commercial. Specifically, in Physicians Mutual's case, putting a phone number on the screen and having the commercials be a drive for viewers to call that phone number.

Dennis with a local commercial mascot for one of his clients. Dennis was the face of literally dozens of companies during the upcoming years, and his contributions helped many smaller clients grow and thrive.

Chapter Seventeen: Here When You Need Him

"Initially, we hired three spokesmen and had all of them doing commercials. One was Doug Pledger, who was a classical music disc jockey in San Francisco. The second was a man named Lee Jarreau. The third was Dennis. We were tracking the amount of incoming calls when the commercials aired, and by far, Dennis' commercials got the biggest response, so Physicians Mutual did the logical thing and just had the guy who was getting the best results do all of the commercials."

Dennis eventually turned Physicians Mutual Insurance from an employer into a client. It began with him offering some constructive criticism after being tapped to be the company's spokesman. The first ad he shot for them was, he felt, somewhat schlocky; it presented him speaking to the viewer while sitting on the roof of a house. He steered clear of attention grabbers for the most part whenever he had been left on his own to whip up commercials. The occasional picture of his two boys while advertising cereal was about as much of a gimmick as he ever employed. Dennis was always a strong advocate for the no-nonsense approach. A warm smile, and a friendly voice, some key talking points from a spokesman who had clearly bothered becoming familiar with the company were enough. Especially for a service like insurance, who's going to buy insurance from the company with the spokesman who talks to you from a rooftop?

Dennis talked Physicians Mutual Insurance into releasing him from his contract as spokesman so that he could then turn right around and sign them as a client of his own business, and he took full control of the television advertising for the firm. The relationship lasted for the rest of his life. He arranged a remarkable contract with Physicians Mutual Insurance. The company agreed to pay a base fee just for having him shoot the commercials and endorse their product. In addition, the company, which generated most of their new clients by telephone, would always put an 800-number at the bottom of the screen in their ads. In addition to the base fee for making the commercials, he also received a bonus of $1 per incoming call to that 800-number—*every* incoming call, whether the person bought insurance coverage or not. In an average year, he collected about $1 million just from his Physicians Mutual Insurance commercials.

A good example of how Dennis' commercial production business worked. He posed for dozens of generic photos of himself in a variety of poses, like holding money, picking up a telephone, or pointing somewhere. In addition to appearing in local commercials, his clients received these photos, which they were free to use however they saw fit for print advertising to tie with the television campaign.

Gary Lortz says, "I led the production part; that was my main contribution. There are different laws in different states about insurance, and I would have to edit the language in the commercials so that it could air in multiple states. The guy who really drove the business and got people calling that number was Dennis. He brought believability into it. He brought his heart and soul into every commercial he did. I've worked with a number of paid

Chapter Seventeen: Here When You Need Him

spokesmen over the years, and I hate to admit this, but yes, many of them just read the cue card and cash their check. Dennis was more than a spokesman. He had to believe in the product or else he didn't do it. He researched the company, he became familiar with the products and services offered, and he presented that information in his own language. Whatever the copywriters wrote, Dennis would go through the script and tweak it just to make it sound like he was the one saying it. He'd alter a word here and there, and usually he'd add 'Okay? Okay!' at the end. And he was great at re-writing these things, he really made the commercials believable just by picking exactly the right words for every point he had to make."

Dennis actually had a long-term impact on Physicians Mutual. Gary Lortz explains, "Dennis really had strong beliefs about advertising. It wasn't just a gig for him. He really put thought into what he was doing. And one of his beliefs was that a commercial needed to offer a benefit not being offered. Physicians Mutual was doing well but wanted to do better. And Dennis said we needed to ask ourselves 'Is there something that you do differently that can convince a viewer to go with *us*?' Dennis believed that if we don't specify a way that the company is different, then you're just telling the viewer that insurance is insurance. Not just insurance, but this is for all businesses: It's important to know why yours is different from the rest.

"So Physicians Mutual held focus groups and really did a detailed exploration looking for how our company was different. And actually we did find a difference; we found that Physicians Mutual handled a lot of their cases very quickly. When customers had claims, they got pay-outs from their policies much faster from Physicians Mutual. And that actually led to a new slogan: 'We're here when you need us.' That slogan came from the focus group. And we changed the ads for a time and Dennis began very, very strongly pushing the speed with which claims were handled. And it helped the company grow. We got out of that plateau."

In 1969, Dennis spent a weekend doing two of his favorite things, golfing and raising money for charity. He and a number of celebrities were hitting the links for a fundraiser. In the process, he unintentionally launched the career of a long-struggling.

Foster Brooks dropped by for a visit. In his late fifties, his career received an unexpected boost from his friendship with Dennis. His sixties would be the most successful decade of his life.

Foster Brooks was a fifty-seven-year-old journeyman broadcaster, who had, at some point in his life, been a singer, then a disc jockey, then a newscaster. He had mostly worked in Louisville, Kentucky and upstate New York, but in 1960, at age forty-eight, he suddenly moved to Los Angeles to try to start a career as an actor. He struggled so badly that he had to keep himself afloat by working as a deliveryman and as a security guard at Dodgers games. He would also later admit that, during this period, he had taken to drinking, perhaps far too heavily, during the weekends. One night, a friend bet him

Chapter Seventeen: Here When You Need Him

$10 that Brooks couldn't go the entire evening without taking a drink. Not only did he win the bet, but to his own surprise, he never felt the urge to drink again.

Micki says, "I really don't remember how Dennis and Foster first crossed paths. In the beginning, when Dennis and I began socializing with Foster and his wife, they really weren't doing very well. They were living in an apartment building, where Foster was the manager."

Brooks became close to Dennis and the family. Every year at Christmas, young Brad was encouraged to "call Santa on the phone" to let him know that he'd been a good boy that year and clue Santa in on what he was hoping to get for Christmas that year. Unbeknownst to Brad for many years, "Santa" was actually Foster.

Foster had another bizarre secret identity that he hid from Brad. Whenever the James family traveled, Brad got a call on the phone inside the hotel room from "Sarah," a little girl who was trying her very best to track him down. It didn't really scare Brad, it just drove him crazy trying to figure out who Sarah was. It was Foster Brooks doing a surprisingly convincing little girl voice.

Although Foster no longer drank, Dennis found that he could be a little unpredictable on the golf course. They spent plenty of time playing together, including a day when Foster's ball went off course and he couldn't find it. After an exasperating search, he finally found his ball, but he was so annoyed by the struggle that he pulled out a concealed handgun and fired at it. Dennis immediately dove behind a tree. Foster was so surprised by the move that he dove behind the tree too.

Dennis lost his temper. "Christ, Foster! If the bullet ricocheted, you could kill one of us!"

Aside from the occasional near-miss, Dennis enjoyed Foster's company and found him to be a pretty funny fellow. During some downtime during the charity golf tournament, Dennis was worried that the crowd might be starting to lose interest, so he approached Foster and offered him $50 if he'd just tell jokes for a few minutes to keep the audience engaged. Foster, on a lark, told his jokes under the guise of being drunk. Drawing from his own experiences, and drawing from a childhood memory of his dad doing drunk shtick to make him laugh, he did jokes while stammering, swaying, hiccupping, and belching. The audience roared with laughter, and the struggling actor figured out that he was on to something special.

Friends in high places. Dennis and legendary singer/actor Dean Martin.

Micki says, "A little while later, Dennis was invited to Perry Como's golf tournament and he asked if he could bring Foster along. Foster wanted to go further in show business but he didn't have any representation. Dennis really took it upon himself to represent Foster for a while, just as a favor. Perry agreed and Foster wound up being a big hit at the golf tournament. A

Chapter Seventeen: Here When You Need Him

few weeks later, Perry Como's agent calls Dennis and he says he wants the contact information for Foster's agent. Dennis told him Foster didn't have one, and Perry's agent says, 'Well, Perry has a booking in Vegas and he wants Foster to open for him.' And opening for Perry Como in Vegas meant that Foster's career was really going to take off. It wouldn't just be a matter of Dennis doing favors for him anymore. So, when Dennis learned that, he set Foster up with a man named Lee Karsian at William Morris Agency."

Foster, for the rest of his life, became something of a professional drunk. It was always an act; he truly never touched another drink after winning that bet, but whenever he appeared on talk shows, game show panels, or stood at the microphone at a comedy club, he stayed in character as a drunk through the whole thing. For a time, he was the go-to actor for playing the role of a drunk character on TV sitcoms.

The act also played a wonderful unintentional dividend. Unlike Dean Martin, who similarly maintained a drunk persona but always portrayed himself as a carouser, a smooth talker, and the life of the party, Foster's drunk act was extremely unglamorous. He wore shabby, disheveled clothes, mixed up his words, slurred his speech, struggled to maintain his balance, squinted, and gagged. It was actually a very embarrassing depiction of alcohol addiction. As Foster's popularity swelled, he was stunned at the amount of fan mail he received from recovering alcoholics who said they decided to quit drinking after watching a Foster Brooks performance.

Foster's once-ailing career made a full recovery, and he owed it all to Dennis and golf.

CHAPTER EIGHTEEN
DENNIS IS RIGHT

As with any person's life, Dennis and Micki's happy world was occasionally invaded by sadness. On the morning of April 24, 1970, they were awakened by the bedside alarm clock radio.

Micki remembers, "The very first words we heard out of the radio were, 'Herb Shriner and his wife Pixie were both killed last night in a single car accident.' Herb and Pixie had moved their family to Fort Lauderdale, Florida in the 1960s to live the kind of life they really loved. And they died that day, and their children, Indy, Kin, and Wil lost their parents. We were extremely shocked, and terribly saddened. And at the same time, we were grateful to God for all the wonderful times we spent with them. For the rest of Dennis' life, we would talk so often about all the adventures that we had with Herb and Pixie."

For all the mountains, all the deserts, and all the national parks that the James family saw on their motor home excursions, the one that left the biggest mark on Brad and Randy was a visit to Las Vegas.

Randy frequently encountered the celebrities that his father dealt with at work. As a kid, he wasn't really star struck by many of them, but there was one celebrity encounter that happened during the trip to Las Vegas that left its mark.

He described it to Stu Shostak: "I'll tell you when it first became a big deal to me. My dad worked for sixty years, so he knew everybody in the business ... The moment when I was really impressed was when we went to see Elvis in Las Vegas. And we were sitting up close to the stage. And my dad never said a word to us about Elvis, nothing about knowing him or crossing paths with him, or anything else. But women are surrounding us and screaming and throwing panties on the stage. And Elvis kneels down and gets real close to my dad and says, 'Hell of a way to make a living, isn't it, Dennis?'

"And I remember looking at my dad and thinking, 'Oh my god!'"

Brad added, "At one point, Elvis begins talking about a special guest in the audience, and honestly, I think all of us were thinking something like, 'Oh, is Bob Hope in the audience? Who is it?' And Elvis announces 'Ladies and gentlemen, here's Dennis James! Dennis, stand up!' And he had my dad stand up and wave to the audience and take a bow."

Randy continued, "When the show was over, Colonel Parker comes over and says, 'Dennis, Elvis would like to invite you and your family backstage for dinner if you'd like a bite to eat.' We went back to Elvis' dressing room, Elvis came out, we had dinner together in his dressing room, and it was one of the coolest experiences of my life."

Chapter Eighteen: Dennis Is Right

Dennis was acquiring clients from all across America with his growing local commercial production business, taping dozens of commercials for clients in businesses spanning from banking to baking, clothing, and correspondence courses. He was always cautious to put his own stamp on everything he did—he was fully aware that the clients were coming to him specifically because he was Dennis James, after all—he ended every one of those commercials with "Okay? Okay."

To Brad's amusement looking back, those dozens of commercials every month were having a subliminal impact on his father. "My dad didn't realize he was saying it sometimes. Once, he sent me to my room, and he literally said 'Brad, you're grounded! Okay? Okay!'"

Dennis' aptitude for doling out a whole stage's worth of prizes caught the eye of game show producer Bill Todman. A temporary gig filling in for Monty Hall would unexpectedly put him back on prime time TV.

Game shows were experiencing a renaissance in the early 1970s. There were two big reasons for this: for starts, the FCC had instituted a new regulation called "prime access time," in which the networks had to surrender 7:30 p.m., commonly considered the opening half hour of prime time, to local stations. The intent was to give local stations an opportunity to produce their own prime time programming to generate more local interest and, hopefully, more income, but most stations in the country lacked the resources to produce their own prime time programs and sought out syndicated programs to plug the newly-created holes in their schedule. Game show packagers got right to work, producing a slew of new game shows to offer local stations.

At the beginning of 1972, CBS appointed a former NBC executive, Bud Grant, to take control of the CBS daytime schedule. Grant handed down the word that he was tired of seeing reruns of prime time programming on the daytime schedule. Both of these events would have a direct effect on Dennis' next career move.

Monty Hall fell ill one day and called on Dennis to guest-host a five-episode taping of *Let's Make a Deal* in his place. Dennis happily accepted the gig on behalf of his friend and got to work. *Let's Make a Deal*, while a simple program in the eyes of a viewer at home, was a fairly complicated game from the standpoint of the host. Many of the deals offered were dilemmas that could go in many directions. The host hands the contestant a wad of cash and offers them a box of some common grocery item on a tray beside them, with the caveat that there might be something extra in the box. The contestant gives the cash back but is now shown a curtain nearby and must choose the grocery item or the curtain. Whatever the contestant rejects could then be won by another member of the audience chosen that moment by the host. The crew of *Let's Make a Deal* was always made aware of how deals were supposed to play out. However, they were also given strict instructions to do exactly as the host commanded, even if they were aware that it was a mistake. The proper execution of *Let's Make a Deal* was on the host's shoulders, more so than the host on a typical show.

Geoff Edwards, another revered host of game shows, said in 2006, "*Let's Make a Deal* is the hardest show to do, as an emcee."

Dennis, who had been thrust into the show on twenty-four hours' notice, handled it beautifully, and somebody noticed, too—Bill Todman.

Chapter Eighteen: Dennis Is Right

Bill Todman was semi-retired by this point. Goodson-Todman Productions had expanded their operations to the west coast by this point, but Todman didn't even have an office in the west coast complex. He seldom went to work in the east coast office, actually. Most of his duties had been assumed by Executive Vice President Giraud Chester, but Bill Todman still carried the clout that came with having his name in the company's name, so the Goodson-Todman staff listened when Todman said he wanted Dennis James to host the company's new project.

Dennis explored the haul up for grabs on *The New Price is Right*.

The new project was an old favorite, actually. The company was developing a revival of *The Price is Right*. The game, originally hosted by Bill Cullen, had been an immensely popular program for NBC, dominating its daytime slot for seven years, while a prime-time version climbed as high as #8 overall in the Nielsen ratings. In the years immediately following the scandals, it was, by far, the most popular game show on television. An ill-advised 1963 move to ABC (at the time, a much smaller, weaker network) killed the show slowly, and it was off the air in 1965. By 1972, Goodson-Todman felt the time was right to give it another go, although with the company slowly migrating west, he handed down word that the new version was going to be done in Los Angeles, not in New York as the original version. Bill Cullen opted not to host the new version because, at the time, he was appearing regularly on two game shows based out of New York, plus a weekend radio show and a local commercial endorsement. It was too much money for Cullen to even think of moving.

At the same time, Goodson began expressing concern that *The Price is Right* wasn't a game suited for 1972. The original premise—present a prize, four contestants place bids on it, the one closest to the actual retail price without going over wins it, repeat for thirty minutes—was so aggressively straightforward that Goodson didn't think it could survive a nation of eroding attention spans. Over a matter of months, the Goodson-Todman staff fashioned a new format consisting of many games within a larger game. Contestants pulled from the studio audience would quickly bid on a prize in a very scaled down version of the original show's format. The winner would then join the host on stage to play a "pricing game" for a chance to win more prizes. The show would have a regular rotation of many pricing games with unique rules and goals.

When Todman happened to tune to *Let's Make a Deal* that day, Dennis got his attention. Yes, he was good, but there was more than that... he was good with contestants pulled straight from the audience... in a game that consisted of multiple smaller games mashed together. Dennis James was the guy. Goodson likely needed some extra convincing after the ugly falling-out that led to Dennis' premature departure from *The Name's the Same*, but eighteen years was apparently all the time that Goodson needed for healing old wounds. He gave *The New Price is Right* to Dennis.

Dennis and Goodson even managed to collaborate right at the very start. To sell local stations on *The New Price is Right*, as it would be called, a fifteen-minute film was made of Mark Goodson and Dennis James presenting a sales pitch. In a room containing only a desk, they explained how the

Chapter Eighteen: Dennis Is Right

new show would work. Dennis showed prototypes of some of the pricing games that might be seen on *The New Price is Right*, with Goodson serving as contestant pro tempore for the demonstration games. To conclude, Goodson showed a segment of *Let's Make a Deal*—the very segment that won Dennis the job, in which a married couple pulled from the audience tried to win a car by playing a game involving guessing prices of small items.

Dennis in front of one of the iconic big doors on the set of *The New Price is Right*.

The sales pitch worked. Goodson-Todman formally announced the new series during the week of February 14, 1972. By mid-April, *The New Price is Right* had been cleared for air in thirty-four television markets.

As all of this was going on, Goodson-Todman's big plans had caught the attention of CBS daytime boss Bud Grant, who thought that *The New Price is Right* sounded perfect for his ambitious new daytime schedule. Grant initially bought the show with the expectation that he was getting a new version of Bill Cullen's hit show from NBC. When Goodson began to lose confidence in the old format and decided to make changes, he went to Grant and explained what was happening to the show that his staff was now tinkering with.

Grant had full faith in the Goodson-Todman staff and gladly encouraged them to do whatever they felt they needed to do to deliver a successful game show.

Dennis once lamented to a reporter, "So many people look down on emcees. An actor with a series will get more respect and recognition... It takes more innate ability to be an emcee than it does to be an actor."

The average person didn't appreciate what a tough job Dennis had, but at the very least, the producers and the staff in charge of game shows all recognized that his was a tricky job, so it stung particularly hard when Dennis found himself in a gig where, he felt, the producers and the staff were looking down on him, too.

Dennis and a contestant contended with Bonus Game, one of the many pricing games featured on *The New Price is Right*.

"A fortune in fabulous prizes could be won by these people tonight, if they know when... The Price is Right!"

Those words uttered by Johnny Olson in 1972 ushered in what would become the most celebrated game in television history. Dennis began hosting *The New Price is Right* in the fall of that year, with Bob Barker hosting the Monday-through-Friday daytime counterpart for CBS at roughly the same time. Under Barker, *The Price is Right*, as it ultimately became known, became an institution, and Barker became synonymous with it. It became surprisingly easy to forget that for five seasons, a different host was at the helm of *The Price is Right* at nighttime, when a much larger audience was seeing it.

To start each show, Johnny Olson called four audience members to "Come on down!" (an Olson ad-lib that became the show's best-known catchphrase) to Contestants' Row, where they were shown a single prize. Each contestant placed a bid, and the one closest to the actual retail price came on up to the stage to play a pricing game. At the start of the show's run in 1972, there were five pricing games:

- Any Number: A board conceals the prices of a car (four digits in the price), a smaller prize (three digits in the price) and the dollars and cents in a piggy bank (three digits in the price. The contestant calls out any number, 0-9, and every number appears somewhere on the board once and only once. The contestant wins the first prize to be fully revealed).

- Grocery Game: The contestant is shown five grocery items and may "buy" any quantity of any item, attempting to run up a grocery bill that falls between $6.75-$7.

- Double Prices: The contestant is shown one prize and two prices, and must pick the correct price.

- Bullseye: The contestant has seven chances to guess the exact price of a car, with Dennis helping by telling them if their next bid should be higher or lower.

- Bonus Game: The contestant is shown four smaller prizes, each with a wrong price attached. The contestant must guess if the correct price for each is higher or lower. Every correct decision captures one of four windows, and if the contestant captures the one window concealing the word "BONUS," a much larger prize is awarded.

Three pricing games were played on each episode. The two contestants who won the most during the show returned for the Showcases. Each contestant was offered a Showcase of fabulous prizes and had to place a bid on the combined total of all the prizes. The contestant closest to his or her own Showcase price without going over won that Showcase.

The show, in daytime and nighttime, was an overnight success. The CBS ticket department was deluged by mail from eager viewers who were on their way to Hollywood and wanted to make sure there was a seat in the studio when they arrived.

Dennis explained the somewhat obvious reason that so many people were writing in for tickets. "Take a show that has ticket requests backed up for two years. That's because people think they might get something if they come. Contestants are motivated by greed. All you have to do is see our show and you'll see it."

The blunt use of the word "greed" made other game show hosts and producers bristle when it came up in interviews. Monty Hall viscerally disputed any critics who used the word when they wrote about *Let's Make a Deal*, but Dennis had no such reservations. He felt greed was, in its own way, important to a game show. It kept things interesting.

"People who win hug me and grab me. But if they lose everything, that warmth isn't there. Some are poor losers, some are not. There are shades of greed. Some people don't have anything, and anything they get they're thrilled to receive. I like genuine people. I don't like contestants who think they're helping me by being overly extroverted. You know, you ask someone where he's from and he says 'From hunger.' If a contestant starts mugging he's going to lose people."

Dennis would remain with *The Price is Right* for several years, but Micki remembered it as an unhappy experience for him. "Dennis was never very happy hosting that show. It taped on Sundays and he dreaded Sundays. *The Price is Right* was really the only job that he never looked forward to."

The man in charge of the nighttime version of *The Price is Right* was

Chapter Eighteen: Dennis Is Right

Frank Wayne, a longtime general in the Goodson-Todman army that had earned plenty of respect from his peers. He had designed most of the stunts used during the eleven year run of the original *Beat the Clock*. He created *The Match Game*. He had produced *Password*.

Dennis looked in amazement at the airplane being modeled by the lovely Janice Pennington. "And that airplane can be all yours... if the price is right!"

The Boston-born Wayne also had a reputation somewhat similar to Dennis, a thorough professional, but for sure, one who preferred doing things his way. Wayne had a specific vision of *The Price is Right* that everybody, including Dennis, had to conform to. Dennis' lack of enthusiasm for the Sunday tapings probably had its roots in an incident that took place in one of the earliest tapings of the program.

Roger Dobkowitz, a production assistant on the nighttime version (and later a producer on the daytime version), recounted the incident for interviewer Stu Shostak in 2009. "It was fun working with Dennis James if only because it was fun to hear Frank Wayne yelling at Dennis James... There was a car in the game; I think we were playing *Any Number*. And Dennis had to introduce the prize. And he said, 'How about THIS piece of junk!'

"And he was trying to be cute, and the doors open up and it's a car. And I remember Frank Wayne coming out of the booth and yelling at Dennis, "Don't you *ever* call any of our prizes 'a piece of junk' again! All of our prizes are great! Dennis says, 'I was just joking!' Frank says, 'I don't care if you were joking! You're never going to call a prize that again!'"

It didn't become physical like the dispute with Mark Goodson at *The Name's the Same*, and the result was very different this time. Dennis faced Wayne and realized he was facing a tough man who was as unafraid to raise his voice as he was. Dennis sized up the situation, apologized, and took the input to heart. He never said "piece of junk" again.

Micki says, "Well, Frank Wayne seemed tough, anyway. He worked for Mark Goodson, so he was always was representing what Goodson wanted. Goodson was the one in that company who was tough, Frank was just the one who acted tough. Eventually, we became good friends with him and his wife, 'Frankie,' we called her. We socialized a lot."

Ironically, the longer Dennis stayed with *The Price is Right*, and the more successful it became, the more insecure he became about his future with the show. He never really became sure-footed at *The Price is Right*. This was largely because, as Dennis would concede, one man who could do it better.

Bob Barker handled *The Price is Right* just beautifully. Bill Cullen, who had hosted the original NBC and ABC incarnation, gracefully conceded to Goodson-Todman staffers once that he couldn't deliver Barker's kind of per-

Chapter Eighteen: Dennis Is Right

formance—saying he could only deliver "hop, skip, and fall on your face" in the format of the new version—and calling Bob Barker "Mr. Smooth." As the months wore on and turned into years, the show's staff quickly created more and more pricing games and added them to the rotation of games that viewers would see. By 1975, there were more than twenty pricing games in that rotation, and day after day, Barker astounded viewers and even the show's staff with how easily he adapted to a show that literally changed rules every time it came back from a commercial break. Each pricing game had its own rules, its own unique staging, and its own terminology. Barker seldom made a mistake, and even on the blue moon occasions when he goofed up, he couldn't be more charming about it, riffing about the mistake and sometimes incorporating it into the way the rest of the game played out.

"These gifts from Radio Shack can be yours, too, if . . . ."
Well, you know by now.

Of course, Barker had a handful of advantages over Dennis when it came to *The Price is Right*. By the time the game show started, Barker had sixteen years of *Truth or Consequences* behind him—a show that similarly changed rules with every segment, five days a week. It gave Barker a malleable mind that adapted to the only-slightly-different *Price is Right* format very easily.

Also, by sheer necessity, Barker was in the studio more often with his five-a-week version, whereas the nighttime *The Price is Right* with Dennis James was a once-a-week offering. Barker had plenty of time to get familiar with the games, inject his own personality into them, and master each one thoroughly.

This wasn't to say that Dennis was delivering a poor performance by any means, but even Roger Dobkowitz, in the same interview, admitted that in a way, the show's staff felt "spoiled" by Barker's presence. It was hard to notice what a tough task hosting *The Price is Right* was when it happened that it was being done by the one guy who could make it look easy. Dennis delivered the best performance he could, but it gnawed at him when he occasionally made a mistake that required stopping tape, being corrected by a staff member, and restarting so he could have another crack at it.

That added to Dennis' discomfort, according to Micki. "Dennis always felt like Barker was nipping at his heels. He always felt like Goodson-Todman was just looking for any excuse to bump him off and give the nighttime show to Barker, too."

Dennis felt like he firmly knew where he stood in the Goodson-Todman camp once in late 1974, when he got the call to fill in for Bob Barker on the daytime version.

Barker was still hosting *Truth or Consequences* for five days a week in syndication. At that point, Barker's schedule from week to week was that on Monday through Wednesday, he'd tape a total of five episodes for *Truth or Consequences*. On Thursday and Friday, he'd tape multiple episodes of *The Price is Right*.

One week, on a Monday, Barker showed up at *Truth or Consequences* looking seriously ill with a cold, fever, and dizzy spells. He barely made it through the taping, but he was in such bad shape that the Tuesday taping was cancelled. When Goodson-Todman got word that Barker was sick, they told him to stay home and called Dennis to come in and host the daytime *Price is Right*. Dennis taped four episodes on Thursday. Late that day, Barker called the office and said he was feeling much better and that he'd be in the studio the next day.

Chapter Eighteen: Dennis Is Right

Dennis studied the board for Any Number,
one of the *Price is Right* pricing games.

A few weeks later, Dennis curiously turned on CBS and watched *The Price is Right* episode that Barker had taped on that Friday, his first episode back after Dennis' four episodes of pinch-hitting. Barker opened the show by saying, without even mentioning Dennis' name, "Before we get started today, I just want to remind our viewers that here at *The Price is Right*, we tape multiple episodes each day, so even though I haven't been here for several shows, I want to make it clear that I only missed one day of work. Now, here's the first item up for bids...."

A friend of Dennis' called the house and asked, "Dennis, did you see that just now?"

Dennis answered, "Yeah. God, what a jerk."

Dennis got much more fulfilment from the Cerebral Palsy telethons. The 1973 *Celebrity Parade*, a 19 1/2-hour extravaganza in which Dennis was joined by Jane Pickens, Bob Hope, Florence Henderson, Robert Reed, Ann B. Davis, Jack Klugman, Monty Hall, Vic Damone, Meredith McRae, Ted Knight, Paul Anka, Steve Lawrence, and Eydie Gorme, raised $2,070,180 for Cerebral Palsy. It was the first time more than $2,000,000 had been raised.

Dennis admitted, "It's great satisfaction. It's ego. One of the kicks I get is that each telethon I've done in an area has brought in more money than the one before. In a way, you get to hoist on your own petard. You try for more money. It's an ego trip."

Peter Marshall, who speaks from experience, adds, "I did a number of telethons over the years, and if you're a true professional, it's an easy job. The first thing you do is hone up on the organization and the cause. Devour as much information as you can so if anybody asks you any questions, you're ready to talk about it. And as you learn more, it's easier and easier to talk about it. And Dennis was a professional, so for him, it was easy. He cared enough to learn about his cause, he was surrounded by a well-organized crew, and twenty-four hours on the air sounds daunting, but if you care and if your crew cares, it's no sweat."

Tom Kennedy, another telethon veteran, agrees. "Once you've had twenty years' experience in broadcasting, a 24-hour telethon is such an easy job. You know your way around, you know how to ad-lib, you know what you're talking about, and you can just talk. The average person couldn't just do it, but experience makes it easy. And of course, Dennis' passion for it was just the icing on the cake. UCP succeeded in raising funds so much because of Dennis. His heart was as big as his body. He was so devoted to the cause."

Monty Hall adds, "It's important to be surrounded by people who care just as much as you do. If they care, and they assemble a lot of great entertainment, and a lot of interesting guests who can hold up their end of the conversation, it's a piece of cake."

By 1974, Dennis estimated he had hosted at least a hundred telethons, which was actually an extremely conservative estimate, given the sheer number of gigs he worked throughout the 1950s and 1960s, crisscrossing the country for local telethons, never for any more compensation than a plane ticket and a hotel room, going out of town so often that he and his family lost track of the last time that he had a weekend off. He had no intention of slowing down either. As grueling as it could be to host twelve to twenty-four straight hours of television programming, Dennis was actually asking for so very little.

"As long as they have my hot water and honey on stage, then I'm ready to go out and do my best."

CHAPTER NINETEEN
TUNE IN, TUNE OUT

IN 1974, DENNIS explained, "Everything works in cycles, and right now game shows are the hottest things around. Networks know they are tried and true entertainment; that's why they are brought back."

That's also why Dennis continued actively pursuing new gigs, even while his side business producing commercials and pitching for local companies was going strong. Game shows had been a successful pursuit for him, and with game shows more popular than ever, why not keep pursuing that work? In 1974, veteran producer Ralph Edwards secured the rights to a venerable game from the 1950s, *Name That Tune*, and prepared to launch a new daily version for network television, plus a weekly version for nighttime syndication.

The original version, hosted at times by Red Benson, Bill Cullen, and George DeWitt, was created and produced by bandleader Harry Salter. In that incarnation, *Name That Tune* pitted two contestants against each other in a simple game where a live orchestra played a song. The contestants, stationed across the stage from a large ship bell, raced across the stage to "Ring the bell and name that tune!" The winner of the game then played a bonus round, Golden Medley, in which the contestant had thirty seconds to name seven tunes for a grand prize of $1,600. During the peak of the quiz show craze, the show's bonus round expanded into the Golden Medley Marathon, in which contestants returned for a series of five consecutive weeks to name seven more tunes each time, for a top prize of $25,000. One of the contestants, who made it to the end of the rainbow and won the full $25,000, was a young pilot named John Glenn.

Dennis actually disliked the original series strongly, later admitting, "Those old ladies running down the aisles turned me off."

When Ralph Edwards called, saying no was difficult. Dennis accepted the role of host for the daytime version, which would air Monday through Friday on NBC. Tom Kennedy, best known at that point as host of *Split Second* on ABC, and as host of the popular *You Don't Say!* on NBC in the previous decade, got the nod to host the nighttime version.

The new version of *Name That Tune* was met with a surprising amount of backlash from NBC viewers. NBC daytime programming boss Lin Bolen picked *Name That Tune* to serve as a replacement for *Dinah's Place*, a long-running and very popular talk/variety show starring Dinah Shore. When *Dinah's Place* started showing signs of wear against the competition from CBS, the game show *The Joker's Wild*, NBC pulled the plug on Dinah Shore, who promptly launched a new version of her show, simply called *Dinah!*, for first-run syndication. It would run for another six years.

Dennis, who was actually a friend of Dinah's away from the TV business, assured viewers that there was no animosity between the cancelled show and the replacement, saying, "I spoke to her when I learned we'd replace her and wished her well. She's a performer and doesn't resent it."

Dennis conceded to the drive for young viewers by keeping his collar unbuttoned on *Name That Tune*.

While Ralph Edwards was happy to have Dennis on board, Dennis didn't quite have the full faith and support of NBC. NBC Vice President of Daytime Lin Bolen was trying to give the network's daytime line-up a facelift. When she arrived in late 1972, she felt that much of the schedule, including long-running, venerable games like *Jeopardy!* and *Concentration*, just felt out of date. She wanted all of the daytime programming, but particularly the game shows, to start looking younger. She wanted bigger, brighter, more elaborate sets, and she wanted youth up front. The new game shows on NBC included a new generation of hosts, Jim McKrell, Alex Trebek, and Geoff Edwards, whom Bolin half-jokingly referred to as "young studs."

Dennis couldn't really hide his age, nor did he want to. He wasn't ashamed of being fifty-seven years old. He used it as a point of pride when talking about his employment history. "This must be some kind of record, when you think of the number of actors unemployed, but I have never been off the air a week except when I was in the war."

Here was a man who gladly told reporters the story of the night that he hosted a television show and the one competing channel was airing a speech by President Roosevelt. Lin Bolen made it abundantly clear that if Dennis was going to host *Name That Tune*, he was to do all he could to fit into that mold.

On orders straight from the boss, Dennis got himself a younger wardrobe, casting away some of the neckties in his collection and hosting *Name That Tune* in butterfly collars and leisure suits. He grew out his hair a little bit thicker, and for a brief period, when facial hair was slow to come in, he even wore a pair of artificial sideburns.

Dennis personally thought the drive for youth and the abandonment of older viewers was a bit silly. He gave an interview about the new version of *Name That Tune* that touted some of the newer, hipper aspects of the show, but with an addendum that probably didn't make Lin Bolen terribly happy.

"Game shows are hot again. Young kids go for them. So do young marrieds. Our music will span middle of the road—the Jimmy Webbs, the Burt Bacharachs. No hard-rock stuff. Ralph Edwards bought the rights to it, and because of his track record, it should draw older people."

Name That Tune debuted on NBC July 29, 1974. The new version was something of a blend of *The New Price is Right* and the old *Name That Tune*. Two contestants were called from the audience at the start of each episode, and they competed against each other in a series of three mini-games.

The starting game, simply called "Ring The Bell," was substantially the same as the original series; the contestants heard a series of tunes and rang a ship bell for the chance to name it; three out of five tunes won the round.

Next, they played Melody Roulette, a large wheel displayed categories, or sometimes names of singers. Dennis spun the wheel five times and the orchestra played a tune from the appropriate category or singer. Three tunes won the round.

Chapter Nineteen: Tune In, Tune Out

I gotta be me. Dennis put his tie back on for a while.

The final round was the legendary Bid-a-Note round. The contestants heard a clue and then bid on how little help they needed from the orchestra's pianist ("I can name that tune in four notes.") Three tunes won the round.

The winner of the day played the Golden Medley round for $2,000 in cash and could return again and again for a maximum of five Golden Medleys, for a total of $10,000.

In an attempt to win over Dinah Shore's displaced audience and get the show off to a hot start, the debut week was billed as a salute to the "Fabulous Fifties," with a different guest star appearing each day to sing a couple of songs. For the premiere, Johnny Mathis sang "Chances Are," A Certain Smile," "Wild is the Wind," and "Wonderful, Wonderful." Later in the week, Rosemary Clooney, Dick Haymes, Della Reese, and Fabian joined the program to sing some of their signature tunes.

Dennis absolutely put his foot down when Lin Bolen insisted that he sing, too. Dennis wasn't a singer, which he more than adequately proved one day when he attempted to join the audience in a sing-along and missed the proper key so badly that it stopped the sing-along cold and the audience dissolved into laughter. He wasn't embarrassed in the least—he already knew he couldn't sing—but it seemed to prove the entire point that he was trying to make to Bolen.

No less an authority than Frank Sinatra would later tweak Dennis' nose by telling him, "That was when they changed the name of the show to *Maim That Tune*."

Micki, watching at home with her mother, could only say, "This is never going to work."

Butting heads with Bolen might have been overwhelming for Dennis, but he depended on his family to keep his morale up, and they were more than helpful. His home life was a happy one, punctuated by lapping and floating in the backyard swimming pool, tending to the garden, and grilling up weekend dinners at the barbecue. Once in a while, he got lucky, and the taping schedule for the local commercials, *The Price is Right*, and *Name That Tune* were spaced out enough that he planned for four straight days off. Whenever he had that much time off, he loaded up the motor home with trail bikes, and took the family for a trip to the mountains or to the desert. When the boys had school, Dennis headed to the Lakeside Country Club and played eighteen holes with Bob Hope and Andy Griffith. Sometimes, he just stayed home and made oil paintings with Micki.

Name That Tune, the NBC version, at least, met its demise on January 3, 1975, after barely just five months on the air. Tom Kennedy's nighttime version was a success and had plenty of success to come; it would stay on the air for seven seasons, even expanding to two and then three nights a week later in its run. At the height of its popularity, NBC tried another five-day-a-week *Name That Tune*, this time with Tom Kennedy hosting. That version only lasted six months.

The show was a glitzy, grand program. How could it be anything less with a sixteen-piece orchestra? To Tom Kennedy, that was the undoing for the daytime version; it seemed too big for daytime.

Johnny Mathis joined Dennis for *Name That Tune*.

He later said, "I think the show was just too rich for five days a week, it was like eating ice cream every day. Too much of a good thing."

Dennis' version wasn't a total loss. In an unusual turn of events, two contestants from his version of the show ended up with the completely unexpected bonus prize of employment on Tom Kennedy's nighttime version. Bruce Fisher and Fern Barishman, had both auditioned for the program in the summer of 1974. Both of them passed the show's test, and won over the people in charge of picking contestants. Ultimately they both appeared as contestants. Bruce won his, Fern lost hers.

A few months later, Ralph Edwards Productions needed a new contestant picker for Tom Kennedy's version and placed an ad in the paper. Bruce answered the ad and, during his interview, made the reasonable argument that since he got picked himself, surely, he had a good idea of what Ralph Edwards Productions was seeking in a contestant. He got the job. Harvey Bacall, *Name That Tune*'s staff musicologist, who was in charge of selecting and arranging the songs to be used on each episode, asked for an assistant. Producer Ray Horl remembered that one of the contestants on the daytime version was a former music teacher. He went through the show's files, found Fern's contact information, and hired her.

Dennis also received an intriguing offer later in 1975. The former Governor of Georgia, Jimmy Carter, was preparing for a run at the Presidency of the United States. Carter was considered an unlikely winner, given the considerably wider name recognition of the other candidates going for the Democratic nomination, including Governor Jerry Brown, Senator Robert Byrd, Ambassador Sargent Shriver, and Governor George Wallace. Carter, feeling that he needed all the help he could get gaining recognition, recruited Dennis to become his television adviser, guiding all of Carter's campaign appearances from behind the scenes, coaching the candidate on how to present himself and deliver his message.

Dennis politely declined. Ever cautious of his image, he was worried of doing damage to his ability to pitch a product or drive donations if he turned off half the country by publicly declaring an allegiance to a specific candidate. He wasn't alone, either. A number of the companies that Dennis endorsed had contracts that prohibited their spokespeople from endorsing political candidates. Things worked out just fine for Jimmy Carter, though.

Dennis safely straddled the fence, remaining cordial with politicians on both sides. He even attended a dinner at the Century Plaza one night to hear a speech from President Gerald Ford. Seated at the same table as Dennis were Los Angeles County Sheriff Peter Pitchess and Dennis' golf buddy, Foster Brooks. Foster had nothing in mind but to get a rise out of Dennis. He opened his jacket to show Dennis a gun crammed into a waistband.

Dennis instantly ratted him out to the sheriff, telling Pitchess, "Foster has his gun."

Pitchess, wanting to avoid any catastrophe, accidental or intentional, began bargaining with Dennis to get him to take the gun away from Foster and hand it over himself. Dennis just looked at Foster the way that Oliver Hardy sometimes looked at Stan Laurel. It was "another fine mess" that Foster got him into.

Dennis welcomed contestants to a new season of *The Price is Right*.

Dennis continued hosting *The Price is Right*. His relationship with the staff became much warmer in the years since those shaky freshman year tapings. Not only had Frank Wayne stopped screaming at him, but he and Dennis had actually struck up a nice friendship. They had family dinners at each other's houses, with Dennis always greeting Frank with an exaggerated display of bowing, kissing the ring on his hand, and addressing him as "Godfather."

In 1975, Bob Barker's daytime *The Price is Right* expanded to 60 minutes, and the show worked so much better as a one-hour offering that its popularity skyrocketed. Dennis' nighttime version didn't follow suit, because it was specifically being offered for that prime access slot. It was more or less beholden to a 30-minute running time, but because the daytime version was clearly so much better in so many ways—even if they were ways that honestly didn't have anything to do with the quality of the host—it only strengthened Dennis' concern that eventually, he was going to be edged out of the show.

The Price is Right had introduced a slew of new pricing games since in debuted in 1972, expanding from the five they had started with to well over twenty by 1976. All of the pricing games found their way to both Bob Barker's version and Dennis' version.

One of the most famous pricing games of the series was introduced in 1976. The game was called Cliff Hangers. The contestant was shown three small prizes (each valued at well under one hundred dollars) and guessed the price for each item, one at a time. Next to Dennis and the contestant was a cartoonish-looking mountain with twenty-five steps marked. At the bottom of the mountain was a mountain climber character, drawn with lederhosen and a walking stick topped with a pickax. When the contestant gave a bid on an item, the mountain climber took one step upward for every dollar separating the contestant's guess and the retail price. The object of the game was to bid accurately enough to prevent the mountain climber from taking a twenty-sixth step, which would send him over the edge of the mountain.

The mountain climber didn't actually have any name, but Dennis, taking note of the German appearance that the designer had given him, decided one night to give him one. As a losing contestant looked on and the mountain climber went over the edge, losing the game, Dennis called out, "There goes Fritz!"

Model Janice Pennington went straight backstage into her dressing room and sobbed for the rest of the taping. Her husband, Fritz Stammberger, had disappeared a year after their marriage and had never reappeared. She had already complained about the Cliff Hangers game to the production staff when it was originally introduced. The show's other model, Anitra Ford, was always the model who handled the prizes when Cliff Hangers was played. Meanwhile, the show's production staff repeatedly tried to assure Janice that the game hadn't been created to make fun of her terrible plight. It was a coincidence.

Dennis and model Anitra Ford showed off their well-coordinated wardrobes. In 2014, Ford wrote on Facebook, "Dennis loved these patchwork jeans I brought back from my vacation in San Tropez . . . He requested a photograph of us together with me wearing the latest from Paree."

Dennis blurted out "There goes Fritz!" Dennis had unknowingly opened up a wound that the staff had already worked hard at unsuccessfully closing. He hardly knew Janice, and certainly couldn't be faulted for his ad-lib, but once again, he had attempted to add just a little bit of color with his choice of words and it had ended in disaster. He felt terrible about what he had done, and even though, deep down, he knew nobody was blaming him, it certainly didn't help that nagging feeling that the show was waiting to get rid of him.

In 1977, when the nighttime show was up for renewal, Viacom, which sold the show for syndication, negotiated a new deal that would switch the show over from NBC-owned and NBC-operated stations to CBS-owned and CDBS-operated stations. CBS made it known that if they were going to air the nighttime *The Price is Right*, they preferred the host that was already hosting that show for the network. It took five full years, but Dennis' nagging suspicion finally came true. Goodson-Todman let him go, and Bob Barker became the host of the nighttime version, which would run for another three years.

It was a milestone for Dennis, though he didn't realize it at the time. He would never again host a game show. The combination of a new generation of broadcasters, plus the veteran hosts, who were virtually guaranteed future work because their current shows were hits, meant that Dennis, the veteran of veterans in broadcasting, was slowly being edged out.

In the summer of 1977, Dennis turned sixty years old, and given how unabashedly he had acknowledged the sheer amount of time he had spent in the business, it was only natural that people would begin asking him about retirement.

The question struck him as somewhat funny, because he realized that, in his case, retirement wouldn't look that different than the life he already had. "I hope to go along for another few years, and then maybe I can relax and play more golf."

One of Dennis' frequent golf partners was Gary Lortz from Physicians Mutual, who shares this tale: "We would golf for a dollar a hole. We were part of a foursome one day and Dennis tallies up the scores and says 'We need to have a playoff. We'll chip off the eighteenth hole.' And we have a circle of caddies around us, and Dennis looks at the caddies for a second, and then gives us a look and says 'Let's make it interesting. A thousand dollars for the hole.'

"Dennis hits the ball and it lands about six inches from the pin. Great shot. But I beat him and the caddies went crazy about it. Those of us who knew Dennis knew he was kidding about the thousand dollars, but the caddies didn't. Dennis paid me his dollar and later in the day we hear the caddies talking about the bet they had watched. About a year later, we're at the golf course again, and we come upon the same group of caddies, and the funny thing is, not only are they still talking about it, but somehow, the prize apparently grew with every re-telling of the story, and they were talking about how I had won $10,000 on a single shot at the eighteenth hole. Dennis loved that, he thought it was so funny the way that fib grew."

Dennis also added another golf tournament to his perpetual list of commitments. Comic actor Harvey Korman, best remembered for his years on *The Carol Burnett Show*, organized an annual competition to raise scholarship funds for children with learning disabilities.

Korman's son, Chris, remembers, "My dad played at Lakeside Country Club and that's how he crossed paths with Dennis. Show business is funny, if you're in it long enough, you'll cross paths with everybody else in show business two or three times, but my dad knew Dennis through the country club, and Dennis just needed so little incentive to help. My dad asked him once if he'd be master of ceremonies. Just once. Dennis responds 'Of course! What's the date? When do you need me?'

"And the plans got a little bigger and Dennis had no problem with it, no matter what my dad asked him. 'Hey Dennis, can you stick around and host a banquet afterward?' 'Yes!' 'Dennis, we've decided to do a silent auction the night before.' 'No problem, I'll be there.'

"My dad's tournament really was a big event, because we had things going on the night before the tournament and then the actual day of the tournament. The night before, we had a silent auction. Dennis would introduce the teams, and everybody secretly placed a bid on the team that they predicted would win the tournament. The next day was the tournament. All the money from the auction went to the scholarship funds, and then American Airlines, which sponsored it, would give a trip to Europe to the highest bidder for the winning team. And after the tournament there was a black-tie affair. Hal Linden, Gene Barry, and some other stars would sing and dance for the entertainment."

Peter Marshall adds, "I hosted a celebrity golf tournament for a number of years, and a very successful one. We built two Ronald McDonald Houses with the funds raised. It's hard to understand how popular golf was at that time, but that's the reason there were so many of these celebrity golf tournaments and the reason they were all so successful; at that time, absolutely everybody played golf.

"They were wonderful events for everybody. James Hampton, the actor, and I, would do comedy bits at the tournament. If it was a tournament where Dennis was at the helm, I would sing. Dennis loved my singing, which meant a lot to me, and he'd always ask me to do that for his tournaments. We all got to perform, we all got to play our favorite sport, and a worthy cause got a bundle of money from it. How wonderful is that?"

CHAPTER TWENTY
TELETHON AND ON AND ON

1975 HAD MARKED Dennis' twenty-fifth year of hosting telethons for United Cerebral Palsy. As the years climbed, so had the donations, and the first twenty-five telethons accumulated a grand total of over $50 million.

Dennis took the telethon as personally as ever, in part because of the harrowing circumstances of Brad's birth twelve years earlier, but the same traits that had served Dennis well as a commercial pitchman had also impacted his relationship with UCP. Like the products he advertised, he had taken it upon himself to become educated about cerebral palsy, causes, effects treatments, and current research. He had even gotten to know some of the children who appeared in prior telethons. During one interview in advance of the twenty-fifth telethon, he excitedly boasted that a child who appeared on the telethon ten years earlier now weighed 190 pounds and had started competing in weightlifting contests.

In the ensuing years, a backlash began surfacing against telethons, not just the annual *Celebrity Parade*, but the very concept of the telethon. When the 1976 *Celebrity Parade* rolled around, Dennis flew to New York and headed into the Ed Sullivan Theater on Broadway. Along with guest stars Paul Anka, Carol Lawrence, Lynn Redgrave, Howard Cosell, and many others, he led the drive for donations over the course of the 20 ½-hour event. Outside the theater, more than twenty protestors, nearly all of them in wheelchairs or on crutches, held up picket signs, with slogans such as "PITY DOES NOT BEGET CHARITY," and one spoofing Dennis' signature song, reading, "LOOK AT US, WE'RE PEOPLE."

The protestors told the press that they were against the way that victims of cerebral palsy were reduced to stereotypes by the telethons. The feeling was that cerebral palsy victims were made to look helpless, unable to do much more than walk and talk. The truth was that many cerebral palsy victims were capable of living functional, active lives.

The protestors particularly expressed disgust with the Children's March, a staple of the UCP telethons in which children with the affliction crossed the stage.

"It's a degrading, exploitative experience for the children," said one protestor.

Micki retorts, "The producers didn't feel that way, and that was certainly not the purpose. The families didn't feel that way or else they wouldn't have shown up. There will always be critics of anything connected to children and how it's handled. Dennis really loved to have the children onstage. He liked

Chapter Twenty: Telethon and On and On

to talk to them and connect with them. If they were shy, he had a way of bringing them out of their shell, and show that they were not different from other children."

The UCP *Celebrity Parade* became a family affair. Son Brad began joining his father onstage during the 1970s.

To say the least, the protestors who lashed out at the *Celebrity Parade* were in the minority. Crowds of hundreds stood outside the theater, hoping to see a glimpse of the stars as they exited. Still others had brought their own children along; they didn't see it as exploitation. Some kids and parents had shown up hoping to be a part of the telethon. Some didn't even want that. They showed up as a show of support and gratitude for an organization that was doing all they could to help. For them, just standing outside during the telethon and keeping their own high-energy vigil had turned into a tradition.

Many members of that assembled throng, including the adults and kids who grew into adults, showed up year after year. The swarming crowd in

1976 was so overwhelming that Brad got separated from his parents as they left the theater and headed for the limousine that had been sent for them. Dennis had to reach for him, grab him, and pull him past the police officers standing on guard to get him into the car.

Micki says, "The song that my husband sang as the children walked around the stage—'Look at us, we're walking, look at us we're talking, those of us who never walked before'—upset some people. The telethon began getting mail about exploiting the children. The children who appeared on the telethon wanted to be there. Their families wanted to be there. They wanted to be on television. They were always very excited about it, especially if the child had improved in any way. They wanted to show off.

"I do want to say, though, I remember in 1976, the protestors made one point that we found reasonable. When they complained that the telethon exploited children, they tried to prove that point by saying that we didn't feature adults with cerebral palsy on the telethon. UCP actually took that criticism to heart—the telethons began talking about adults who were affected and featuring them as guests on the show. And again, the adults with cerebral palsy who appeared on the telethon were there because they wanted to be there."

Dennis was unscathed by the criticism, only because it never seemed to reach his radar. Brad remembers, "You have to remember, there was no internet back then. My dad was insulated from these criticisms, and nobody ever confronted him with it. Some of us were aware of the criticism of the *Celebrity Parade*. All I can say personally is that the kids loved it and they showed up to participate. They wanted to be there."

Micki recalls, Dennis *was* aware of the criticism, it just didn't faze him. "He understood the message that they were sending, but he also understood the message that UCP was sending. If anyone didn't get it, that was their problem."

Author Paul K. Longmore, in his book *Telethon*, lodged a complaint about the severity with which the effects of Cerebral Palsy were depicted by the telethon. He wrote, "Year after year, Dennis James recited 'Heaven's Very Special Child,' a saccharine poem about a council in Heaven that urges God to carefully choose parents for a 'very special' child who would have a disability."

In response, Brad says, "In later years, I would interview clients who had cerebral palsy. Some faced grave challenges, and some would talk about living independent lives, going to school, and going to work. Certainly, the severity of the condition varies from case to case and person to person, and we really tried to get that point across in the telethons. Also, please keep in mind, research was being done on cerebral palsy through all these years as we continued the telethons, and it certainly altered the way that we presented the information. I would have to say that the telethons progressed and matured through the years. A criticism of how we did things in the 1950s may not be true of how we did things decades later."

Frank Sinatra joined Dennis for the UCP *Celebrity Parade*.
Gavin MacLeod and Charo couldn't hide their awe at the star
power of the man who decided to just drop by.

Longmore also protested that the telethons provided misleading information about cerebral palsy. Most egregious was using "sickness" terminology to refer to this. One telethon guest said that research "has done a lot to curb this dreaded disease," while another said that money raised could lead to research that could "help prevent the spread of this dreaded malady."

Longmore wrote, "As with so many disabling pathologies, cerebral palsy was a catch-all term for a number of conditions rather than a single disease. Indeed, it was not a disease in the sense in which most people used that word. Although it was not contagious, over the years some UCP stars promised that research would stop its spread."

Brad says, "My father was always very diligent about presenting cerebral palsy accurately. I can tell you I never heard my father use a word like 'sick' or 'disease.' He knew perfectly well what it was. I would always hear him refer to it as an injury to the motor section of the brain. Now in terms of a cure, my father would often say that by the year 2000, perhaps no child would be born with cerebral palsy. The research being done on cerebral palsy found that many cases of children being born with cerebral palsy had to do with doctors using forceps during the delivery, or doing something that might cause oxygen to be cut off. Information about those effects was becoming widely available and many doctors were changing the way that certain things were done during childbirth. Forceps aren't used anymore, and doctors are more vigilant about the supply of oxygen. This is what my father was referring to.

"Now, often, they would have celebrities come on and make pitches, be it in Los Angeles or New York, and they were obviously not as well-informed. And the guests would sometimes call it a disease or an affliction. I can tell you that my father, if he heard a guest use those terms, would always very diplomatically try to correct them."

Micki adds, "Dennis was disciplined about it when he was on the air. At least once in every hour, he made it a point to explain the correct medical facts about cerebral palsy, as well as it was understood at that time, and about the mission of UCP. Unfortunately, the hope that 'after the year 2000, no child would be born with cerebral palsy' did not come true. However, statistics show it is not as common as it was a few decades ago. And research is being done all the time. You've now heard the story of how our son Brad was born with several factors that contributed to CP, and that the doctors were able to prevent it with blood exchanges. A blood exchange was a new concept when it was done for Brad, and we're actually at a point where doctors don't do blood exchanges anymore because they've found better ways. The telethon presented hope and offered help. Part of our mission was to finance research that led to those better ways.

"Now it is true that we could be a bit overblown with it. We wanted to show that hope for people with cerebral palsy, so some years, Dennis would bring out children who had made enough progress that they could throw away their crutches. And we would emphasize teenagers' accomplishments and adults who had jobs and independence. Good things have happened."

Indeed, Dennis was trying to keep the audience well-informed about what exactly cerebral palsy was. During one telethon, he interviewed a mother and son who both had cerebral palsy. Dennis repeatedly reminded viewers throughout the segment that this was a coincidence. Cerebral palsy wasn't contagious, nor was it genetic.

Dennis often tried to stimulate donations by referring to them as a form of insurance. He was criticized for this approach, in which he admonished viewers that they, some day, could be affected by cerebral palsy, and that their donations were aiding in research and treatments that could very well come around to benefit them when that day came.

The critics who lambasted Dennis for this approach had no way of knowing that he spoke with a voice of experience when he told this to viewers. He was literally describing the birth of his third son. For over a decade prior to 1963, he had been giving everything he had at every telethon to gather donations, and after Brad's eventful birth, he had been told that the very funds he had helped raise had prevented Brad from developing cerebral palsy.

Okay? Okay! Dennis James' Lifetime of Firsts

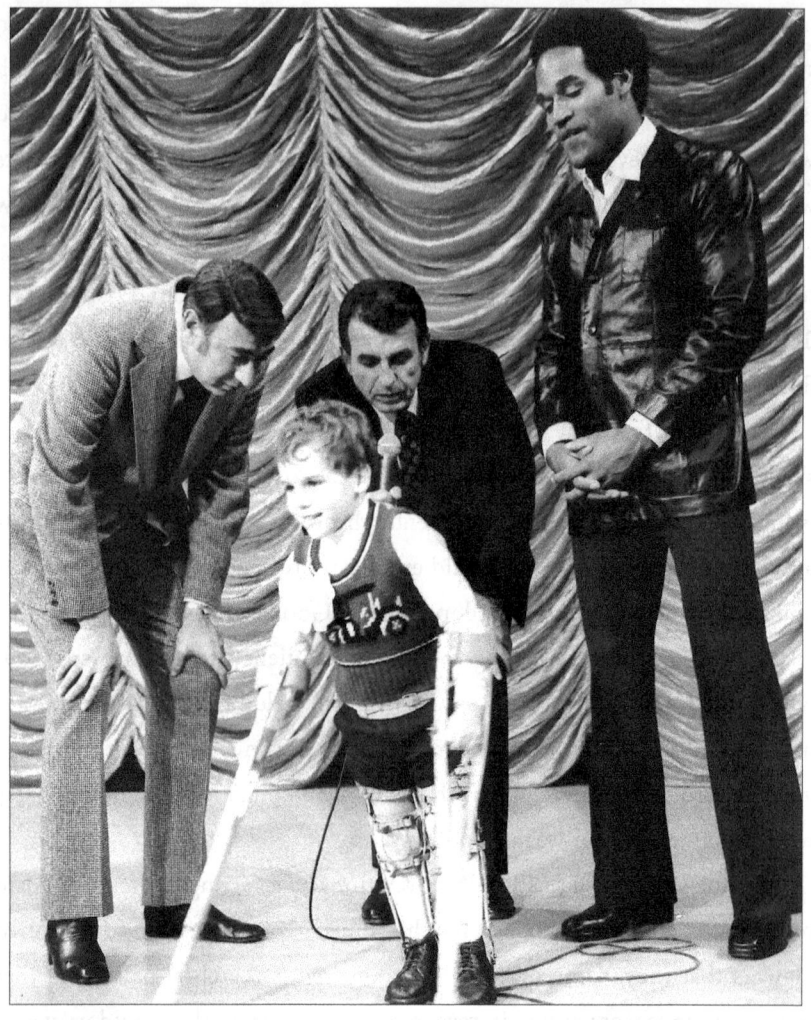

Dennis with his guests at the UCP *Celebrity Parade*. At the time, Howard Cossell was the most infamous figure on the stage.

Brad stands by his father's insurance-based tack for donations. "You or I could develop cerebral palsy tomorrow. It could be a car accident. It could be falling and hitting your head on the sidewalk. There will always be incidences of cerebral palsy, and that constant development of treatments and that constant research is going to be vital because there's no way of predicting where or when."

Chapter Twenty: Telethon and On and On

One thing worth mentioning to Dennis' credit is that he held United Cerebral Palsy to just as high a standard as anyone who might make a donation, even holding them to a high standard to the detriment of "happy moments" that a telethon might strive for. A standard feature of virtually every telethon has always been the moment when the host goes to the tote board to see how much money has been pledged so far. Dennis refused to go to the tote board until he was personally satisfied that the math had been done correctly. The staff of volunteers may have been eager to announce the exceptional sum that they had tabulated, but he didn't see any benefit to announcing wrong information, even if it was uplifting wrong information.

That's why Dennis was so irritated when a "happy moment" at one telethon went so wrong. A prank caller lied about his identity and got himself on the air for a live phone call with Dennis and co-host Florence Henderson to announce a phony $50,000 donation, then revealed the prank and hung up abruptly. Dennis seethed on air, lashing out at the prank caller. What viewers didn't realize was that it was such a frustrating moment particularly for him because for years, he had warned the staff that this kind of thing might happen. He didn't want to take unverified phone calls on the air unless the caller's identity could be confirmed. He let himself be talked into taking this call on the air, and it backfired exactly the way that he had anticipated.

Over the years, the good far outweighed the bad. Dennis graciously began sharing hosting duties for the UCP telethon with actor John Ritter. Ritter joined the endeavor at the height of the popularity of his sitcom *Three's Company*, and in addition to being a red-hot name at the time, he brought some deep personal experience to the telethon. He had a brother with cerebral palsy, and, like Dennis, he was able to speak knowledgably and sincerely about the benefits of the research and the available treatments. The hosting duties were split from coast-to-coast to make the telethon a truly nationwide affair. Ritter hosted segments live from Los Angeles, while Dennis hosted the show live from New York.

Micki says, "Dennis and John Ritter were never what you would call close, but they were friendly with each other, and Dennis was glad to have him be part of the organization. Every year before the national telethon, they would go to Marty Pasetta's house—Marty was the director for the telethon—and they just had a friendly evening together. It wasn't business or a rehearsal. But that turned into a nice annual routine for Dennis and John."

Brad met the Chairman of the Board on *Celebrity Parade*. Because of the events surrounding Brad's birth, Dennis felt a deep personal attachment to the telethon and its cause, and passed that passion along to his son.

Every now and then, pleasant surprises happened during the telethons. The atmosphere backstage was incredibly loose, and in New York, it became something of a custom for stars of Broadway shows to stop over at the telethon for a few hours after their own show had ended for the evening. Dennis

Chapter Twenty: Telethon and On and On

and UCP liked the lax attitude toward backstage guests because it drew so much extra attention to their cause. Droves of people showed up outside the theater because they knew stars would be drifting in and out as the telethon progressed.

There was the night in New York that the telethon staff noticed a Burt Reynolds look-alike wandering around backstage. This was at the apex of Burt Reynolds' stardom. His face was in the lobby of movie theaters and on the covers of magazine, but there was certainly no reason he would be at the United Cerebral Palsy telethon. His name wasn't on the schedule and he wasn't performing on Broadway, and it made no sense that the biggest movie star would just show up on a whim.

Everyone just ignored the Burt Reynolds look-alike as he wandered around backstage. If anything, the staff felt like this wannabe was in the way. Randy, who worked as an ABC page and was helping with the telethon this year, examined the guy from a distance, and felt a little more bothered by him than the rest of the staff.

When the telethon paused for a break, Randy walked onstage and approached his father. "Dad, there is a Burt Reynolds look-alike backstage. Well, everyone says he's a look-alike. But I gotta tell you, I think it's really him. If not, he's the best damn look-alike I have ever seen."

Dennis nudged his son aside and told him, "I can tell you in two seconds if it's Burt Reynolds or not."

He walked backstage and examined the stranger for just a split second. His face broke into a broad smile, and he opened his arms for warm embrace. Burt simply told him, "I was watching television in the back of my limo. I saw the telethon and decided I'd drop by."

Dennis was delighted. The staff looked on in horror as the reality sank in for all of them that they'd been ignoring and pushing past the real Burt Reynolds.

CHAPTER TWENTY-ONE
ACTING UP

DENNIS WAS PROUD, and justifiably so, of how much steady employment he had enjoyed from television, often saying "I haven't had more than a week off except for my time in the Army."

After a game show pilot called *Passport* failed to make it on the air, and after the end of Dennis' tenure on *The Price is Right*, he noticed that his calendar was significantly more open than it had been in years past. He actually had an optimist's approach to that free time. Some years earlier, when he had moved to Los Angeles from New York, he had expressed hope that he could pursue acting. Holes in his schedule quickly became few and far between, and that goal was cast aside. As the 1970s drew to a close, he realized that he could now carve out enough time to commit to script studying, rehearsing, and performing. He began acting once more.

"You know what I'd really like to do?" he daydreamed as an interviewer listened. "I'd love to play a heavy on *Police Story*. That would be fun. First I'd have to overcome my identity as a game show host. People don't think of me as an actor."

Although Dennis could hardly complain about pigeonholing, it certainly appeared that many of his acting roles in the coming years were written with him in mind. He played the host of a telethon on an episode of the drama *Rich Man Poor Man*. In 1978, over a quarter-century after his big screen debut, he finally landed a second film role, playing professional wrestling commentator Dennis James in *The One and Only*. Directed by Carl Reiner, *The One and Only* starred Henry Winkler as an aspiring but struggling Broadway actor in the late 1940s, whose career takes a wild detour, leading him into the world of professional wrestling. The film's climactic scene is Winkler's character making his debut in a new persona, "The Lover," a peroxided, flamboyant sissy inspired by Gorgeous George (Winkler had taken the role primarily because it was such a drastically different look from the role of Fonzie on TV's *Happy Days*, and he was fearful of typecasting).

As the film's plot is laid out, the scene is supposedly the first time that wrestling has ever been seen on television, so it was a rather nice touch of realism for the film to have Dennis involved. He sports a tuxedo and takes his seat at a barebones set-up of a wooden table and some crude audio equipment at ringside, surrounded by a New York City crowd consisting largely of Damon Runyan-style ticketholders.

Dennis stepped onto the set of the film, stepped back in time, and brought much of himself into the role, not just by name. As he had done with calling the actual matches in the 1940s, the Dennis James of *The One

Chapter Twenty-One: Acting Up

and Only tweaked and teased as he called The Lover's lavish entrance into Madison Square Garden.

"Well, if you folks just tuned in, this is not *Queen for a Day*. This is wrestling from Madison Square Garden, believe it or not, and this is what the well-dressed wrestler will wear this year."

One of Winkler's opponents in the film is a character named Leatherneck Joe Grady, played by an actual pro wrestler, a young up-and-comer making waves on the west coast. His birth name was Roderick Toombs, but he was becoming a star in the wrestling world under the name Rowdy Roddy Piper.

Dennis also pursued summer stock, starring in *The Impossible Years* as Dr. Jonathan Kingsley, a psychiatrist and professor raising two teenage daughters. The older falls in love with Dr. Kingsley's teaching assistant. The performance was so well-received that Dennis reprised it several times for different theaters along the east coast for five more summers.

Micki says, "Dennis never actually took any formal training for acting once he pursued summer stock. Most of the shows he did were light comedy, so it didn't require any really heavy acting. And truth be told, he was never that passionate about acting. He wanted to do it, but always from the point of view that it might be fun to try or a neat thing to say that he did it. He didn't really care about acting.

"I think the reason acting didn't really appeal to him was because it required memorizing so much and it required rehearsals. Dennis loved his broadcasting work because most of it required ad-libbing and minimal rehearsal, sometimes not even the rehearsal. Dennis liked acting, but he liked it in low doses. It was fun for him as long as it was a summer stock gig or something similar, where it was just for a few weeks at a time."

Dennis took on another movie role, and it was darn familiar territory by this point. He was playing a wrestling commentator named Dennis James for the 1983 feature film, *Rocky III*. Sylvester Stallone, who played the title role, was born in 1946 and spent his formative years in Hell's Kitchen watching the wrestling and boxing matches on TV. The memory of those early broadcasts stayed with him into adulthood. For Rocky III, a film about boxer Rocky Balboa gradually getting lured into the trappings of celebrity, Stallone penned a scene in which Rocky steps into the ring for what he expects to be a total farce, a boxer vs. wrestler charity fight against a wrestler named Thunderlips.

Stallone remembered that the same man called the first boxing and wrestling matches that he had seen on TV and thought it would be humorously appropriate for that commentator to call the Rocky/Thunderlips fight. Dennis James got the ultimate bragging right. He had landed a movie role because Stallone had personally requested him.

Brad told Stu Shostak, "I went to the set with him. I remember the entire cast and crew being very gracious toward him, particularly Stallone. Sylvester Stallone was very kind to him."

Like *The One and Only*, the casting for *Rocky III* made use of an actual professional wrestler. Thunderlips was played by Terry Bollea, who had become a major star in the New York, New England, and Midwest wrestling circuits under the name Hulk Hogan. Hogan's star grew as a result of his role in *Rocky III*, ultimately triggering the wrestling boom of the mid-1980s. Wrestling peaked in 1985, largely on the strength of Hogan's feud against Rowdy Roddy Piper; the two of them battled in February of that year on a live MTV special. The month after that, they competed again in a tag team match at the first Wrestlemania event. Six weeks later, NBC aired a 90-minute late night special, *Saturday Night's Main Event*, featuring Hulk Hogan and Rowdy Roddy Piper, among others. It was the first time professional wrestling had aired on network television since Dennis James signed off from Dumont for the last time.

In the 1940s, Dennis James' voice had ushered in a golden era of popularity for professional wrestling. In the twilight of his career, Dennis James' voice that was there to usher in the second golden era.

Into the 1980s, Dennis continued focusing his efforts on commercials. He was still working with Physicians Mutual, and even with more than a

Chapter Twenty-One: Acting Up

decade of that relationship behind him, he hadn't started coasting. Gary Lortz says, "Dennis was obsessed with analyzing the results of the ads. He talked constantly about it. He wanted data, he wanted progress reports, and he wanted as much information as Physicians Mutual would give him. He would analyze which commercials worked and try to zero in on what made it work. He wanted to know why other ads failed. He wanted to know if the results were divided from region to region. If there was a major city or a state that didn't respond well to an ad, Dennis wanted to figure out why not. And that was what made Dennis so different from so many others; he wanted to really earn his paycheck. He worked for it."

With a much more open schedule than he was accustomed to in television, Dennis filled the gaps in his calendar with theater.

Lortz, by this point, had gone into business for himself, still working for Physicians Mutual but now taking on a side business producing commercials for other clients, including National Geographic. Lortz says, "Dennis was the best thing that ever happened to my business, because he taught me how to work with my clients. He taught me loyalty. He taught me believability. And he taught me to be honest. I learned not to BS anybody. I have told potential clients 'This isn't going to sell.' I've turned down quite a few clients and some possible paychecks because I felt they didn't have a solid business plan and I told them so. I learned that from Dennis.

"And what I appreciated about Dennis was that, long after I had struck out on my own, we maintained a relationship that helped my business. Even though we weren't working together at this point, we could go golfing, and Dennis was somebody I could trust and talk to. I like to call him my business father. 'Dennis, I got a problem with this client, here's what's happening.' He always, at the very least, led me in the right direction, and ninety percent of the time, his suggestion was right on target."

Dennis' impact on Lortz' business went even deeper. Dennis had an eye for even slight problems that could have disastrous results, and he passed that skill along to Lortz. "Dennis would look at a commercial after we finished filming and he'd say 'Wait, we need to reshoot that. That lamp is right above my head. The viewers aren't going to be looking at my face, they're going to be focused on that lamp.' And after all these years, I notice little things like that in commercials all the time. It's actually very frustrating sometimes. But Dennis was so good at spotting minutiae like that and getting rid of it."

Dennis was still producing commercials for local businesses well into the 1980s, and it was still quite successful, although he had unknowingly done some harm for his own effort. He once boarded a plane and found himself seated next to Ed McMahon, the perennial second banana for Johnny Carson on *The Tonight Show*. Despite being best-known for that role, Ed, like Dennis, was always looking for other gigs. Like Dennis, he did commercials, game shows, talent shows, and occasional acting roles. The two seasoned broadcasters spent the flight discussing what they had been doing for a payday lately.

Dennis mentioned doing commercials for businesses in Florida and North Carolina, which puzzled McMahon because Dennis was a national

Chapter Twenty-One: Acting Up

star. Dennis explained the ins and outs of Dennis James Productions—the way he'd set prices on a sliding scale depending on the size of the city, sign contracts promising not to endorse a competitor in that market, and stepped in front of the camera to shoot commercials for multiple clients in the span of a day. Ed was intrigued by Dennis, who made no secret of what a successful enterprise it had been for him.

Dennis with co-stars Virginia Mayo and Alan Young during a promotional appearance for their upcoming play, *Murder at the Howard Johnson's*.

About six months later, Dennis learned of a new business producing commercials for local markets. Ed McMahon endorsed companies in any city, setting a price on a sliding scale depending on the size of the city, signed contracts promising not to endorse a competitor, and shot commercials for multiple clients in the span of a day. Dennis was making small talk on an airplane and accidentally created his own competition.

Craig MacEachern joined Dennis James Productions in 1982, as a director and producer. "I remembered Dennis from the Kellogg's commercials when I was a kid, so it was interesting working with him now that I was an adult. I remember being impressed early on with two things. First of all, very professional. He was extremely early for the shoot, and we always knew where he was. We never got into a predicament where somebody had to go find him. The other thing that impressed me was his warmth. He was very approachable, very friendly, and really made you feel like his business was a team effort. He was personally familiar with everybody in the studio, made them all feel at ease, and really conducted himself as if he was just one member among this entire gang putting the ads together."

Dennis had been doing commercials for the past forty years, in business for himself for about fifteen. By this point, it was a finely-tuned machine that he had orchestrated for cranking out these ads, and Craig was impressed by the process. "Most of us showed up at 10:00 in the morning to start prepping the studio. Dennis would arrive at noon.

"By that point, most of Dennis' clients were men's clothing stores, and the contract was that Dennis would do two commercials a month for them. Every month, a shipment of suits would arrive from each store with a note about what Dennis was to wear for each commercial. An ad agency would send us the script, and I got familiar with Dennis' style very quickly, so I would read the script out loud at Dennis' speed to make sure it fit into thirty seconds.

"Dennis would shoot the commercials in front of a green screen. We would have Dennis in the foreground with a display of suits, and the green screen would have a photo or video footage of the store's interior. Dennis was amazing. After he arrived at noon, he'd go straight in front of the green screen. We had the script loaded onto a teleprompter. Dennis would go through the script once just to get familiar with it and sometimes he'd tweak it a little bit to put more of himself into the delivery, maybe add an 'okay, okay' in there somewhere, and then we'd roll tape. We'd rarely do a second take. Dennis was just amazing at doing what he needed to do in one take. We had ten clients to shoot two commercials apiece for. We'd shoot two commercials, change the display of suits, change the picture on the green screen,

Chapter Twenty-One: Acting Up

shoot two more commercials, and barring a technical glitch, we were finished in two hours. Dennis didn't even need time cues. He would do exactly thirty seconds. If it was a Physicians Mutual commercial, which had to be two minutes, he'd do exactly two minutes. If the Physicians Mutual commercial had some extra 7-second bit with actors or a graphic, and Dennis' part had to be exactly 1 minute and 53 seconds, Dennis would talk and deliver exactly 1 minute and 53 seconds. No time signals. He really had a clock built into his head. It was amazing."

Even with theater and a healthy business producing commercials, the UCP telethon was still priority #1. Dennis was joined by Robert Goulet, Florence Henderson, and Scott Baio.

MacEachern, who would later become a Vice President of Marketing Production for the Lifetime cable channel, says that working for Dennis was one of the best learning experiences he ever had about marketing and advertising. "Physicians Mutual wanted to do an advertisement with a close-up of a newspaper, because the advertisement was promoting a Sunday newspaper insert that they had coming up soon, so we shot the commercial at Dennis' house so we could get a shot of him walking onto the front porch, then cutting to a close-up of the newspaper with the insert, and then Dennis walks through the door and finishes his pitch. And that kind of commercial was actually the exception and not the rule with Dennis.

"He really disliked gimmicks in advertising. He didn't even like cuts. He had to be talked into that close-up of the newspaper. He felt that, number one, you lost touch with the audience when you cut from one camera to the other too much. The camera was, in a manner of speaking, the viewers' eyes, so cutting from shot to shot means you aren't maintaining eye contact with the viewer.

Dennis shooting a commercial in the 1980s.

"The other problem was that he felt that gimmicks could distract from the message. We had another client once who had an idea for a commercial involving a classic car. They needed an antique, classic car for this commercial for some reason. And the ad would begin with Dennis saying, 'Beautiful, isn't it?,' and he'd talk about the car for a little bit, and tie it into another point about the client's product. I had all these shots lined up of the car. I was going to shoot it from different angles and do some lighting techniques to really make it an eye-catching series of shots. Dennis looks at the script and he says 'Now listen to me, I'll say the thing about how the car is a beauty, but that's IT!'

"Dennis felt if the attention was on the car, the viewer would remember only the car. He wanted just a short shot of the car, and then a cut straight to his face and he rewrote the advertising copy so he tied the car to the selling point much sooner. He wanted very straightforward advertising copy. He hammered this into me—Feature, benefit. Everything Dennis said fit that structure. Feature, benefit. Feature, benefit. Feature, benefit. Here's what the product has, here's why it's a good thing that the product has that.

"And that really stuck with me. Over the years, I'd keep doing Physicians Mutual commercials with him, and I would choreograph them, in a way, because they were each two minutes long and they were so straightforward that I had to come up with something to make them different. So, we'd shoot a commercial with a large easy chair, and then one with Dennis in front of a bookcase, and then one with Dennis in front of a window. We'd do a commercial where he crossed to the right, and then one where he crossed to the left. But I was always mindful not to get too elaborate. Dennis was cautious about not doing anything that distracted from the information. He felt that information presented well worked better than gimmicks."

Dennis was still looking to sell Dennis James as much as he was looking to sell the clients' products. And even in a business where ageism can sometimes lead to ungracious exits, he thought that his age actually gave him an advantage for one project that he wanted to get off the ground. He wanted to host a talk show called *Seasoned Citizen*, in which he'd talk with some of his older friends from the business about all of their experiences. The project never got off the ground.

As Dennis began turning the corner from his sixties into his seventies, he decided that this lack of work might not be the worst thing in the world.

CHAPTER TWENTY-TWO
THE WORK NEVER STOPPED

IN 1980, BRAD, in his late teens by this point, visited Palm Springs with a buddy and loved it so much that he implored his parents to give the area a look for themselves. Dennis and Micki liked it so much that they found a second house and bought it, while keeping their place in Encino. They didn't move into the Palm Springs residence right away; Dennis had landed a role in a summer stock production of *Murder at the Howard Johnson's*.

Murder at the Howard Johnson's had flopped on Broadway the previous year, closing after only four performances, but ended up being quite popular in regional performances, like Dennis' production in Lubbock, Texas. It's a story consisting of three very long scenes between a husband, a wife, and the wife's lover, all in a Howard Johnson Motor Inn. Each scene consists of two characters plotting the murder of the other character. Dennis played the role of the husband, lured to the motel room on the promise that several stolen cars were there for his taking.

This review appeared in the *Lubbock Avalanche-Journal*:

> "James, an actor with more than forty years in the entertainment industry, shows the value of such experience with a truly admirable sense of comic timing. He is quick with a comeback, knows how to milk a laugh (moving about while tied to his chair) and manages to keep a straight face in the funniest of situations. For example, upon being told his wife is killing him to run away with her dentist, he only expresses disappointment at the fact that there are really no hot cars to purchase.
>
> "But as happens so many times, the 'star' in an equity production once again unselfishly gives of himself and winds up being upstaged a good deal of the time by his supporting cast." –William D. Kerns, *Lubbock Avalanche-Journal*

Dennis, Micki, and Brad all moved to Las Vegas for three months in the summer. Once they were back, Dennis and Micki settled into the house in Palm Springs. They also owned a lot on a golf course on Lake Havasu, with thoughts of building a house there someday. They never quite got around to

Chapter Twenty-Two: The Work Never Stopped

it; instead, Dennis and Micki took the motor home and the speedboat and parked them on the lot for extended camping trips.

During the 1980s, Dennis' workload became significantly lighter. He was primarily doing commercials for Physicians Mutual Insurance and voluntarily hosting the *Weekend with the Stars* telethon for United Cerebral Palsy. He still found acting work. He played a drunk sportscaster sitting at ringside on *Oh Madeline!* starring Madeline Kahn.

There's a doctor in the house. Dennis received his Ph.D. in 1988.

With so much money in the bank after so many years in front of the camera, living life in thirteen-week cycles wasn't really a concern for him anymore, and he didn't hunt for employment as fervently as he used to. The local commercial business was working just fine.

Age even seemed to cool down his temper. Three decades after grabbing Mark Goodson by the neck and shoving him against a wall, Dennis walked into a studio to record a Physicians Mutual commercial.

The young director in charge of the shoot didn't like what he saw in the first take, and said, "Dennis, let's do it again, but this time let's try—"

Dennis interrupted him by holding up a single hand, and very calmly said, "I've been doing these ads for the client for twenty years. I know what I'm doing."

End of discussion.

Peter Marshall remembers, "If you didn't know Dennis, you would probably view him from a distance and think he was a pain in the ass. But he was a wonderful man, and he was a strong force. He had a way that he wanted things done, he believed in his way, and his way worked. He was right to be as strong-willed as he was."

In 1988, Dennis celebrated his fiftieth anniversary in television, and his alma mater, St. Peter's College, commemorated the milestone during its graduation ceremony that year. Dennis received an honorary Ph.D. for his work in the development of television and his impressive list of accomplishments in the medium. His parents were no longer there, but the occasion put a smile on his face when he realized what a perfect compromise had been struck by the honor: he got to do the work in television that he always set out to do, and his parents got the doctor in the family that they had always hoped for.

Dennis continued with his philanthropic efforts, even lending his name to a charity golf tournament in the San Diego area that would be held annually for twelve years.

Brad and Randy were both long out of the house. Brad became a telecommunications broker, overseeing James Communication Corp. Randy became a talent manager. Dennis Jr. was across the country practicing law. With three kids, who had formed happy and productive lives for themselves, Dennis took a look at his own life. He was in his late sixties, and the man who lived life in thirteen-week cycles decided that it would have been extremely optimistic for a man in his late sixties to wait for the next phone call from the producers of a new game show pilot or a network executive seeking a prime-time talent show. A new generation was running television, and they

Chapter Twenty-Two: The Work Never Stopped

were hiring a new generation of talent. That was the nature of the beast. He didn't resent that for a moment. He and Micki settled into a cozy life with more golf than ever.

Micki remembers, "Dennis really enjoyed the golfing life in his later years. He traveled all over the country to play in charity tournaments and I often went with him. We had many friends playing the 'circuit,' like June and Fred MacMurray. Those were good times. We went to Morocco for the Kings tournament. Andy Williams hosted a tournament, Bob Hope, Dinah Shore, Danny Thomas, and Frank Sinatra. We always attended.

"To be honest, as competitive as Dennis was when he played, he never really considered himself a good golfer, but he loved the game. Some days he got lucky, like his hole-in-one in St. Croix, or the time he outscored Tom Weiskopf. He got to play with Jack Nicklaus, too. He had pictures and notes from those two made into plaques for his office wall. He was so pleased that he got to do that!"

Welcome to the 1990s. Dennis, Florence Henderson, and Ben Vereen welcomed *Weekend with the Stars* performers, The New Kids on the Block.

Dennis sometimes called it retirement, but Brad and Randy smirked whenever their dad mentioned that word, and for good reason. As Brad told Stu Shostak, "We'd go down there [to Palm Springs] on weekends, and every Friday, Saturday, and Sunday, he was putting on his tuxedo."

Back in 1980, word seemed to spread quickly through Palm Springs that Dennis had moved into town and his calendar filled up instantly. He was hosting or helping with seemingly every charity function in the area. He was doing the Bob Hope golf tournament, the Frank Sinatra golf tournament, Variety Club with his friend Monty Hall, Childhelp, and everything else.

Micki says, "Dennis had been part of a group called the Childhelp ambassadors. One day a letter comes in the mail from the founders of Childhelp, and the letter says that they're lobbying for Dennis to get a star on the Hollywood Walk of Fame, because they know about his television accomplishments and because Dennis had done so much public service for so many organizations. And then another letter comes a few weeks after that, telling Dennis that he's getting the star."

The ceremony took place on September 10, 1992. A group of 300 spectators showed up, along with Bob Hope, Foster Brooks, honorary Hollywood Mayor Johnny Grant, and dozens of Dennis' co-workers from on and off camera.

Among the invited guests was Craig MacEachern, from Dennis' commercial production team. "I loved that Dennis saw fit to invite me. I was so touched that he felt my work with him merited that. What I remember about that ceremony was chatting it up with all of the other invited guests and spotting the same quality in everybody that I spotted in Dennis. That genuineness. You got the feeling that everybody was sincere, everybody was being their authentic self. I think you can judge people by the company they keep, and meeting Dennis' peers really cemented the way that I already perceived him. Dennis was a real, genuine, warm man. And you saw it that day.

"As an aside, because I think this is another story that sums up what Dennis was like . . . I had dinner with him and Brad once. We were in the

Brown Derby on Vine Street. A woman recognized Dennis and approached him, and he was so gracious to her, of course. She just curiously asked who he was with. Now—I understand why Dennis did what he did here, because explaining who exactly I was would have been a little complicated, so Dennis took a short cut. He says to this woman, 'These are my sons, Brad and Craig.' Again, it was easy to see why he said what he said, but I just never forgot that he introduced me that way. That always stuck with me."

Dennis and Micki joined by Bob and Dolores Hope, two of the guests that watched him receive his star on the Walk of Fame.

Dennis was later honored on February 29, 1996, with a star on the Palm Springs Walk of Fame. Walk of Fame stars were one thing, but Dennis got another honor later in the year that acknowledged his contributions more personally; it used his name, it used his favorite pastime, and it helped his favorite cause. United Cerebral Palsy approached him in 1996 to let him know about a new fundraising effort that they were planning: The First Dennis James Celebrity Golf Classic. They had come to Dennis seeking permission to use his name.

After what UCP described as "two seconds of thought," Dennis said yes, on the condition that he could help produce. After all, a golf tournament would be like anything else he had ever attached his name to: it had to be a product that met his satisfaction.

He organized a golf tournament that did exactly that. Monty Hall, Tom Bosley, Peter Marshall, Joe Pesci, Tom Poston, Howard Keel, James MacArthur, Hal Linden, Jerry Vale, Gary Muledeer, and more than twenty other stars hit the links on behalf of United Cerebral Palsy. Dennis got to see the fruits of his labor. He saw that first Dennis James Celebrity Golf Classic. It would be the only one he'd see, but the day was such a rousing success that he left secure in the knowledge that it couldn't possibly be the only.

In January 1997, Dennis returned to New York to co-host another Weekend with the Stars telethon with Florence Henderson. After returning to Palm Springs, he noticed a slight but persistent cough, and went to his doctor for answers. By February, the diagnosis had been made: lung cancer.

Dennis was the first to recognize the irony. At the dawn of television, he had been the face of a cigarette company, and the size of his contract renewals at the time indicated that he had been a darn good one. In the ensuing years, as information about tobacco and nicotine addiction became more widely available, he began to regret more and more how he had built part of his fortune.

When talk of his cigarette pitching years came up among family and friends, Dennis often said, "I wish I had the money to buy back every cigarette I sold."

On the same day that Dennis was diagnosed with lung cancer, he competed in the Frank Sinatra Golf Tournament. He and Monty Hall co-hosted a charity auction that night. The only thing that Dennis knew to do was keep going. A month after the diagnosis, he entered the Dinah Shore Classic. He had never missed that golf tournament before and he didn't miss this one. He broke a rib on the course while taking a backswing, but finished in third place.

Chapter Twenty-Two: The Work Never Stopped

Chris Korman says, "He came to our golf tournament. I hollered at him 'Take a rest!' because I was worried about him. Dennis insisted he was fine. All he wanted to do was golf. He didn't want sympathy. He didn't think about how sick he was. He just wanted to play."

Dennis even continued making commercials. As long as he could get out of bed, he didn't see lung cancer as a reason to miss a contractual commitment for a client. He even made plans to have a wig made to match his own hair so he could keep making the commercials after he began chemotherapy.

Dennis joined by friends Foster Brooks and Mike Connors at a charity golf tournament. Dennis remained devoted to his hobbies and causes to the very end.

Dennis' battle with lung cancer would be an unexpectedly short one. It took its toll quickly, and he recognized that he wouldn't survive. In his final weeks, he felt there was one urgent piece of business that he needed to tend to. Dennis, raised in the Catholic faith, suddenly became very concerned by the circumstances surrounding his marriage to Micki. He had been married and divorced before meeting her, and his wedding to Micki hadn't taken place inside a Catholic church. He became concerned that their marriage wasn't valid. He called a priest and asked him to come to the house.

Once the priest arrived, Dennis explained his concerns in detail. The priest listened attentively, and asked for clarification on one detail. "How long have the two of you been married, again?"

Dennis answered, "Forty-six years."

The priest nodded. "Yeah, in the eyes of God, you're married. Don't worry about it."

Dennis died in his home on June 3, 1997. Age: 79. Children: 3. Grand total raised for United Cerebral Palsy: $700,000,000.

David Narz remembers, "My father, Jack Narz, had a second home in Las Vegas, which was where I was living at the time. And Dad was very melancholy one day and told me that he just heard Dennis had passed away. And my dad talked about when he and my mom divorced. For a time, Dennis and Micki opened their home to him and my dad stayed there for a little while, and my dad just never forgot that Dennis and Micki did that."

Tom Kennedy says, "I thought about a lot of the stories he used to tell. He would reminisce about working in the early days of television and they were great stories. Dennis would do run-throughs for new shows in a basement somewhere in New Jersey. I loved listening to him talk about that. I had nothing but the deepest respect for him. He brought energy and excitement to everything he did. His eyes were always wide open, he as always looking around, he was so effusive. A wonderful talent and a terrible loss."

Chris Korman says, "I thought back to one of the first times I met Dennis, and we had a good long conversation. I remember noticing this at that moment when I was a kid and I thought about it when I learned he was gone—that long conversation was almost entirely about me. Dennis didn't talk about himself. Dennis wasn't interested in himself. He didn't talk about working in TV, he didn't talk about his long list of 'firsts' or anything. He didn't care. He just liked meeting people and talking with them."

Monty Hall says, "We really lost a gifted broadcaster. He was articulate, smooth, good-looking, quick on his feet... he was everything you're looking for. So, it's a personal loss—he was a good friend—but it was also a loss for the broadcasting industry. You hate to lose anyone who brings that much to the field."

Peter Marshall agrees. "A lot of broadcasters keep it in neutral. They're essentially just hired to be a face, but they have their teleprompter, they have their cue cards, a lot of the newer emcees even have an earpiece so they can be fed instructions. So, when you look back at someone like Dennis, who could go out there and wing it, and put his true personality into it, and knew what he was doing and always knew what he was talking about, you realize there just aren't enough people like that on television. That's a shame."

Dennis' death was so sudden—he was gone only four months after being diagnosed—that plans hadn't been fully made for how to handle some details of his business when he was no longer there. Physicians Mutual Insurance actually continued airing his commercials for the rest of that year.

Dennis and Micki with son Brad. Brad hosted the UCP telethon the year after his father's passing, but the changing economics of television were making it tougher to do large scale telethons, and UCP shifted its focus to other forms of fundraising in the coming years.

Peter Marshall says, "When Physicians Mutual finally got themselves collected and decided to figure out how to replace Dennis, a number of us among his friends were asked to come in and audition. I auditioned, Tom Kennedy auditioned, and Physicians Mutual finally decided, 'We can't replace Dennis.' There was a lot of truth to that. So, they took their advertising in a completely different direction."

Thanks to an up-and-coming cable channel, Game Show Network, Dennis would still pop up now and then, on the channel's occasional reruns of *Judge for Yourself*, *Two for the Money*, and *The Name's the Same*, or his appearances with Micki on the celebrity couples game *Tattletales*. The channel even dusted off one of the *Price is Right* episodes that he had guest-hosted for Bob Barker. Between those reruns and the movie channels' periodic screenings of *Rocky III*, Dennis lived on, and quite often.

To the family's delight, the mail indicated after all these years that people were still thinking of Dennis. Brad says, "This was very recent, I actually got a letter from a man who enclosed a photo of three generations of his family. And the attached letter explained that all the men in the family are named Dennis James, and that started because his grandmother was such a big fan of my dad. He got mail about that when he was alive too. There have been hundreds of men over the years with the name Dennis James and they got that name because of him."

UCP, in the next few years, concluded that the annual golf tournament just wasn't enough for the man who had boarded more planes than could be counted, traveled to more cities than anyone could hope to list in one breath, and hosted telethon after telethon after telethon. For all the achievements that UCP had made since the mysterious affliction began finally receiving attention and study in the late 1940s, the feeling was that some more acknowledgment was due for the man who had brought them to that point. In 2000, United Cerebral Palsy of the Inland Empire in California officially renamed their facility: The United Cerebral Palsy Dennis James Center.

David Narz says, "I moved back to California in 2000 and began tagging

Chapter Twenty-Two: The Work Never Stopped

along with my dad for tournaments. The company I worked for sponsored a foursome. And the CEO of United Cerebral Palsy offered me a spot on the board. And then a few years after that the president of the board resigned, and I began board president of United Cerebral Palsy. And one of the big things that enticed me to take that opportunity was how active Dennis' family were and are. His wife Micki was vice president, his sons Randy and Brad were both Board members. I just looked at them and thought 'If these people are involved, I'll be there.' And after all these years, they're still there, and so am I.'"

The Dennis James Celebrity Golf Classic continued year after year. In 2015, at a ceremony commemorating the twentieth Classic, Brad read a list of achievements made by developments made by UCP contributions since the Classic's inception:

Six after-school programs, with a seventh to come.

A bike program that provides individualized, customized bikes for special needs children

A respite program for 300 families

Educational and recreational programs, numbering in the hundreds, for special needs children and adults.

Dennis James was gone, but his name continued working tirelessly for two decades and counting. The man who lived in thirteen week cycles would have liked knowing that.

The Big Record, aka *The Patti Page Show*

APPENDIX
DENNIS JAMES' RESUME

TELEVISION, as himself

Television Roof (W2XWV-TV), host, 1938-1943

Sports Parade (W2XWV-TV), host, 1938-43)

Commentary for football and boxing (W2XWV-TV), 1938-43

DuMont Beepstakes (DuMont game show special), host, May 29, 1946

Cash and Carry (DuMont), host, June 20, 1946-July 1, 1947

Ted Mack's Original Amateur Hour (DuMont and ABC), commercial announcer, January 18, 1948-1955

Sports Den (first-run syndication), host, 1948

Boxing from Jamaica Arena (DuMont), host, September 1948-49

Wrestling from Jamaica Arena (DuMont), host, September 1948-55

Dennis James' Carnival (WCBS-TV), host, October 31, 1948

Okay Mother (DuMont), host, November 1, 1948-July 6, 1951

Stop The Music (ABC), commercial announcer, May 5, 1949-April 24, 1952

Boxing from Sunnyside Gardens (DuMont), host, September 1949-50

The Star Spangled Revue (NBC-TV), commercial announcer, May 27, 1950

The Dennis James Show (ABC), host, September 24, 1951-February 15, 1952

Chance of a Lifetime (DuMont and ABC), creator/host, May 8, 1952-June 24, 1955

Two For the Money (CBS), commercial announcer, August 15, 1953-1955

Judge For Yourself (NBC), commercial announcer, August 18, 1953-May 11, 1954

Turn to a Friend (ABC), host, October 5-December 31, 1953

On Your Account (CBS), host, October 4, 1954-March 30, 1956

The Name's the Same (ABC), host, October 25, 1954-April 4, 1955

America's Newsreel Album (first-run syndication), host, 1955-60

Dollar a Second (ABC), substitute host, 1956

High Finance (CBS), creator/host, July 7-December 15, 1956

Club 60 (NBC), host, March 11-September 27, 1957

What's My Line? with host John Charles Daly

What Makes You Tick? (unsold pilot), host, 1957

The Big Record (CBS), commercial announcer, c. 1957-1958

Treasure Hunt (NBC), substitute host, July 1958

Haggis Baggis (NBC), host, February 9-June 19, 1959

What's My Line? (CBS-TV), commercial announcer for episodes sponsored by Kellogg's, 1960-1967

Appendix: Dennis James' Resume

Your First Impression (NBC), regular panelist, January 2, 1962-June 26, 1964

Beat the Odds (KTLA-TV), host, July 1962-August 23, 1963

People Will Talk (NBC), host, July 1-December 27, 1963

Chain Letter (NBC), host for unaired pilot only, 1964

PDQ (first-run syndication), host, fall 1965-summer 1969

Your All-American College Show (first-run syndication), host, fall 1968-summer 1970

The Price is Right (first-run syndication), host, fall 1972-summer 1977

Name That Tune (NBC-TV), host, July 29, 1974-January 3, 1975

Fantasy Island, with Maureen McCormick

TELEVISION, acting

Kraft Television Theatre (NBC-TV), one episode, 1954

The Dick Powell Theatre (NBC-TV), multiple roles, two episodes, 1962-63

The Farmer's Daughter (ABC-TV), as "M.C.," one episode, 1964

Batman (ABC-TV), as "Chet Chumley," one episode, 1966

Rich Man, Poor Man Book II (ABC-TV), one episode, 1977

Fantasy Island (ABC-TV), as "Beauty Pageant Announcer," one episode, 1978

Oh Madeline (ABC-TV), as "Gibbons", one episode, 1984

WNEW radio in New York, early 1940s

RADIO

WAAT-AM, disc jockey 1938-1939

WNEW-AM, disc jockey c.1939-c.1943

Kate Smith Speaks (CBS), announcer, c. 1939-1941

When a Girl Marries (CBS), announcer, c. 1939-1941

Pepper Young's Family (CBS), announcer, c. 1939-1941

Lawyer Q (MBS), host, April 3-June 29, 1947

Can You Top This? (NBC), host, July 14, 1947-September 25, 1948

Ted Mack's Original Amateur Hour (ABC), announcer, September 29, 1948-September 18, 1952

Appendix: Dennis James' Resume

Red Carpet correspondent (ABC Radio), 1948-1950

Turn to a Friend (ABC Radio), host, 1952-1953

Entertainment USA (Armed Forces Radio), host, 1964-1965

Startime USA (Armed Forces Radio), host, 1964-1965

MOTION PICTURES

Paramount News newsreel series, narrator, 1947-c.1950

I Remember You (short subject), 1949

Cowboy Crazy (short subject), 1950

The Rhumba Seat (short subject), 1950

Mister Universe, 1951

Rocky III, 1982

The Method, 1996

THEATRE

Two for the Seesaw, as Jerry Ryan

Come Blow Your Horn as Alan Baker

Murder at the Howard Johnson's as Paul Miller

The Impossible Years as Jonathan Kingsley

OTHER EMPLOYMENT

Abercrombie & Fitch – salesman, dog department (1938)

BUSINESS INTERESTS

Jersey City Giants – owner of AFL professional football team

Jade Productions – owner of television producing and packaging firm

Dennis James Productions – owner of television commercial producing and print advertising representation firm

BIBLIOGRAPHY

"1st Survey Shows WABD is Higher Than Radio." *Television Daily.* 3 Dec. 1948.

"2 Actors Join Nightside." *The New York Times.* 23 Nov. 1962.

"$413,265 Pledged in Palsy Aid." *The New York Times.* 11 Jan. 1960.

"$655,108 Raised Over TV." *The New York Times.* 8 Dec. 1952.

"ABC-TV Moves to Reduce Overhead." *The Billboard.* 29 Aug. 1953.

Annual Report. P. Lorillard Company. 1946.

Baber, David. "Television Game Show Hosts: Biographies of 32 Stars." MacFarland and Company. Jefferson, North Carolina. 2008.

"Backstage at Lennen and Mitchell." *Sponsor Magazine.* January 1950.

Bak, Richard. "Joe Louis: The Great Black Hope." Da Capo Press. Dallas. 1996.

Barasch, Norman. "The Joy of Laughter: My Life as a Comedy Writer." iUniverse. New York. 2009.

"Behind the Mike." *Radio Daily.* 17 Feb. 1949.

Buck, Jerry. "What Makes Game Shows Work? Greed, Of Course!" *The Tennesean.* Nashville, TN. 27 Aug. 1974.

Butterfield, C.E. "Dennis James Fills Actor Role Expertly." *The Evening Sun.* Hanover, PA. 29 Mar. 1954.

"Cash and Carry." *The Billboard.* 29 Jun. 1946.

"Cash and Carry." *Television Magazine.* Sep. 1946.

"Co-Axial Time." *Broadcasting Magazine.* 3 Jan. 1949.

Cohen, Martin. "Dennis James' Glad Tidings." *Radio-TV Mirror.* July 1956.

"Coming and Going." *Radio Daily*. New York, NY. 19 May 1949.

Crosby, John. "Agony Giveaways Create Welfare Department Work." *St. Petersburg Times*. 9 Oct. 1953.

Crosby, John. "All That Glitters is Not Allen on Fred's Show." *St. Petersburg Times*. 7 Sep. 1953.

Crosby, John. "Dennis James Hits the Top." *St. Petersburg Times*. 24 Jul. 1956.

Crosby, John. "Greed on Kiddy Level Disturbing." *Toledo Blade*. 19 Dec. 1956.

Dailey, Arthur. "Real Honest to Goodness Cinderella." *The Pittsburgh Courier*. 1 Jan. 1955.

Danzig, Fred. "New Show Comes Up with Innovation in 'Intros.'" *The Bend Bulletin*. 3 Jan. 1962.

"Daytime TV Good Selling Media—Gallery." *Broadcasting Magazine*. 29 Aug. 1949.

"Dennis James Cites Super-Stars' Demise." *The Indianapolis Star*. 16 May 1954.

"Dennis James Files Suit for Divorce." *Reading Eagle*. Reading, PA. 22 May 1951.

"Double Lucky Quiz Winner." *Jet*. 16 Dec. 1954.

DuBrow, Rick. "Critic Sees Nixon Scoring Points on TV Panel Quiz." *Reading Eagle*. 20 Jul. 1962.

"DuMont Plant: World's Largest TV Set Factory Opens." *Broadcasting Magazine*. 3 Oct. 1949.

Dunning, John. "On the Air: The Encyclopedia of Old-Time Radio." Oxford University Press. 1998.

Darst, Maury. "Front Row, Section Eight of World War II." *The Galveston Daily News*. 24 Jul. 1983.

"Enlist in Fight Against Cerebral Palsy." *Independent Press-Telegram*. Long Beach, CA. 10 May 1964.

"Finance to Pay Annuities." *The Billboard*. 31 Mar. 1956.

Flynn, Joan King. "Dennis James Cashes in on His Gift of Gab." *The Milwaukee Sentinel*. 7 Oct. 1951.

Forman, Murray. "One Night on TV is Worth Weeks at the Paramount: Popular Music on Early Television." Duke University Press. Durham, North Carolina. 2012.

"For Two Contestants, Jobs Were the Prizes." *The High Point Enterprise*. High Point, NC. 14 Sep. 1974.

Hamm, Thomas L. "A Lifetime Spent Doing What I Loved to Do!" iUniverse. New York. 2008.

Bibliography

Herman, Pinky. "Words and Music." *Radio Daily.* New York, NY. 16 Dec. 1949.

Herman, Pinky. "Words and Music." *Radio Daily.* New York, NY. 9 Feb. 1950.

Herman, Pinky. "Words and Music." *Radio Daily.* 27 Jan. 1950.

Hoffman, Steve. "Dennis James' Firsts Second to None." *The Cincinnati Enquirer.* 25 Aug. 1974.

Hogan, Jr., Martin. "Have to Keep Pace." *The Cincinnati Enquirer.* 21 Aug. 1968.

Hyatt, Wesley. "Short-Lived Television Series, 1948-1978: Thirty Years of More Than 1,000 Flops." McFarland and Company. Jefferson, NC. 2003.

"In Public Service." *Broadcasting Magazine.* 22 Jun. 1953.

"In Review: Club 60." *Broadcasting Magazine.* 25 Feb. 1957.

"In Review: Judge For Yourself." *Broadcasting Magazine.* 24 Aug. 1953.

Irwin, Virginia. "He's Old-Timer in New Medium." *St. Louis Post-Dispatch.* 12 Apr. 1953.

"Is This Really Wrestling?" *Salt Lake City Tribune.* 24 Jun. 1951.

"It's Like an Ex-President Washing Dishes for a Living." *The Owosso Argus-Press.* 27 Sep. 1956.

"James Doubles Area Sale of TV Filters." *Broadcasting Magazine.* 29 Nov. 1948.

"Johnny, Rosemary Launch Quiz Show." *The Herald.* Provo, UT. 22 Jul. 1974.

Kleiner, Dick. "The Marquee." *The Pittsburgh Press.* 27 Jun. 1954.

Lohman, Sidney. "News of Television." *The New York Times.* 10 Jul. 1949.

Lovejoy, Clarence E. "1950 Boating Total to Hit $600,000,000." *The New York Times.* 14 Jan. 1950.

"Main Street." *Radio Daily.* 20 Dec. 1946.

"Main Street." *Radio Daily.* 4 Jan. 1949.

"Main Street." *Radio Daily.* 18 Jan. 1949.

"March of Dimes Drive: Radio-TV Spur Fund Raising." *Broadcasting Magazine.* 5 Feb. 1951.

Martin, Bob. "After 37 Years, Dennis is Still a Winner on TV." *Independent Press-Telegram.* Long Beach, CA. 8 Jun. 1975.

Marvin, Wanda. "Reviews: DuMont Television." *The Billboard.* 31 Jul. 1943.

Marvin, Wanda. "Reviews: DuMont Television." *The Billboard.* 7 Aug. 1943.

Marvin, Wanda. "Reviews: DuMont Television." *The Billboard.* 18 Sep. 1943.

McLellan, Dennis. "Foster Brooks, 89; Drew Laughs with Drunk Act." *Los Angeles Times.* 22 Dec. 2001.

"Mobile TV Latest Creation of Dumont Line." *Television Daily.* New York, NY. 12 Apr. 1949.

"Monty Hall Prefers to Emcee TV Show." *Asbury Park Press.* 4 Apr. 1962.

"Name That Tune, Mondays-Fridays, NBC Television Network." *The Daily Standard.* Sikeston, MO. 23 Aug. 1974.

"Network Accounts." *Broadcasting Magazine.* 8 Nov. 1948.

"Network Program Reviews and Analyses." *The Billboard.* 12 Apr. 1947.

"Nightclub/Vaud Reviews." *The Billboard.* 19 Jul. 1952.

Njeri, Itabari. "He's Second to None When It Comes to Firsts." *Detroit Free Press.* 29 Nov. 1982.

"Not So Hot." *Radio Daily.* New York, NY. 30 Aug. 1946.

"NY Critics Circle Presents Citations." *Broadcasting Magazine.* 24 May 1948.

Orcutt, Maureen. "Celebrities' Day on the Links: They Swing Well and Sign Well." *The New York Times.* 9 Jun. 1960.

Owens, Jim. "Tele Topics." *Television Daily.* 3 Feb. 1948.

Owens, Jim. "Tele Topics." *Television Daily.* 26 Feb. 1948.

Owens, Jim. "Tele Topics." *Television Daily.* 27 Jan. 1948.

Pearson, Howard. "Educational, Newspaper Shows Hold Interest." *The Deseret News.* 11 Oct. 1956.

Pegg, Robert. "Comical Co-Stars of Television: From Ed Norton to Kramer." McFarland and Company. Jefferson, NC. 2002.

"P.S. New Developments on Sponsor Stories." *Sponsor Magazine.* 16 Jan. 1950.

"Quiz Show Films to be Made." *Daytona Beach Morning Journal.* 11 Sep. 1956.

"Radio and Television: Dennis James Will Begin Own Video Show on CBS Sunday—Fashion Story Set." *The New York Times.* 27 Oct. 1948.

"Radio Editors' Top Programs." *The Billboard.* 7 Jan. 1950.

"Report $2,225,500 Price Tag on James' Sterling Drug Pact." *Television Daily.* New York, NY. 16 Dec. 1948.

"Report to Sponsors." *Sponsor Magazine.* 18 Oct. 1954.

Bibliography

Resnik, Bert. "Bert's Eye View." *Independent Press-Telegram.* Long Beach, CA. 4 Aug. 1963.

Reskin, Bert. "TV Experiment Pays Off for Quizmaster." *Independent Press-Telegram.* Long Beach, CA. 21 Apr. 1963.

"Sandra Wins Puppy, $1625 on TV Show." *The Pittsburgh Press.* 14 Jan. 1956.

Scott, Vernon. "24 Years in the Business." *The Pittsburgh Press.* 31 Mar. 1963.

Scott, Vernon. "Dennis James' College Talent Show is Unique." *The Terre Haute Tribune.* 16 Mar. 1969.

Scott, Vernon. "Dennis James Not as Irish as He Sounds." *El Dorado News-Times.* 4 Sep. 1974.

"Second Viewing." *The Billboard.* 20 Jul. 1946.

"Sports Den." *Radio Daily* (special Annual issue). New York, NY. 1948.

"Star Cavalcade Studs Lewis' MD Telespec." *Radio-Television Daily.* New York, NY. 30 Oct. 1962.

"Stars Ham Up Circus for Charity." *The Billboard.* 14 Apr. 1951.

"Sterling Drug to Curtail AM, Try TV." *Broadcasting Magazine.* 6 Dec. 1948.

"Sterling Signs 10-Year Contract for WABD Series." *Broadcasting Magazine.* 20 Dec. 1948.

"Stop Music to Go Off TV After April 24." *The Billboard.* 19 Apr. 1952.

Strassberg, Phil. "Dean of Quiz Has New Show." *Arizona Republic.* Phoenix, AZ. 24 Jul. 1974.

"Telepulse: WABD Daytime Rating High." *Broadcasting Magazine.* 13 Dec. 1948.

"Tele Topics." *Television Daily.* New York, NY. 10 Feb. 1950.

"Television and Radio: Turn to a Friend." *The Billboard.* 17 Oct. 1953.

Tell, Jack. "The Mama's Boy of Television." *The New York Times.* 9 Jul. 1949.

"Test of Personality: Video Performers Must Measure Up to New and Exacting Standards." *The New York Times.* 13 Jun. 1948.

Torre, Marie. "Dennis James Due to Return." *Lawrence Journal-World.* 7 Feb. 1959.

"Toyland Marches, Small Fry Goggle." *The New York Times.* 23 Nov. 1951.

"TV Quiz Whiz Would Be Lawyer." *Sunday Herald.* Bridgeport, CT. 4 Nov. 1956.

"TV Scout Report." *Abilene Reporter-News.* 1 Jul. 1974.

"Web's Shows, Talent Cited During Season." *Television Daily.* New York, NY. 19 Apr. 1950.

"A Week at BBDO." *Sponsor Magazine.* 31 May 1954.

Weinstein, David. "The Forgotten Network: DuMont and the Birth of American Television." Temple University Press. Philadelphia, PA. 2004.

Weiss, Sid. "Behind the Mike." *Radio Daily.* New York, NY. 14 Jul. 1947.

Witbeck, Charles. "Dennis James Keeps Rolling Along." *The Journal News.* White Plains, NY. 22 Aug. 1966.

White, Sid. "Main Street." *Radio Daily.* 28 Feb. 1950.

Wilson, Earl. "Dennis James Remembers Television's Pioneer Days." *The Milwaukee Sentinel.* 12 Oct. 1953.

"Wins Cow and Chicks on TV." *Gettysburg Times.* 26 Dec. 1953.

"Wrestling No Longer a Sport, Magazine Says." *Prescott Evening Courier.* 19 Jul. 1950.

Zieger, Gay Pitman. "For the Good of the Children: A History of the Boys and Girls Republic." Wayne State University Press. Detroit. 2003.

http://slam.canoe.com/Slam/Wrestling/2008/05/13/5550691.html

http://www.nytimes.com/1998/07/14/nyregion/jack-hausman-96-executive-raised-millions-to-combat-palsy.html

http://articles.latimes.com/1985-01-20/entertainment/ca-10627_1_tv-charity

www.lindfuneralhome.com/tributeajax/printobituary.html?id=4130

http://web.archive.org/web/20071224052124/http://www.latimes.com/news/obituaries/la-me-linkletter20dec20,0,3111524.story?coll=la-home-obituaries

http://www.allamericanwatches.com/page/45030

Index

Numbers in **bold** indicate photographs

$64,000 Question, The 154, 158, 163, 182, 183
77 Sunset Strip **204**, 204

Aidala, Artie 152-153
Alexander, Joan **137**
Allen, Fred 75, 132-134, **133**
Allen, Steve 166, 169, 170, 209
Amoroso, Teresa 3, 6, 67, 124
Andrews, Vincent 84, 94, 103

Bacall, Harvey 262
Bailey, Jack **79**
Baio, Scott **289**
Barasch, Norman 146
Barishman, Fern 261-262
Barker, Bob 246, 250-253, 263, 264, 266, 304
Barnhizer, Dave 168
Barnum, P.T. 42, 49, 91
Barrett, Rona 219
Barty, Billy 198
Beat the Odds **200**, 200-202, 204, 211, 309
Belzer, Richard 20-21
Berle, Milton 38, 86, 109, 168, 224

Berry, Ken **223**
Billboard, The 13, 14, 31, 93, 120, 146
Bolen, Lin 256, 257, 258, 259-260
Bowes, Major Edward 6, 57-58
Brennan, Walter 189
Brooks, Foster 219, **234**, 234-237, 263, 298, **301**
Brown, Pat 191
Butterfield, C. E. 109-110

Can You Top This? 38, 310
Cara, Irene 80
Carney, Art **87**, 172
Carpenters, The **225**, 225
Carroll, Diahann 114
Carson, Johnny 126, 200, 286
Carter, Jimmy 262
Carvel, Tom **153**, 154
Cash and Carry
Cates, Joe 180, 181-182
Celebrity Game, The 205
Celebrity Parade for Cerebral Palsy 86-87, 89, 91, 140, 141, 156, 170, 182, 207, 209-210, **211**, 253-254, 270-279, **271**, **273**, **276**, **278**
Chance of a Lifetime 112-117, **113**, 144, 149, 154, 155, 158, 159, 223

319

Charo **273**
Childhelp 298
Club 60 166-168, **167**, **169**, 169, 170, 186, 308
Cohen, Martin 158
Cole, Nat "King" **90**, 120, 128, 168
Como, Perry 194, 236-237
Connors, Mike **301**
Crawford, Marjorie see James, Micki
Crawford, Mildred 156-157
Crosby, John 132-133
Cullen, Bill 164, 243, 244, 245, 250, 256

Daily, Bill 168, 170
Dalton, Abby 219
Daly, John Charles 206, **308**
Danzig, Fred 189
Davis Jr., Sammy **167**, 168
Dennis James Celebrity Golf Classic, The 299-300, 305
Dennis James Show, The see *Okay Mother*
Dennis James' Carnival see *Eyes Have It, The*
Dobkowitz, Roger 250, 252
Douglas, Mike 168, **169**, 170
Dubin, Harry 34-35
DuMont 10, 12, 13, 14, 15, 16, 17, 18, 28, 29, 31, 33, 34, 39, 40, 42, 50, 51, 58, 59, 63, 64, 69, 70, 71, 72, 83, 91, 99, 110, 111, 112, 142, 165, 284, 307
DuMont, Dr. Allen B. 1-3, 8, 10, 12, 14, 15, 17, 28, 42, 63, 71, 110
DuMont Beepstakes 29, 307

Edwards, Geoff 242, 257
Edwards, Ralph 188, 255, 256, 257, 258, 262
Edwards, Vince 50

Eisenhower, President Dwight 120, 211-212
Elliott, Win 134
Ern Westmore Show, The 118, 120
Esterlin, Malcolm 38
Eyes Have It, The 61-62, **61**

Farnsworth, Dr. Philo T. 1-2
Farrakhan, Louis 60
Fates, Gil 29
First Row, Section Eight 25, **25**
Fisher, Bruce 261-262
Ford, "Senator" Ed 38
Ford, Anitra 264, **265**
From Here to Eternity 128
From This Moment On 191

Gabor, Zsa Zsa 154
Gallery, Tom 69
Gallichio, Joseph 168
Garabaldi, Gino 49, 101
Gleason, Jackie 86, 120, 172, 184
Godfrey, Arthur 91, 144-146, 168, 226
Goldenson, Leonard H. 84, 85, 86, 89
Goodson-Todman 129, 130, 132, 133, 134, 136, 137, 138, 163-164, 185, 189, 243-244, 245, 246, 249, 250, 252, 266
Goodson, Mark 74, 129, 132, 133, 138-139, 142, 244-245, 250, 295
Gotch, Frank 43
Gould, Jack 63
Goulet, Robert **289**
Grant, Bud 242, 245-246
Greene, Marion 24, 26, 217

Haggis Baggis 180-182, 308
Hale, Jr., Alan 197, 198
Hall, Monty 83, 184, 187, 190, 202,

Index

204, 212, 215-216, 242, 248, 253, 254, 298, 300, 302-303
Hampton, James 268
Hatos, Stefan 188, 191
Hausman, Jack 84-86, 89
Heatter, Merrill 188, 204, 205, **212**, 213, 214, 222
"Heaven's Very Special Child" 87-88, 273
Henderson, Florence 253, 277, **289**, **297**, 300
Hewett, Tarzan **44**
High Finance 159-163, **161**, **163**, 179, 308
Hill, James 63
Hogan Jr., Martin 221
Hogan, Hulk 20-21, 284
Hollywood Squares, The 206, 222-223
Hope, Bob 86, 188, 196, 210, 224, 240, 253, 260, 297, 298, **299**
Hope, Dolores **299**
Horl, Ray 262
Hot Properties 20-21

Impossible Years, The 283, 311
It Could Be You! 188, 189

Jackie Gleason Show, The 172
James, Alden 147
James, Brad 207, 209, 210-211, 216, **218**, 219, 226, **227**, 227, 229, 235, 240, 241, 270, **271**, 272, 273, 274, 275-276, **278**, 284, 293, 294, 296, 298, 299, **303**, 304, 305
James, Craig 299
James, Dennis Jr. 26, 100, 157, 217-218, **218**, 296
James, Micki 94-103, **96**, **97**, **99**, **102**, **105**, 105-108, **111**, **121**, 121-123, 124-125, 126, 127-128, **127**, 130, 131-132, 134, 137, 142, **145**, 149, 150, 152, 154, **155**, 155-157, **157**, 158, 168, 171, 173, 174, 177, 186, 193-194, 196, 198, 199, 207, 213, 217, 218, 219, 226, 235, 236-237, 239-240, 248, 250, 252, 260, 270-271, 272, 274-275, 277-278, 283, **293**, 293, 294-295, 297, 298, **299**, 301-302, **303**, 304, 305
James, Randy 158, 165, 170-171, 173-174, 176, 193, 210, 217, **218**, 219, 226, 240, 279, 296, 298, 305
Judge for Yourself 132-134, **133**, 136, 304, 307

Keaton, Buster 189
Kellogg's 156, **171**, 172, **173**, 175-177, **176**, 179, 182, 184, 206-207, 210, 211, 212, 223, 287-288, 308
Kennedy, John F. 190, 191
Kennedy, Tom 196, 198, 216-217, 219, 254, 256, 260-261, 262, 302, 304
Kent, Herbert 149
Kent, Mrs. 102, **145**, 149
Kirgo, George 188-189, 202
Klein, Robert 60
Knight, Gladys 60
Korman, Chris 267-268, 301, 302
Korman, Harvey 267-268

Lady Luck and the Tiger 83-84
LaLanne, Elaine 196-198, 199, 222
LaLanne, Jack 196-198, 199, 222
LaLanne, John 197
Landon, Michael 205, 213, 224
LaRosa, Julius 145-146
Lawyer Q 37-38, 310
Lee, Ruta 214, **216**

Let's Make a Deal 242, 244, 245, 248
Lewis, Jerry 86, 87, 168, 191
Linkletter, Jack 180
Longmore, Paul K. 272-273, 274
"Look at Us, We're Walking" 88-89, 272
Lortz, Gary 229-230, 232-233, 266-267, 285-286
Louis, Joe 40, 162, **163**
Lynde, Paul **223**

MacEachern, Craig 287-288, 289-291, 298-299
Mack, Ted 58, 59, 60, 63, 80, 82, 93, 105, 111, 112, 223, 307, 310
MacLeod, Gavin **273**
Major Bowes' Amateur Hour 6, 57-58
Mann, Carol 199
March, Hal **90**, 154
Marshall, Peter 196, 205, 214-215, 222, 254, 268, 296, 300, 303, 304
Martin, Dean 224, **236**, 237
Marvin, Wanda 14
Marx, Groucho 130
Mathis, Johnny 259, **261**
McCoy, Bibber 20
McMahon, Ed 286-287
Meade, Julia 67
Mellow-Larks 168, **169**
Mister Universe 50, 311
Moore, Garry 120, 126, 152-153
Moss, Herb 116
Mother O' Mine **54**
Muntz, Madman 226
Murder at the Howard Johnson's **287**, 294, 311
Muscular Dystrophy Association of America (MDA) 87, 191
Myerson, Bess **137**, 140

Name That Tune 154, 255-262, **257**, **261**, 309
Name's the Same, The 136-140, **137**, **139**, 142, 164, 244, 250, 304, 308
Narz, David 302, 304-305
Narz, Jack 196, 219, 302
New Price is Right, The see *Price is Right, The*
New York Times, The 52-53, 63, 83
Nicklaus, Jack 297
Niles, Wendell 223-224, 225
Nixon, Richard 190-191, 197

Oh Madeline! 295, 310
Ohme, William G. 115
Okay Mother 64-72, **66**, **68**, **69**, **71**, 91, 93, 98-99, 106, 111-112, 307
Olson, Johnny 120, 246-247
On Your Account 134-136, **135**, 149, 157-158, 308
One and Only, The 282-283, 284

Paar, Jack 168, 170, 189
Paramount News 40, 311
Pardon My Prisoner 109-110
Parker, Colonel 240
Parks, Bert 74-75, **75**, 152, **153**
Pasetta, Marty 278
Password 185, 205, 249
Patti Page Show, The 172-173, **306**
Patterson, Dick 214, **216**
PDQ 213-217, **214**, **216**, 219, 222, 309
Pennington, Janice **249**, 264-265
People Will Talk 204-205, **206**, 206, 213, 309
People's Court, The 38
Physicians Mutual Insurance 229-230, 231-232, 233, 266, 284-285, 289,

Index

291, 295, 303-304
Piper, Rowdy Roddy 283, 284
Pitchess, Peter 263
Police Story 282
Presley, Elvis 240
Price is Right, The 164, **243**, 243-253, **245**, **246**, **249**, **251**, **253**, 258, 260, **263**, 263-266, **265**, 281, 304, 309
Price, Vincent 197

Queen for a Day 117, 283
Quigley, Bob 188, 204, 205, **212**, 213, 214, 222

Race for Space 217, 223
Radio Daily 33, 82
Rayburn, Gene **87**, 136-137, **137**, 139-140
Reese, Della **223**, 224, 259
Reiner, Carl 205, 282
Reynolds, Burt 279
Rich Man Poor Man 282, 310
Ritter, John 277-278
Robbins, Fred 180, 181
Rocca, Antonino "Argentina" 54
Rocky III 283-284, 304, 311
Rogers, "Nature Boy" Buddy 54-55

Sahl, Mort 166-167
Sarnoff, David 2, 10
Saturday Night's Main Event 284
Scott, Vernon 202, 225
Seasoned Citizen 291
Shearer, Jimmy 7-8, 94
Sherwood, Don 166
Shore, Dinah 202, 256-257, 259, 297, 300
Shostak, Stu vii- viii, 173-174, 219, 240, 250, 284, 298
Shriner, Herb 101, 121, 126, 130-132,

131, **133**, 140, **143**, 152-153, **153**, 239-240
Sinatra, Frank 6, 8, 12, 55, 58, 128, 146, 260, **273**, **278**, 297, 298, 300
Sixteen Whacks and a WAC 25
Sponsor 58-60, 115
Sports Parade 18-19, 41, 194, 307
Sposa, Demitrio 3-4, **4**, 5-6, **123**, 124, 127, 158, 227
Sposa, Frank 3, 4, 158
Sposa, Lou 3, 4, 8, 26, 63, **64**, 67, 99, 158
Stallone, Sylvester 283-284
Stammberger, Fritz 264-265
Stang, Arnold **137**
Stanlee, Gene **44**, 55
Steiner, Aaron 38, 103, 174-175
Stop the Music 58, 74-76, **75**, 93, 106, 107, 112, 154, 307

Tapps, Georgie 134
Tattletales 304
Ted Mack's Original Amateur Hour 58-61, 63, 80-81, 93, 111, 112, 223, 307, 310
Teen Tones, The 60
Television Roof 11-17, **15**, **17**, 18, **19**, 31, 63, 307
Texaco Star Theater 109
Tierney, Gene 128
Tillet, Maurice 51
Tinker, Grant 146
Tirpak, Lila 13-14, **15**
Todman, Bill 129, 130, 132, 133, 134, 136, 137, 138, 163-164, 185, 189, 242-243, 244, 245, 246, 249, 250, 252, 266
Tonight Show, The 166, 169-170, 286
Torre, Marie 182

Truth or Consequences 29, 251, 252
Tufts, Sonny 25
Turn to a Friend **117**, 177-120, 308, 311
Two for the Money 130, 132, **133**, 136, 146, 153, 304, 307
Two for the Seesaw **183**, 184, 311

United Cerebral Palsy (UCP) 86-92, **87**, **90**, 120-121, 140, 141-142, 156, 170-171, 182, 208, 210-212, **211**, 254, 269-279, **271**, **273**, **276**, **278**, **289**, 295, 299-300, 302, **303**, 304-305

Van Dyke, Dick 114, 164
Vereen, Ben **297**
Video Village 188, 204

Waring, Fred 15-16, 194
Wayne, Frank 249-250, 263
Wayne, John 224
Weaver, George 119-120
Weekend with the Stars 295, **297**
Westmore, Ern 118, 120
What's My Line? 136, 206-207, **308**, 308

White, Betty **185**
White, Sid 70
Whose Line is It Anyway 38
Winchell, Paul 101, 124, 153
Winkler, Henry 282, 283
Winters, Jonathan 114
Witbeck, Charles 213
Wolcott, Louis see Farrakhan, Louis
Wrestling from Jamaica Arena **41**, 42-56, **44**, **46**, **48**, **52**, 59, 62, 63, 64, 66, 70, 93, **99**, 100, **109**, 109, 142, 215, 282, 283-284, 307
Wynter, Dana 215

You Bet Your Life 129-130
You're in the Picture 183-184
Your First Impression 185-191, **185**, **187**, **189**, 190, 193, 194, 202, 204, 211, 309
Young, Alan **287**
Your All-American College Show **223**, 223-226, **225**, 309

Zimbalist Jr., Efram **204**

www.ingramcontent.com/pod-product-compliance
Lightning Source LLC
Chambersburg PA
CBHW060109170426
43198CB00010B/830